IAN WOOSNAM'S GOLF MASTERPIECES

IAN WOOSNAM'S GOLF MASTERPIECES

Classic tales from the clubhouse

Ian Woosnam with
Peter Grosvenor

SIDGWICK & JACKSON
LONDON

Cartoons by Roy Ullyett
Book design by Alan Chalk

First published in Great Britain in 1988 by
Sidgwick & Jackson Limited
1 Tavistock Chambers, Bloomsbury Way
London WC1A 2SG

ISBN 0 283 99676 5

Photoset by Rowland Phototypesetting Limited
Bury St Edmunds, Suffolk
Printed in Great Britain by
Butler and Tanner Limited, Frome, Somerset

Contents

Introduction   9

Ian Woosnam's Record   23

1. IN THE BEGINNING   25

The Origins of Golf *Michael McDonnell*   25

The Home of Golf *Pat Ward-Thomas*   27

Our Mother, that Sad Old Bitch *Peter Dobereiner*   31

The Best Game Man Ever Devised *Herbert Warren Wind*   33

From Barefoot Caddie to Open Champion *Sandy Herd*   36

2. GOLF IS FUN – OR SHOULD BE   41

Sundered Hearts *P. G. Wodehouse*   41

Golf Gamesmanship *Stephen Potter*   54

Golf in a Dinner Jacket *Walter Hagen*   61

The Wit and Wisdom of Sam Snead   63

You're Supposed to Enjoy Golf – Even with a Pain *Peter Dobereiner*   64

Celebrity Quips   68

3. THE GREAT TRIUMVIRATE *Bernard Darwin*   69

Harry Vardon   70

J. H. Taylor   74

James Braid   77

4. THE IMMORTAL BOBBY AND THE INDOMITABLE BEN   81

Bobby Jones *Bernard Darwin*   81

Ben Hogan *Geoffrey Cousins and Tom Scott*   91

5. HENRY THE GREAT   95

   Banned from Cricket So I Take Up Golf *Henry Cotton*   95

   My Three British Opens *Henry Cotton*   98

   The Master and a Modest Case of Forgery *Henry Longhurst*   108

6. HENRY THE COMMENTATOR   109

   Augusta in April *Henry Longhurst*   109

7. THE BIG THREE   115

   The Million-dollar Shot – How Arnie Palmer Made Boldness His
   Friend *Arnold Palmer*   115

   The Genius of Nicklaus – Greatest of Them All?
   Herbert Warren Wind   122

   Mind Over Matter *Gary Player*   133

   Player's Incredible Last Nine Holes in the Masters
   Herbert Warren Wind   141

8. THE AGONY AND THE ECSTASY   145

   When Just One Shot Can Make or Break a Career *Angus MacVicar* 145

   Tony Jacklin – the Price of Success *Liz Kahn*   149

   How to Lose the US Open *Sam Snead*   156

9. MY FAVOURITE COURSES   161

   Wentworth *Ronald Heager*   161

   A Course to Make a Welshman Proud *Peter Allen*   164

   The Very Irish Hazard of Maggie Leonard's Cow *Pat Ward-Thomas* 166

10. SOME MODERN HEROES   169

    Tom Watson *Peter Alliss*   169

    Super Mex on the British *Lee Trevino*   176

    Seve – the Car Park Champion *Peter Alliss*   185

    Steady as She Goes – The Way to Win the Open *Nick Faldo*   190

11. HEROES WITH PROBLEMS   193

    The Yips – and How to Beat Them *George Plimpton*   193

How to Give up Golf Without Really Trying *Henry Longhurst*   200

My Cure for the Yips *Bernhard Langer*   203

How Not to be a Club Thrower *Greg Norman*   207

12.   THE CADDIE   211

My Favourite Caddie *Gene Sarazen*   212

A Caddie-ish Trick *Henry Longhurst*   218

The Caddie who Out-earned the Open Champion *Sam Snead*   219

Caddie Backchat   220

13.   GOLFING INTELLIGENCE   221

It *Does* Take Brains to Play Golf – or Does it? *Gene Sarazen*   221

Introduction

In this anthology I have tried to express some of my love of the game and just how much I owe to it. The more you play and think about golf, the more you marvel at the demands it makes not just on your physical skill but also on your temperament. The moment you think you have golf licked it comes up behind you and bites you in the rear. I reckon that a quick loss of temper to relieve your frustration – like the time when I snapped a 2 iron across my knee in the Majorca Open – is much better than brooding over disaster and letting it sap your morale. The game can be agony and ecstasy – the title of one of the sections in this anthology – and that's as true for the professional like myself as it is for the 28 handicapper. As one sage put it, 'Golf is like a love affair. If you don't take it seriously, it's not fun. If you do take it seriously, it breaks your heart.' What drives us on? No one expressed it better than that wise golf writer Bernard Darwin, several of whose pen portraits of the great players of the past you can read in these pages. He said, 'It is this constant and undying hope of improvement that makes golf so exquisitely worth the playing.'

Small is Beautiful

Severiano Ballesteros caused a few laughs after I had won the Suntory World Match Play at Wentworth in 1987 with his quip: 'Woosnam will be a great golfer when he grows up.' I have never seen my 5 feet 4 inches as a disadvantage. It certainly would be if I were a basketball player, but in golf the old adage 'A good big 'un is better than a good little 'un' is just not true. Look at Gary Player, barely 5 feet 7 inches; Hogan and Watson are no more than 5 feet 9 inches. Golf is very much a game of balance. The taller you are, the more you are liable to sway and create greater body movement. The smaller you are, the more turn you can get. That is why I am among the big hitters in the game. Sandy Lyle and I have been friendly rivals from the days of our Shropshire youth when he won the junior prize and I was runner-up. I vowed there and then that I was going to beat him one day. 'You'll have to grow a bit first,' Sandy told me. That's the least of my worries.

The subject of my size came up when in March 1987 I was honoured to have lunch with the Queen and Prince Philip at Buckingham Palace. Though members of the Royal Family are not noted for their addiction to golf, the Queen, who is patron of the Royal and Ancient, watches it on television in the evenings. She asked me whether I found it difficult playing in the wind. 'It certainly helps to be small, Ma'am,' I replied, 'because you don't get blown about so much.'

When I turned professional in 1976 at the age of eighteen, I was christened 'the toy bulldog', although I'm also known as 'the mighty atom' and 'the little golfing wizard from Wales'. I am sturdily built for my height, weighing 11 stone, and I have the strength where it matters – in the legs, in the arms and above all in the hands, which is important because I'm a wristy player. As soon as I was old enough for my feet to touch the pedals, I was driving the tractor on my father's farm. There was no power steering then, and that gave me powerful forearms. I would also practise steering the tractor with just the index finger and thumb of my left hand, and in that way developed great strength.

My Back

The only cloud over my fortunes has been my back. I'm not the first golfer to suffer in this way. After years at the top Jack Nicklaus said, 'There has not been a day in the past twenty years when my back hasn't ached.' Like Seve, another back sufferer, he would hang from a trapeze that stretched his back, easing the pressure between the vertebrae. Langer also suffers periods of back pain and Lee Trevino has had surgery. I have had back trouble pretty much since I became a pro; it doesn't hurt when I'm actually playing, but I feel it afterwards. Sometimes the muscles go taut and I can't get to sleep, or I manage to sleep and wake up aching. And when I get up on the morning of a tournament it's sometimes so bad I can't even put my socks on.

One rheumatologist told me that I had spondylitis, a progressive disease of the spine in which the vertebrae start to fuse. It can be caused, or aggravated, by constantly leaning forward to hit golf shots. I was in real pain after all the rain in Hawaii where Dave Llewellyn and I won the World Cup for Wales at the end of 1987. It didn't seem like a happy omen for my trip to Sun City immediately afterwards for the Million Dollar Challenge. Happily, the weather was much warmer and the facilities laid on for us there were extensive. A chiropractor who specializes in muscle and joint problems gave me exercises to do, lying on a bed and lifting my feet up. I went on to win that week and to date his advice has worked wonders. Oddly enough, it is being so small that helps contribute to my back problem. If I sit up in an ordinary chair or even an aeroplane seat my feet sometimes don't quite touch the ground, and on aeroplanes especially I put a briefcase under my feet to give support to my back.

My Ambition

My ambition is to be number one golfer in the world and to be remembered alongside the real greats of the game – Tom Morris, Jack Nicklaus and my two special heroes, Tom Watson (who has such style) and Gary Player (because he's such a great fighter). I've had this competitive urge at sport ever since I can remember and I think it comes from my father, Harold. He's not a golf professional like Sandy Lyle's father, who gave Sandy a lot of painstaking tuition. Whereas Sandy always had a course outside his front door to play on, I had to make a 15-mile trek.

My own swing is more or less self-taught. What my father taught me was never to know when I'm beaten. He's so competitive at everything he does that he would spin a scrabble game out for two days to get the very best possible score if we let him.

My Early Days

At Rhyn Park School my main interest was sport, not study. I wanted to be the best at soccer, boxing, swimming, anything sporting. My father tells a story about a family holiday at Butlin's during which I earned the nickname Tiger for my ring heroics. 'They could never find anyone Ian's size, but he still beat them,' he recalls. 'He even won the swimming and we didn't think he could swim. It just shows how competitive he's always been.'

I had ambitions to play soccer for England, though never so strong as my ambitions in golf. When I left school I suppose it was touch and go whether I would opt for soccer or golf. I was in the local football team and used to play very hard, always getting stuck in. My father told me that if I carried on like that it wouldn't be long before I wasn't able to play football again or even golf. He says he just had to step in because he knew I would hurt myself.

So golf won, and anyway it's a sport in which you can go on longer. At the age of thirty I'd now be over the top as a footballer, whereas I know that the best of me is yet to come as a golfer.

I swung my first golf club when I was seven and my father says that even now he still

picks up the balls I hit on the farm when I was practising. He took up golf in his thirties and at one time played a very competitive game off a 5 handicap though nowadays it's nearer 8. We played at the Llanymynech Club where fifteen holes are in Wales and three in England. That's a bit like me. I was actually born on the border, just in England, at the village of St Martin's near Oswestry, but I regard myself as a Welshman through and through (as much of a Welshman as Lloyd George, who was born in Manchester).

I have two brothers and one sister. The eldest brother, Keith, a central heating plumber, is four years older than me and plays off 11. He was born in a hospital in Wales, as was my sister Julie who is two years older than me. My brother Gareth is nine years younger. He plays off 4 and could be a very fine golfer if he had more time to practise.

I played most of my early golf at Llanymynech and by the time I was thirteen I was down to a 6 handicap. I was always badgering the members to play me for £1, even though I hadn't any money in my pocket. Fortunately, I didn't often lose. Then I slumped a bit and was only down to a handicap of 1 when I turned pro in 1976.

When I was sixteen I left school and took a job with Albert Minshall at the Hill Valley Club near Whitchurch. First of all I helped in the pros' shop, but that was too quiet for me. So after a couple of weeks I joined the green staff, a 7.30 a.m. to midday job which gave me plenty of time for practice in the afternoons, though I probably spent more time playing than practising. Playing is the real way to improve your game, by which I mean getting round in fewer strokes. You can learn far more by playing than by practising, as I'll explain later.

Early Struggles as a Pro

I was eighteen when I turned pro in September, 1976.

I spent three seasons at the players' school at Foxhills, Chertsey, in Surrey. My first important win was in the *News of the World* Under-23 Match Play, when I beat John Hay in the final. I also acquired the nickname of Bertie because of the rather remote similarity of my surname to that of P. G. Wodehouse's famous character, Bertie Wooster. A special dinner was held for me to raise some money to get me to Portugal and we called it Bertie's party. The name has stuck.

I borrowed my father's old Volkswagen caravanette for the tour. It was white going off-white so I painted it blue to make it look a bit more respectable. It became a real home from home as we travelled round. We slept in it, dried our clothes in it, and ate our rather monotonous fare of crisps, soup and endless tins of baked beans.

I never had much trouble getting a good night's rest in the van, but moving around in it presented more problems. I just prayed it wouldn't break down because I had no money for repairs. I remember that it took me more than three days to drive to Milan. Once there, the old banger began to splutter and choke and slowed down to an embarrassing 10 m.p.h. crawl, its top speed. I hawked it about from one garage to another, fearing that the engine had broken up. How on earth was I going to find several hundred quid for a new one? No one seemed to be able to diagnose the trouble till at last I found a Volkswagen dealer. He fixed it in moments: a tube had come off the carburettor, and once it was back on the VW ran like a bird. I came ninth in the Italian Open so at least I had enough money for the petrol home.

I wasn't always so fortunate. Very often I didn't make eating money. Another time I was down to my last £2 after filling up in Lyons. Credit cards weren't generally accepted in France then – not that I had one anyway – and I just hoped and prayed that a full tank would get me all the way to Calais. Crossing the city boundary with the needle at empty I breathed a sigh of relief, only to have the van splutter to a dry stop just 1 kilometre from the ferry. If you've ever tried buying a couple of litres of petrol from a French garage with only £2 in English money in your pocket, you'll know just how difficult that can be. I trudged around with a can till finally I found a guy who would take English pound notes and I was spared the indignity of having to push my vehicle on to the boat.

Soon after that things got a little easier financially. I was still too poor to fly, but I could afford a bed and breakfast place. A group of us – David Russell, Joe Higgins, Martin Poxon, Mike Inglis and myself – took two cars, sharing petrol costs, to drive to the Italian Open. I shot an 87 and failed to qualify, as did Mike Inglis. The others, however, did qualify, and Martin generously lent us his wreck of a Triumph Dolomite so that Mike and I could seek our fortunes in the French Open.

This was another of those occasions when our driving troubles began well before we got to the tee. The wretched vehicle broke down in Nice and required a new head gasket. As usual, we had no money and were limited to drawing £50 a day each with cheques backed by cheque cards. Finally, after a couple of days, we scraped together enough to pay for the repairs and set off for Paris, only to have the shock absorbers go. Buzzing down the autoroute in that hair-raising old car which bobbed about like a cork on the ocean was not the ideal preparation for the French Open and not surprisingly we failed to qualify. The only consolation was that Martin Poxon agreed to pay for the repairs to the shock absorbers.

That was what life was like at the bottom end of the professional circuit. We had a lot of laughs and a lot of fun, but quite a lot of heartache too. No one would endure that kind of perdition and frustration for many months unless he was really determined to succeed, and I was. In 1979 I was 122nd in the order of merit and won £1,049. Often I had to quit the tour and get a part-time job as a barman or labourer to gather together enough money for another stab at it – anything to scratch a few bob together.

In 1980 I struck it rich: all of £3,481, and I was number 87 on merit. Then in 1981 it all fell apart when I slipped back to 104th and earnings of only £1,884. I couldn't seem to qualify and I felt like giving up the tour. I was going to apply for the pro's job at Oswestry Golf Club. I spent two weeks feeling very sorry for myself. Deep down I still wanted to be the best golfer in the world, but there were times when that objective became submerged. I got stuck: I couldn't even see what I was doing wrong; I could hit the ball as well as the rest of them, *but I wasn't scoring*. Yet something inside me told me to hang on in there.

The Breakthrough

In 1982 a chance encounter changed everything for me on the eve of the Nigerian Open. I was on the practice ground with Yorkshireman Gordon Brand Senior. While I was hitting the ball well, he looked awful: pushing one over the fence on the right, pulling the next one yards left. But while he got round in 68, I was taking 76. Suddenly it clicked: *bad shots didn't worry him*.

All he worried about was getting a good score on his card. I thought it was a great attitude. It changed my whole outlook on the game and also my life. I just went out and never worried about my bad shots again. I stopped putting myself under too much pressure by trying to hit perfect shots all the time, and adopted the oldest adage in the game: 'It's not how, but how many.'

By finishing third in the African Safari Tour money list in 1982 I became exempt from qualifying in Europe and that was the start of the big time. After that I got my temper under control: no more putters smashed in anger, no more clubs hurled in a rage. I went on to win the Swiss Open, my first big victory, and came second in the Italian Open. I didn't have to pre-qualify now; I won £48,794 and finished eighth in the European order of merit. I was on the road from golfing pauper to golfing millionaire, or so I hoped.

The other parts of my life began to come together as well. In 1983 I married my childhood sweetheart, Glendryth. Before we married she wanted to do her own thing and came to London to one of the teaching hospitals where she trained to become a State Registered Nurse. That gave me my first taste of London life. To be with her I bought a flat in Maida Vale which I later sold: it would certainly be worth a lot now. But I'm not a townee, though I wouldn't mind a place in the Wentworth area. I'm really still a country boy with no desire to give up my first home at Oswestry.

In 1984, in a thrilling head-to-head last-round contest with Sandy Lyle, I won the Scandinavian Open. When Glendryth gave birth to our son Daniel in the following year, that was another incentive to be successful. Winning is an infectious habit: it brings confidence. Success breeds success. I started with a win in the Zambian Open in March 1985, had ten top-eight finishes in the European tour and was placed fourth in final Order of Merit with earnings of over £80,000.

During the Ryder Cup of that year Paul Way and I beat Fuzzy Zoeller and Hubert Green by one hole on the first day, and then by four and three on the second to help Europe to their first victory in twenty-eight years, and that gave me as much pleasure as anything I'd done in golf up until then.

If I win in the early part of the season, I'm confident. If I start badly, I get a bit anxious. Although I don't have to worry financially, that doesn't mean I've lost the desire to excel, to be number one. I'm a good loser, I like to think, though I hate to lose. But every time I go out now, I feel that I can win.

Coping with the Pressures

1986 was a good year for me with winnings of £111,799, even though my putting was in poor shape for half the year.

At the Open at Turnberry I wasn't put off by the appalling conditions. Someone joked that at my height I operated 3 feet below the wind! I had a great first round of 70 to lead the field, then made 74, 70 and 72 on the final day when the weather had returned to normal. I finished third and won £35,000.

I was still struggling on the greens, however, until halfway through the third round of the Lawrence Batley TPC when I decided to line up my putts differently and promptly birdied four out of the next six holes to finish with a round of 66 and then 69 to win by seven shots, incidentally ending the Belfry's seven-year wait for a British winner.

Golf is full of hidden problems which can creep up on you unawares. But where there's a will there's a way.

Look at Bernhard Langer. He had the dreaded 'yips' – that involuntary jab or twitch that sends the ball wide on short putts – worse than anyone in the world; and the yips have driven other men out of the game, but not Bernhard. He conquered the problem by changing his method, adopting the reverse grip for close putts, and most of all by sheer guts and determination because he wanted so badly to overcome it.

There are lots of great players out there who have never won anything really big like a major. Maybe the pressure gets to them. Even now, when I'm close to winning, my heart is pounding and my hands are shaking, probably most of all on the greens. When you've learned to play through nerves like that, you've almost cracked it. Nerves can be a hindrance and nerves can be a help. But you can never play to the peak without some nerves. Nerves set the adrenaline flowing and get you pumped up. Great footballers like Sir Stanley Matthews used to be physically sick before a big game. The tempo of soccer is very different from that of golf, of course, in that once you're on the football pitch the game is so fast and so demanding you haven't got time to feel nervous (except during set pieces such as a crucial penalty). The player who is a bag of nerves before a Cup Final can go out and play the game of his life once he's on the pitch.

In golf, with long gaps between shots, the pace is obviously different, and that's where the other essential comes in: concentration. Because I need to concentrate I don't talk to my partners or opponents as I used to. When I played Sandy Lyle in the final of the Suntory World Match Play in 1987, I suddenly realized that I was in danger of blowing it because I was talking to Sandy too much. It was either him or me who would become the first Briton to win the trophy. So I kept quiet and the competitive edge returned.

Inevitably, after years of competitive pressure, there has to be a reaction at some point, as Tom Watson has shown. He's done everything and you can't last at the top for ever. Nicklaus, however, is different. His extraordinary win in the Masters in 1986 was a triumph of determination, as if to say, 'I want to win to prove that I still can win'. But I feel that maybe Jack should have retired at that point, going out right at the top. Jack and Tom Watson are both very nice guys. Usually the best players are the nicest, because they are at ease with themselves.

Money has changed my life to an extent, but for me the trophies of wealth are much less important than the success itself. I bought my five-bedroom house in Oswestry for a six-figure sum, that is peanuts by London or New York standards. Mind you,

Glendryth and I have put a lot into the house, with a specially built snooker room and bar, a jacuzzi and a sauna. The drawing room is bulging with Waterford crystal from various prizes.

I have a few of the badges of wealth, such as my Porsche with its personalized number plate – PRO IW. It has a car phone, which is a bit of a toy really and a damn nuisance when I leave it on by mistake and it runs the battery flat. I've got a compact disc player in the car and a TV dish in the garden to pick up those transatlantic golf programmes, because I'm addicted to watching golf. It can teach you so much. But extravagance will never come easily to me.

1987 saw me become the first player to top £1 million in tournament winnings. The year had got off to a whirlwind start when I won the Hong Kong Open with a four-round total of 275, four shots ahead of David Feherty and Sam Torrance who shared second place. I was the first Briton to win the tournament in its 29-year history, which pleased me a lot. After that came victory in the Jersey Open and the winning streak was well and truly on. In the Madrid Open at Puerto de Hierro I clipped one shot off the 270-stroke championship record set by Ballesteros seven years before. In July I had my third victory of the European tour by winning the Bell's Scottish Open at Gleneagles with seven shots to spare, having led from start to finish. The Lancôme Trophy gave me my fourth European win of the season and I was on the crest of a wave when I joined the European Ryder Cup team at Muirfield, Ohio. We were defending the trophy we had won at the Belfry two years before and playing in the four balls and foursomes with Nick Faldo we achieved 3½ points out of a possible 4. To be the first European team to win on American soil was a very emotional experience. Just as emotional was winning for Wales with David Llewellyn in the World Cup, where I had a 14 under par for the best individual score. The icing on the cake was victory in the $1 million 'Winner takes all' tournament at Sun City, the richest prize in golf. So what do I do for an encore in 1988? Win one of the majors, I hope.

Some Thoughts on Practice and Pacing Myself

This may shock generations of golfers but if things are going well I try to practise less, not more. Even today I don't like to practise more than forty-five minutes at a time unless there's some specific problem to work out. Practice sometimes leads to fiddling, to experimenting with different gimmicks and ideas, and that can be positively damaging. As the Americans say, 'If it ain't broke, don't fix it.' And that applies to a golf swing which is working well.

Before a big tournament I will arrive about an hour before tee-off and hit about eighty shots, largely just to loosen up. I then finish off with about half an hour's chipping and putting to get the feel and the pace of the greens.

Although I had some tuition in the early days – much of it was from the professional Cyril Hughes, a disciple of Henry Cotton – basically I'm a self-taught player. I learn from watching myself on video and from watching others whose swing I admire, notably Tom Watson and Gary Player. And, of course, I can always take a tip. Sam Torrance says, 'Clear your hips quicker on the down swing.' If it feels good and it looks good when I see it on video, I can believe in it. Sam's father, Bob Torrance, taught me to get my weight transference on to my right side on the back swing, which is very important.

If I'm not playing well, I settle down to watch myself on video: it usually works. In the European Open at Walton Heath in 1987, for example, I shot a poor 73 and then watched the television recording. I soon spotted the fault. My legs were too straight at the address. I was coming up on the ball too much and either pushing or hooking. Next day I made sure that I flexed my knees a bit and I shot a 65. The following week I went on to win the Lancôme Trophy in France. I know pretty well what works for me now and I generally know how to put myself right, though it's usually necessary to watch a video because that shows you exactly what you *are* doing rather than what you think or feel you are doing. I have a set method of addressing the ball, an identical set-up and stance, and I always grip the club in the same way. I usually hit the ball at 90 per cent power with woods and 85 per cent with irons. If I hit the ball more softly I can still put it off-line.

Many people are amazed to hear that I don't play regularly in the winter months and I don't want to either. In the winter of 1986–87 I played only seven times in three months. After Sun City in early December 1986 I didn't play again until mid-February, but last winter I had only three weeks off after Sun City before going to Australia. However, I still made some space for myself before that. For instance, after winning the World Match Play I had a good two weeks off before going to Hawaii for the World Cup, and after that I enjoyed a clear break, no play for five days, before flying to Sun City. After two practice rounds I was back in the game. Unfortunately, my stomach wasn't. The night before the last round my son Daniel, then not quite three, was up all night, and I had a tummy bug too. For the first nine holes of the last round I didn't know how to contain myself. I was hitting the ball everywhere but somehow managed a 35 for 1 under par. I felt much better on the back nine and thanks to an eagle 2 at the 17th I shot a 33 to beat Nick Faldo. I've seldom played better and seldom felt worse. It was a strange way to win the first million-dollar cheque in tournament golf.

I like to rest and I need to rest from golf. I believe it's very important to pace yourself. It's very easy when you have a big success to overdo it, to accept too many offers and engagements. Then you get tired and stale and lose your zest and enthusiasm for the game. That way lies premature retirement. You won't catch me making that mistake, nor Seve. He plays only about twenty times a year now and he still knows how to score.

Mind you, I swing the club quite often without the ball to make sure that I'm in the groove. Mostly I do it in the kitchen at our house at Oswestry, choosing the right time on a winter's evening when Glendryth is not cooking and Daniel isn't somewhere underfoot or demanding attention. I line myself up so that I'm reflected in the kitchen window (it's like a mirror at night-time) with the central strut of the window exactly bisecting my head. At the end of each swing I make sure that my head is still in the same place, bisected by the strut. If that sounds like rather a primitive practice facility for a man who won £1 million last year, I can only say that it suits me.

When I hit a bad patch in 1988 many commentators were saying that I shouldn't

CHIP PAN in the kitchen!

have changed clubs to the Japanese-made Maruman clubs in place of the ones that I had used during the great year of 1987. It's true that some adjustments had to be made to the new clubs – basically metal was shaved off the heels to flatten the lies – before I felt fully at home with them. But I never blamed the clubs for my loss of form. The real problem was in my swing. I went through what I can only call a nightmare and the problem was still not solved after I'd practised until my hands bled. After missing my second successive cut in America I spent three hours on the practice ground without learning a thing. Practising became like a drug that I couldn't stop, but I was only practising the wrong things. The solution came when I stood in front of the mirror in my hotel bedroom. I saw that my hips were in the wrong position when I addressed the ball. Consequently I was swinging the club from out to in. By putting more weight on my right foot and changing the position of my hips, the old rhythm started to come back.

Usually I know precisely what I want to achieve or correct. That is one of the things that distinguishes the professional from an amateur, who will often knock the ball around on the practice ground without much thought. But, and this may console the handicap golfer, just like an amateur the professional can hit a bad patch and not know the reason why. Sometimes it's a technical fault, sometimes a mental one. Then, as Seve says: 'It can all change. You wake up one morning and you feel different and know you're ready. Sometimes you just don't know when it will happen.'

A strong left hand and wrist is very important for control but I try to *hit* the ball with the right side. Being a wristy player, I want to feel my right side and hand coming into the ball. Seve tends to use the right side more now and to do that he's trying for a flatter swing. There's more to Seve than most people know. He's changing his swing so as to last longer and he doesn't hit the ball so hard now.

I am very precise about just how far I hit the ball with each club. In average conditions, I use a driver for 270 yards; a 1 iron for 235 yards; a 2 iron for 215 yards; a 3 iron for 200 yards; a 4 iron for 190 yards; a 5 iron for 180 yards; a 6 iron for 170 yards; a 7 iron for 155 yards; an 8 iron for 145 yards; a 9 iron for 133 yards; and a wedge for 125 yards.

I certainly haven't conquered putting but I'm probably unique among top golfers in not having a settled putting style. I keep changing my method, thinking I've found the secret, and it works very well for a while. Then, as with all such 'secrets' in golf, you go on doing it, exaggerating it perhaps, and quite suddenly it doesn't really work very well any more. So then it's time to turn to a new secret. At one time I used to line the ball up facing the hole square, then I'd move round, leaving the club face where it was. Another time I used to try reaching out for the ball.

Then David Llewellyn, my partner in the World Cup, said that I should lengthen my back swing. At the moment I favour a crouching style, right arm well bent, no wrist movement, hitting the ball on the up (so as to impart top spin and steady line) with the right hand. Next year it might be something different. Perhaps I should stick to one thing, but I've yet to pick the style that works well all the time, even though I've been a pro now for twelve years.

My Wobbly Friend

An essential part of my life is Wobbly. That's what we call Phil Morbey, my caddie, because of his rather unusual walk. He's a curly-haired 23-year-old Yorkshireman who used to stack goods in a Selby supermarket. Now he helps me stack up some good scores on the tour, having been with me for just over a year, and he's a real friend. When I won the Suntory World Match Play at Wentworth, we both had tears in our eyes. My achievements are his too. As he says, 'I'm involved in all the pressures and the action. It has all been happening to me as well as to Ian out there.'

Wobbly had a lot of experience working for David Jagger, David Russell, Ian Baker-Finch, Howard Clark and several others before joining me. He is very good at clubbing me. Quite often – as happened in the Match Play, for instance – Phil suggests a different club from the one I have chosen, and he is right. But he only volunteers information when I ask him. Sometimes I know just the right club and pick it for myself. We get together on the putts and usually we agree on the line. I want him to see the putt the way I see it. If he doesn't, I tell him to go and stand by the edge of the green.

They say that to be a great player you have to have a good golfing brain. In some ways because I've gone all out for golf I have a sort of tunnel vision. I don't want to clutter my head with information that doesn't help my golf career. I'd much rather listen to music on my car radio, Neil Diamond for preference, than to news or current affairs programmes, which I find mostly gloomy.

I can understand figures but big words fool me. I'm not much of a one for books, unless they are about golf. I'm proud of what I've achieved, but I don't dwell on it too much. In fact, I try to forget my scores, even the successful ones, because I'm concentrating on the future. I have to think if asked how many holes I've done in one: it's about six. The important thing in golf for me is now to win a major tournament.

If I had another ambition it would be to play snooker. I have a full-size table at home and spend a lot of happy hours on it already. The challenge is fantastic, the skills, the thinking behind a big break. The best I've managed so far is only 45, but I'm working on it. Challenge is what I thrive on. Perhaps in fifty years' time I'll be the fastest man in the World All-comers Wheelchair Race.

In the pages that follow I have tried to tell something of the history of golf through the personalities of the great players who have adorned it, from the Triumvirate of Vardon, Braid and Taylor at the turn of the century to the Big Three – Palmer, Nicklaus and Player – who dominated golf in the sixties and on into the seventies. Then come the younger giants including Greg Norman, Tom Watson, Bernhard Langer, Seve and Sandy. Of course, equipment has changed out of all recognition even since the war, so you cannot but marvel at, say, Henry Cotton's round of 65 at Sandwich when he won the 1934 Open (the round which gave the Dunlop 65 its name).

Despite developments in equipment and in the level of prize money the mental pressures are almost exactly the same: how not to choke when you're ahead, how not to let the bad shot get to you. This book, like the game of golf itself, is intended for

After 40 dedicate myself to snooker.

addicts of all abilities. And the long-handicapper can console himself or herself with the words of A. A. Milne: 'Golf is so popular because it is the best game in the world at which to be bad . . . at golf it is the bad player who gets most strokes.'

Ian Woosnam's Record

Country: Wales

Born: 2 March 1958

Height: 5 feet 4 inches

Turned pro: 1976

Married: Wife Glen, son Daniel (born 1985)

Hobbies: Fishing, snooker and sports generally

Tournament Victories

1979   *News of the World* Under-23 Match Play Championship
1982   Swiss Open
1982   Cacharel Under-25s' Championship
1983   Silk Cut Masters
1984   Scandinavian Enterprise Open
1985   Zambian Open
1986   Kenya Open
1986   The Lawrence Batley Tournament Players' Championship
1987   Hong Kong Open
         Jersey Open
         Madrid Open
         Bell's Scottish Open
         Lancôme Trophy
         Suntory World Match Play
         World Cup (Wales)
         Sun City

Order of Merit Positions

Year	Position	Winnings	Year	Position	Winnings
1979	122	£1,049	1983	9	£48,164
1980	87	£3,481	1984	6	£68,126
1981	104	£1,884	1985	4	£82,235
1982	8	£48,794	1986	4	£111,799
			1987	1	£253,717

Miscellaneous

Ryder Cup	1983, 1985, 1987
Hennessy Cognac Cup	1982, 1984
World Cup	1980, 1982, 1983, 1984, 1985
Dunhill Nations Cup	1985, 1986
Nissan Cup	1985, 1986

1

IN THE BEGINNING
The Origins of Golf

Michael McDonnell

Till recently the Scots were confident that they had invented golf; now that claim is disputed by the Dutch. Certainly there is far more literature about the early game in Scotland. It was several times declared illegal there in the fifteenth century. 'Ye futball and ye golf be utterky cryt donne and nocht usyt,' said James II's ban of 1457. And Mary Queen of Scots made history as the first golfing widow – though not in the usual sense. She was severely criticised at her trial for heartlessly playing two days' golf after the murder of her unloved husband, Darnley. Here a distinguished golf correspondent gives his verdict on the controversy – by coming down on both sides!

I.W.

Even the Romans found a certain fascination in hitting a small ball with a curved stick. Their game was called *paganica*, referring to the leather ball stuffed with feathers, which in fact was to remain the form of the golf ball until the advent of the *guttie* in the mid-19th century.

Throughout the intervening centuries, variations of a game in which a ball was hit across open countryside have appeared in different countries, under different names and rules. The ancient French played a game called *jeu de mail* in which a wooden mallet (*mail*) hit a ball over a course about half a mile in length to a marker, the winner being the player who took fewest strokes.

Much later the Belgians and the French played a game called *chole*, clear evidence that the pastime was popular there in the mid-14th century, almost 100 years before any reference to the game in Scotland. However, there was a combative element to this form of play: it involved a team aiming to hit a cross-country target in a predetermined number of strokes, while their opponents were given specified opportunities to hit the ball in the opposite direction to any difficult hazard they could find.

The paradox is that golf, such an exact game in terms of skill and conditions of play, should have no verifiable record of its origins and has therefore become the subject of rival claims between the Dutch and the Scots as to who actually invented it.

While forms of stick-and-ball games were always popular in continental Europe, there is evidence that a game called *cambuca* – a feather-filled leather ball hit with a stick to a target – was also played in England in the 14th century and the stained-glass east window in Gloucester Cathedral depicts the figure of a man wielding a club at a ball.

When considering the game as we now know it, the main issue is whether 17th-century Scottish traders copied it from their Dutch counterparts along the seashore, while waiting for their ships to be unloaded, or whether in fact the Scots exported it.

The origins of the word do not help much either. The Scottish word *gouf* means 'to strike'. The Dutch word *kolf* means a club used to strike a ball.

That said, the Scottish parliament banned football and golf in May 1491 ('or uther sik unprofitabill sportis') because the populace was obsessed with those pastimes and not devoting enough time to archery practice. By 1513, Catherine of Aragon, Henry VIII's first wife, wrote to Cardinal Wolsey saying that the King's subjects seemed 'to be busy with the golf, for they take it for pastime, my heart is very glad to it'.

But the Dutch claim is strengthened by research work of historian Steven Van Hengel, who died while attending the 1985 British Open. Van Hengel traced a stick-and-ball game, using an iron-headed club back to 1300. It was popular with children and became such a nuisance in town that it was moved to open countryside.

The famous 1688 Adriaen van de Velde painting entitled 'A Frost Scene' clearly depicts a kilted man playing a form of golf in Holland. It adds to the debate about who invented golf, although there is no question that golf today owes its popularity to the Scots who taught the world to play.

From *The Complete Book of Golf*
by Michael McDonnell
(Kingswood Press, Surrey, 1985).

The Home of Golf

Pat Ward-Thomas

There's not much doubt that St Andrews and the Royal and Ancient are the home of the modern game. But there are rival views on this traditional old links course – modified though it now is. Sam Snead disliked it – and the icy wind, and even more the £150 prize money – despite winning the British Open at St Andrews in 1946. The late Pat Ward-Thomas, of the *Guardian*, was plainly a lover of this 'capricious mistress'; not so Peter Dobereiner of the *Observer*, in very acerbic mood in the second of these two pieces.

I.W.

The origins of golf are obscure. Whether it evolved from the Roman game of *paganica*, *kolven* in Holland or other pastimes few would dispute that St Andrews has long been the home of golf. For centuries the aged city has been renowned as a seat of learning and religion but to golfers the Royal and Ancient Club and the Old Course are the heart of its fame. No place on earth where a game is played has attracted more pilgrims and no other golf club has as many members from so many countries, nor as great an influence on the game.

The Royal and Ancient is a unique institution. It is a private members Club but has no course of its own. At the same time it is a governing body with supreme authority for the Rules of Golf, the organisation of the Open and Amateur Championships, and numerous other international affairs.

At any Autumn or Spring Meeting of the Club golfers gather from the far places of the world; the fires in the Big Room glow and the pictures of famous men look down upon the lively scene. The originals of the portraits might be surprised to find that claret is no longer a common beverage, and meals are not banquets.

On quiet days when nothing of moment is afoot and a few members drowse in their deep chairs one might look through the tall windows and dream awhile. So peaceful is the scene, so silent the room that it is hard to believe that almost every great golfer in the game's history has stood on the tee below and looked down the long fall of fairway to the hills beyond; and that on an upper floor the processes of guidance and government are constantly under way.

The Club's stature in the game was an accident of history. Had the Old Course not existed early in the 18th century, in whatever primitive a form, the Club might never have come to life. There would have been no cause for the historic meeting on 14 May 1754 when twenty-two Noblemen and Gentlemen assembled, doubtless over a substantial repast. Admiring the game as a healthy exercise, and having the interest and prosperity of their ancient city at heart, they decided to contribute five shillings each for a Silver Club to be competed for every year. The St Andrews Society of Golfers, subsequently the Royal and Ancient Club, was born, but the progenitors could not have imagined what would grow from the tiny seed of their inspiration.

For a hundred years and more after its foundation the Society had no particular powers. It was content to follow the original code of rules which had been devised in 1744 by the Company of Gentlemen Golfers in Leith, but when the fortunes of that Society fell into temporary decline in the 1830s there was a gradual growth of the Club's influence. Eventually, out of more than fifty countries, the United States and Mexico alone did not take their lead from the Royal and Ancient in matters of the Rules of Golf and of Amateur Status.

Of the millions who watch the Open Championship every year many are unaware that its promotion and organisation are solely the province of the Royal and Ancient. No professional golfing body is involved in any way. The Championship Committee, composed entirely of amateur golfers and assisted by a small club staff under the Secretary, bears the whole responsibility for the success or failure of an event which has become a substantial business undertaking.

The profit from the Open or other activities is devoted to the general welfare of golf and not shared among its members. For generations the Club has been a trustee for the game, its spirit and its customs. By using powers to guide rather than to dictate an effective form of democratic authority has grown. There have been no threats to the Club's stature from without, and no lasting turmoil within. It has moved peacefully into its third century, its foundations as secure as those of the grey stone Clubhouse.

The Old Course

For generations golfers have journeyed from afar to visit the Royal and Ancient Clubhouse and meet the timeless challenge of the Old Course. Throughout the ages it has tested the finest golfers, all save Hogan who, alone of the great masters, never competed there. And, particularly for golfers from overseas, there is a special satisfaction in being able to say that they have been in the Club and played the course, no matter how many strokes it may have cost them. For many the experience could match a garden party at Buckingham Palace or an audience with the Pope.

The visitor will not readily forget the first impression of the place – so intimate are its policies on the very fringe of the old university city. The clubhouse, massively implanted, sombre and yet serene, is at the crest of a quadrangle, encompassing the first and last holes, flowing down to the Swilcan Burn and the long ribbon of the links beyond. On the one hand shops, houses, hotels and golf clubs form a grey terrace; on the other a vast putting green rolls towards the curve of the bay where the tide trails its silver chains. The prospect could not fail to quicken the heart of any golfer as he faces a test the like of which he will find nowhere else.

The Old Course has no parallel anywhere because its fashioning owes more to nature than to the hand of man. In the beginning there was no plan, no architect; the holes simply evolved and by some miracle have stood the test of time with little need for change except for occasional lengthening here and there to counter the power of modern equipment.

The shape of the course is much the same as it was centuries ago when the citizens of St Andrews were granted the right to include golf among their pastimes. It runs over gently crumpled linksland out to the Eden estuary and then swings back along the 8th and 9th holes, giving it the shape of a billhook. Linksland, common to the coasts of Britain, was formed when the sea receded, leaving undulating wastes of sand.

These became resting places for birds whose droppings helped to fertilise seeds borne by the wind, and grasses, gorse and other vegetation grew. In time the links were an ideal breeding ground for rabbits and other animals who wore paths and burrows in the wilderness. Over the years the passage of man widened the paths and when the golfers appeared they found natural fairways, sites for greens and bunkers in profusion. At St Andrews the space between the arable land to the south with its protective banks of whins, and the whins on the other side was so narrow, about 40 yards, that the golfers had to share the same fairways and holes going out and coming home. At first they took the left-hand route going out and returned on the other side, changing about to add variety. The left-hand route was used for the Amateur championship in 1886 and occasionally in recent years for a winter competition at a time when the Course is being rested.

The early golfers started from a tee west of the present 18th green and played to the 17th. This must have been a formidable hole. The land which now lies to the north, with its embankment and putting courses, had not then been reclaimed from the sea wherein a sliced tee shot could easily vanish. The present first green was made in 1870, some years after Tom Morris had created the 18th, the green which now bears his name.

Long ago the gorse was thinned and cut back but the Old Course, running between the Eden and the New courses, rarely measures more than 100 yards across, and its total area must be the smallest of any championship course in the world. All the while golfers cannot help but trespass on each other's fairways and indeed on the seven double greens introduced in 1832. Only the 1st, 9th, 17th and 18th have a green to themselves; the remainder are huge, rippling surfaces, some almost an acre in area. Many are on plateaus, a providential blessing, starkly exposed to the elements and fearsome places for the man whose putting touch is amiss. As Nicklaus remarked once, 'You can feel so lonely out there, missing a short putt'. Nowhere does the classic excuse for an indifferent score, that of taking three putts, sound less convincing. The golfer may find green after green, although not always his own, and leave himself putting from 30 yards and sometimes much further. Judgement of distance is of the essence in scoring well unless the player can survive a great burden on his short game. However well a man may think he knows the holes there are times when he can be far out in his reckoning. The undulating land often makes the flags look much nearer than they are.

The legend of the 'Old' as a capricious mistress, all deceitful wiles, is less true than it was before the age of watering. When the ground was baked hard and the ball running fast, short approaches needed the utmost delicacy of touch, and the little slopes and falls had to be studied and known. There was too no question of firing approaches to pitch near the flags. The course still demands unceasing vigilance and rarely does it forgive thoughtless attack, faint-heartedness or lack of perception.

The winds can be flirtatious with the movement of the tides, so much so that it is possible to play out against the breeze and face it again coming home, but it is the subtler changes of angle that can alter strategy. Within the hour, or even minutes, what was a safe line can become a dangerous one mainly because of the bunkers. They are nowhere near as plentiful as when they were holes from which sea shells were dug or places for sheep to shelter, but they are numerous enough to dictate the strategy of play on every hole, save the first and last, and to tantalise the golfer. Many are not at once visible to the striker and can be totally unexpected hazards for those ignorant of their presence. Thus contentment can swiftly turn to fury and frustration. And yet, Thomas H. Peter, in his reminiscences was moved almost a century ago to declare that 'Bunkers which gave such interest in old times now scarcely form hazards at all'. They must have been fearsome.

From *The Royal and Ancient* by Pat Ward-Thomas
(Scottish Academic Press Ltd, Edinburgh, 1980).

Our Mother, that Sad Old Bitch

Peter Dobereiner

It was a matter of historical accident that decreed that a round of golf should be played over eighteen holes. In the early days of the game's development there was no standard number of holes. The available land was the governing factor. Holes were laid out according to convenience on the linkland; the waste common ground which bordered the sea. Some courses could accommodate nine holes only, others fourteen or more. It so happened that at St Andrews the players found it convenient to hole out eighteen times as they played out to the farthest promontory of their narrow strip of links and returned, using the same greens in many cases, to the starting-point. And as St Andrews developed as the most influential centre of the game so eighteen holes became accepted as the norm.

The reputation of the Old Course also set the standards for golf course layout and even today there are people who believe that links golf is not just the best but indeed the only true form of the game. It is a point of view with which I have little patience. Apart from the selfishness of denying that those who play inland are real golfers, it ignores the fact that golf is developing. New equipment has changed the game entirely and, in any case, St Andrews is no longer the course it used to be. This part of the coast of Fife is subject to silting and whereas the Old Course used to be right alongside the shore it is now nearly a mile inland. Changes in the character of the turf have been largely accelerated by modern techniques of course management. Artificial fertilisers have enriched (and coarsened the grass) and automatic water-sprinklers have softened the greens. These innovations have been introduced in the name of progress but the result, in my opinion, has been the destruction of the Old Course. Instead of being a monument to the pioneers of the game, St Andrews today is an unhappy mixture. The matriarch of golf has been tarted up in lipstick and mini-skirt. The dignity of antiquity has been lost and her character compromised. She is a sad old bitch of a golf course, grotesquely old fashioned by modern standards and hopelessly raddled to those who loved her as she was. The city of St Andrews is established as the home of golf and is the Mecca of enthusiasts from every corner of the world. The city fathers are conscious of their responsibility to the past and to the present, but in my view their compromising does a gross disservice to both.

How much more satisfactory it would be if they let the Old Course revert to as near her original condition as nature allowed. Take away the automatic-sprinklers and allow the greens to become as hard and fast as glass. Let the fairways be so that once again a golfer might be able, as the American Craig Wood once did, see his drive kick into a bunker some 400 yards distant down the wind. And, for good measure, provide pencil-case quivers of hickory clubs so that visitors could get an idea, if a sketchy one, of what the game was like during the genesis of golf. In other words, make St Andrews a living museum.

From *The Game with the Hole in it* by Peter Dobereiner
(Faber and Faber, London, 1970).

At no place but St Andrews would such hazards be acceptable; on the old course they are as natural as the grey stone of the houses which line the closing hole.

Robert Trent Jones, golf architect.

Say, that looks like an old abandoned golf course. What did they call it?

Sam Snead, on first seeing St Andrews in 1946.

Know what I really feel about St Andrews? I feel like I'm back visiting an old grandmother. She's crotchety and eccentric, but also elegant and anyone who doesn't fall in love with her has no imagination.

American Tony Lema, Open Champion at St Andrews,
in 1964.

Those greens on St Andrews used to be so crisp that you could hear the crunch your spikes made when they cut into the turf. Oh, they were fast!

Bobby Jones in 1968.

The Road Hole, the seventeenth, is the most famous and infamous hole. . . . As a planner and builder of golf holes worldwide, I have no hesitation in allowing that if one built such a hole today you would be sued for incompetence.

Peter Thomson, elegant Australian, five times winner of
the British Open, one of them at St Andrews in 1955.

The reason the Road Hole is the greatest par-four in the world is because it's par-five.

Ben Crenshaw in 1984.

My first impression of St Andrews was one of strange ambiguousness. I didn't like it, nor, for that matter, did I hate it. I've never been so puzzled after a first practice round in my life.

Tom Watson in 1984.

It finds you out. If there is one part of your game not right, no matter how you try to hide it – to protect it – the Old Course will find it during the championship.

Peter Thompson in 1984.

There is no place in the world that I would rather win a championship.

Jack Nicklaus in 1984.

Daniel, then two years old, celebrates his father's Suntory World Match Play win with Ian. (*Express Newspapers*)

Ian, at Sun City, becomes the first golfer to win a million dollar cheque. (*Associated Press*)

The putt that didn't get away. Ian explains how he narrowly beat Sevé Ballesteros in the World Match Play semi-finals in 1987 and then went on to win. (*Matthew Harris*)

Ian with Daniel and his wife Glendryth – a typical close family scene. Not having his family with him in America upset his form. (*Phil Sheldon*)

The modern greats (Woosnam and Greg Norman) beat the ancient greats (Nicklaus and Trevino) in a sudden death play-off in the $300,000 Desert Scramble in Arizona. (*Associated Press*)

The victorious European Ryder team after their win over the USA in September 1987. From left: Sevé Ballesteros, Gordon Brand Jr, José-Maria Rivero, Ken Brown, Sandy Lyle carrying José-Marie Olazabal, Ian Woosnam carrying captain Tony Jacklin, Nick Faldo, Bernhard Langer, Sam Torrance, Eamonn Darcy and, kneeling, Howard Clark. (*Popperfoto*)

Sevé says it with bubbles, missing Jacklin's open mouth. No matter, a Ryder Cup win is champagne in itself. Torrance and Langer share the joy. (*Peter Dazeley*)

A million-dollar shot. With this 7 iron pitch which he holed for an Eagle 2 on the 17th at Sun City, Ian ensured his million-dollar victory over Faldo. (*Associated Press*)

Another triumph in his great year of 1987, Ian holds up one of the many trophies he won at individual and team competitions. Honours for Wales (with fellow Welshman Dave Llewellyn) in the World Cup tournament at Kapalua, Hawaii on Maui. (*Associated Press*)

Dave Llewellyn demonstrates a crisp follow-through. (*Peter Dazeley*)

The Best Game Man Ever Devised

Herbert Warren Wind

Herbert Warren Wind is one of the great American golf writers and a good enough golfer to have competed in the British Amateur at St Andrews in 1950. When he wrote this short perspective of the game in 1954, President Eisenhower was in the White House (on those rare occasions when he wasn't on the golf course) and the game was enjoying a spectacular post-war boom on both sides of the Atlantic which still shows no signs of diminishing.

I.W.

Ever since golf began – Scottish historians have settled on the year 1100 as a reasonable date of birth – the game has been an enigma. For those who have steered clear of its clutches, the devotion it commands from its followers looms as one of the great absurdities of the human race's supposed progress. There are moments when every golfer agrees with this verdict. If he could only have back in one lump all the time, money, energy, and anguish he has spent on golf and invest it towards some sensible goal, why, there is no knowing the heights of happiness he might reach. Then he plays a good round in congenial company on a sunny morning, and his golfer's balance returns. If there is one thing he is certain he has done right in his life, it has been to play golf, and his only regret is that he hasn't given the game more time. He might have become better.

Beyond the fact that it is a limitless arena for the full play of human nature, there is no sure accounting for golf's fascination. Obviously yet mysteriously, it furnishes its devotees with an intense, many-sided, and abiding pleasure unlike that which any other form of recreation affords. Perhaps it is, as Andrew Carnegie once claimed, an 'indispensable adjunct of high civilisation'. Perhaps it is nothing more than the best game man has ever devised.

In comparatively modern times, the spread of golf's popularity has come on by waves. The first big one broke just about a century ago – in 1848 – when the gutta-percha ball was introduced and rapidly replaced the 'feathery', the leather-cased ball packed tight with feathers, for centuries the standard equipment. Until the coming of the 'gutty', Scots living in Scotland had been the only golfers, but the new ball changed all that. It made golf a much better game. A player no longer had to be a technician of considerable skill to nudge the ball nicely off the ground and send it flying a good distance in a relatively straight line. The gutty required a powerful swing and a well-timed hit, but when it was struck cleanly, it could be propelled tens of yards farther than the feathery, and the essential thrill of 'distance' entered the game for the first time. This revitalised kind of golf swept south of the Scottish border into England, then to the European playgrounds of the international set of that day, and, by the turn of the century, it had made its way to every continent. Wherever golf was taken, it took. It arrived in the United States in 1888 – that, in any event, was the year the first American golf club was founded – and so instant was its contagiousness that twelve years later the number of American golfers exceeded a quarter of a million.

Golf – gutty golf – undoubtedly would have gained more and more adherents, but it is questionable if it would have made quite the conquest of man's leisure hours as did the rubber-core ball, the revolutionary modification of the gutty which made its appearance in 1898. This new ball – its core wound tightly with strips of rubber, the cover of gutta-percha – was the impetus behind golf's second great wave of popularity and ushered in the present version of golf, the game eight million people play today. The new ball was superior to the solid glob of gutta-percha in almost precisely the same respects which the gutty had been to the feathery: it would, on the average, go some fifteen yards farther when struck correctly, and, more important, it would go *someplace* when not struck right on the button. It was just what was needed to make the average player feel like a golfer and not like a well-dressed labourer. The invention of the rubber-core ball is usually credited to Coburn Haskell, of Cleveland, and for all that American ingenuity later did for the game, it undoubtedly stands as our outstanding technical contribution to the advancement of golf.

Then the waves began to come closer to each other. There was a mighty one in 1913. In our National Open Championship that September, an unknown home-grown amateur, Francis Ouimet, a remarkable twenty-year-old ex-caddie from a family of medium means, astounded the golf world as it had never been astounded before or afterwards by first tying with and then defeating in a dramatic play-off two acknowledged masters from Great Britain, Harry Vardon and Ted Ray. Until Francis' epochal victory, most non-golfers in America had viewed the game with hostility as the pampered pastime of the wealthy, the elderly, the would-be Continental, the unrugged – and they were welcome to it. After Francis' victory, this stigma was removed once and for all, and the base was laid for golf's development in this country as a genuinely democratic sport, whatever the inevitable social overtones of the clubhouse. Hundreds of thousands of reformed golf-haters rushed to the golf courses, and it was only a matter of months before they viewed with suspicion anyone who didn't play their game.

The majestic personalities of the 'twenties completed golf's ascendancy to the status of a major American sport. First there came Walter Hagen. Until Walter made the British Open his personal property – he won it first in 1922 and three times later – British golfers, despite Ouimet's one break-through, had continued to rule supreme in international competition. Walter's exploits abroad and at home eradicated our national inferiority complex, and they were achieved with a dash and bravado that captivated the Great American Sports Fan who had been bred on baseball, football, and boxing heroes. Hagen was a guy he could understand, and he took to golf through him. Another dimension was added when Gene Sarazen, the son of an immigrant carpenter from Italy, came bolting out of complete obscurity to win the

National Open in 1922, the first of his many championships. And then there was Jones – Robt. T. Jones, Jr., Atlanta, Ga. Even in the Golden Age of the 'twenties when every sport had its heroic-sized champion, its Ruth or its Dempsey or its Tilden, there was no other athlete who was consistently the champion that Bobby Jones was on and off the fairway. The beauty of it was that Jones's qualities were recognised by everyone instinctively.

Golf is presently on the crest of another wave, the first that has rolled in since Jones's Grand Slam. From the close of World War II on, the game has made tens of thousands of converts annually.

The increase in leisure time available to the average man and woman has been a major factor in this recent expansion. In a way, so has Ben Hogan, by all odds *the* dominant sports personality of the post-war world, the champion who came back after his near-fatal accident and had the stuff to make himself an even greater champion. In the process he became a national hero of such proportions that, during his assault on the British Open in 1953, non-golfers, so green about the game that they first confused Carnoustie with a new wax for motor-cars, followed his progress with the same proud concern that veteran golfers did. And, of course, a good measure of the game's increasing popularity derives from the presence in the White House of a man for whom golf is, no question about it, an 'indispensable adjunct of high civilisation'. Today well over five million Americans play some golf every year and there are not nearly enough courses to take care of everyone who would like to play.

Part and parcel of this upsurge of enthusiasm has been a burgeoning interest in what has been written about the game. A great deal has, which is not too surprising. Whatever else it may be, golf is the most ruminative of recreations. Play it and you will talk it endlessly and chew upon it at the oddest hours and, apparently, if you have the dormant urge to put your thoughts on paper, golf will bring it out. Over the years, as a result, a vast body of writing about golf has accumulated which far surpasses any other game's for sheer quantity. Forgetting the countless magazines and pamphlets, golf books alone run into the thousands – how-to guides, collections of short stories, poetry (usually of the class that leaves Milton's position intact), memoirs and biographies, diaries, critical essays, involved psychological disquisitions, formal histories, one-act and three-act plays, all varieties of humour, travel reports, over a score of full-length novels, and 'golf translations' of Shakespeare, Horace and Omar Khayyam. While a large part of this outpouring falls a good distance short of that standard of writing we call literature, no other game has acquired a literature that compares with golf's. Men write extremely well about it, and sometimes wonderfully.

From *The Complete Golfer* by Herbert Warren Wind
(Heinemann, London, 1954).

From Barefoot Caddie to Open Champion
Sandy Herd

Sandy Herd (1868–1944) was a great Scottish character, famous for his 'waggles' when addressing the ball. 'All the time the club waggles in my hand I am getting my wrists supple and shifting my feet inch by inch till I know everything is right for the shot,' was his explanation. He won the British Open in 1902, the first year in which the new American Haskell or rubber-cored ball was used. During practice before the championship, Herd tried a Haskell: 'That was the end of the gutty ball for me. The first drive I ever made with the Haskell was longer than any I ever made with the gutty.' He was the only player not to use the gutty and won by one stroke from Vardon and Braid. Perhaps fortune smiled on him then, as it certainly did not in 1895 after a hailstorm put paid to his championship chances.

Herd was a celebrated teacher, his pupils including Field-Marshal Lord Haig, who occasionally took time off from the mud and blood of Flanders to play golf, the Prince of Wales (later Duke of Windsor) and his brother, the Duke of York (later King George VI). He was a professional at Huddersfield, Coombe Hill and then for many years at Moor Park. But he made his start at St Andrews as a 'bare-fitted' urchin caddie, a golfer of the street who used sticks for clubs and champagne corks with screws (to give them weight) as balls. The lamp-posts on the cobble streets were the flags.

Apprenticed as a baker and then as a plasterer (his mother could see no future in golf which she saw as 'just a life for a ne'er-do-well'), Herd attributed his success to the advantages of a caddie's upbringing. He was one of the first golf professionals to think of making a real career in the game. Before him Jack Burns, Open Champion in 1888, actually preferred the 'security' of working as a platelayer on the railway. When asked how he was playing, Burns used to reply: 'Never better – I haven't been off the line for years.' He, like Herd, was also a plasterer, which made for a few pranks when they were youths.

I.W.

Three Plasterer Champions

It has often struck me as a wonderful thing that out of Andrew Scott's plasterer's yard, where I served my apprenticeship, should have come three Open Champions, Willie Fernie, Jack Burns, and myself. Fernie and Burns were a little before me.

When I was in St Andrews during the last championship week I met Jack Burns and asked him about his golf.

'Never better,' he said. 'I have not been off the line for years.'

The joke was that Burns had been working on the railway line as a platelayer. He won his championship long before I won mine. But Jack did not follow up his advantage. In fact, he played little competitive golf after that.

'I've done what I set out to do,' he used to say, 'and I am satisfied. Now all I want is a steedy job, and I've got that on the railway.'

The winning of a championship thirty-five years ago was not the great stroke of business it is to-day, when a champion is a 'made man,' with the wheel of fortune supposed to be throwing off Treasury notes and American dollars to him at every turn.

Burns probably got about £10 for his money prize. When I won the Open Championship in 1902 the first prize was £50. It is increased since. Throughout the year there were numerous other big prizes, of which at different times I have had my share.

Add to all this the amazing multiplication of golf clubs in this country and America since the beginning of the century, with all the expanding trade in clubs, bags, and balls and the demand for tuition – a profitable branch of the professional golfer's business – and it will be seen what gigantic strides the game has made.

Suppose some obscure young golfer were to come forward to-day and win the Open Championship – not a likely occurrence, I admit, but it might happen. He would wake up next morning to find himself in demand for exhibition matches at increased fees, and his club would find it hard to keep him at home.

The Americans, too, would be sure to want a look at him on a substantial guarantee basis, while clubs on both sides of the Atlantic might bid against each other for possession of him – if only as an ornament!

Anyhow, there would be no danger of his 'going on the line for a steedy job,' as Jack Burns thought it best to do long ago, before Edward Ray and George Duncan had started caddying, or Mr Cyril Tolley and Mr Roger Wethered were out of their nurseries.

James Braid was working in St Andrews as a joiner in my plastering days, but as he was three years my junior and a backward young fellow with little to say, we did not pal up much then. Three years' difference in ages around twenty means more than three years around fifty, where Jimmy and I find ourselves now, he 'daein' awful weel' at Walton Heath and I 'gettin' on fine, thank ye,' at Coombe Hill when telling this story, but at Moor Park when you are reading it.

Together we fought for the honour of Scotland in many a hard battle, mostly against those well-nigh unbeatable Sassenachs J. H. Taylor and Harry Vardon, who for twenty-five years probably won more foursomes than any two golfers in the world.

Not long ago the Americans wanted Braid and me to go across, but Jimmy could not 'gi'e up his business' for golf, and so it fell through. I have heard that when people have expressed surprise to him that he had never visited America, Jimmy's reply was: 'Neither has Mr Lloyd George.' Accompanied by J. H. Taylor, I paid my second visit to America in the summer of 1922. The Americans and I got on finely together.

There were no 'plus 4' knickerbocker suits for professional golfers in my young days. In fact, neither I nor Braid has ever departed from the 'lang breeks' – though now they are tailor-made and pressed, unlike the pair I wore at my first championship, which were mother-made and baggy.

You can imagine me going down to my first Open Championship at St Andrews wearing white fustian plasterer trousers, my working jacket, and a 'dooble peekit' cap, like that worn by Mr Balfour when he played himself in as captain of the Royal and Ancient Club in 1904, with old Tom Morris standing ready to clap his hands, as he did, when the great statesman, who has done more to spread the game of golf than any other amateur, made a very fine drive before a great ring of spectators that September day.

I was frightened to death when I tried my apprentice hand at winning a championship. As I stood up to address the ball on the first tee, I told myself to get well away at the start and the worst of the trouble would be past.

For the life of me I cannot remember now who I was drawn with. You may be surprised at this, but things are apt to get misty in one's memory with a long string of championships and a host of tournaments to sort out.

You see, it did not then dawn on my mind that ever I should come to this – relating my life for others to read. I wonder what my father and mother would say about it if they were alive, as I wish they were.

It may seem a thing hard to believe, but I do not remember having a handicap – I may have had one, but if so I cannot have taken any notice of it. Anyhow, it's a good thing to forget your handicap till the game's finished. I am speaking now of the time when I belonged to the St Andrews Club, not the Royal and Ancient, oh! dear no, the likes of me – a baker, or a plasterer, as I afterwards became – could not enter there.

As I showed no liking for baking I was next apprenticed to Andrew Scott as a plasterer. My parents were desperately anxious to make 'a decent working man' of me. As I had served four years as a baker so I served another four years as a plasterer, at which trade I worked some time as a journeyman. But whether mixing flour or cement my mind ran on golf all the while. At nights in bed I teed up an imaginary ball on the counterpane and drove off into the Land of Nod, where you may depend upon it I returned many wonderful scores, surpassing everything in real life.

Plastering taught me one trick that I laugh now to think of. I used to make a mould of the gutta ball and fill it with plaster of Paris. You could not tell the sham ball from the real. Then I'd get some caddie to tee up with one of my own make. The ball flew off in dust, and I'd watch the fun at a safe distance. I've seen angry old gentlemen chase caddies about the course for playing this trick on them, vowing vengeance on their heads with a club. We were wee devils aye up to some mischief or other.

Four Clubs and No Golf Bag

This much I can remember, that I had only four clubs – a driver, a spoon, a cleek and an iron – no putter and no bag! A younger brother carried my sticks to save caddie fees. Ten shillings a week as an apprentice plasterer put the idea of hiring a caddie clean out of the question.

Of course we played with the gutta ball. I made a very poor show, and went off my sleep for nights thinking that I had not done justice to myself. That is the galling reflection young professionals are often left to torment themselves with, calculating for weeks how many strokes were needlessly dropped.

Nothing but experience can put that right; and some are doomed never to play their best game when it is most wanted. I suppose I had less cause to complain on this score than many others; for I have generally figured pretty well, though my luck has not been of the best. There's aye been a lot of 'ifs' in it.

Had I won the championship of 1895 at St Andrews – as I must have done except for a hailstorm – there is no telling what the effect would have been on me as a champion at twenty-seven. The thought of it haunts me still.

I always flatter myself by thinking that that was the unlucky championship which ruined my chances of winning as many thereafter as Taylor, Braid, and Vardon.

The telling of my story now brings it all fresh to memory and some of the gall with it. Taylor was my conqueror and the first to acknowledge the trick the weather played on me, while it favoured him.

'You had me beaten, Sandy,' he said, 'but for that storm.' It blattered at me for ten holes and stopped when Taylor started out.

From *My Golfing Life* by Sandy Herd
(Chapman and Hall, London, 1923).

2

GOLF IS FUN – OR SHOULD BE

Sundered Hearts

P. G. Wodehouse

As I explained in the introduction to this book, my nickname on the professional circuit is Bertie, partly because of the resemblance of my surname to that of P. G. Wodehouse's famous character, Bertie Wooster. So I'm something of a Wodehouse fan. Certainly no one tells a funnier tale about golf addicts than 'Plum' Wodehouse. His memorable character, the Oldest Member, a venerable sage and clubhouse counsellor to young and old who gave up golf when the rubber-core ball replaced the gutty, regards golf as no laughing matter at all – and contrives to be hilarious in the process. Here is a typical story.

I.W.

In the smoking-room of the club-house a cheerful fire was burning, and the Oldest Member glanced from time to time out of the window into the gathering dusk. Snow was falling lightly on the links. From where he sat, the Oldest Member had a good view of the ninth green; and presently, out of the greyness of the December evening, there appeared over the brow of the hill a golf-ball. It trickled across the green and stopped within a yard of the hole. The Oldest Member nodded approvingly. A good approach-shot.

A young man in a tweed suit clambered on to the green, holed out with easy confidence, and, shouldering his bag, made his way to the club-house. A few moments later he entered the smoking-room, and uttered an exclamation of rapture at the sight of the fire.

'I'm frozen stiff!'

He rang for a waiter and ordered a hot drink. The Oldest Member gave a gracious assent to the suggestion that he should join him.

'I like playing in winter,' said the young man. 'You get the course to yourself, for the world is full of slackers who only turn out when the weather suits them. I cannot understand where they get the nerve to call themselves golfers.'

'Not everyone is as keen as you are, my boy,' said the Sage, dipping gratefully into his hot drink. 'If they were, the world would be a better place, and we should hear less of all this modern unrest.'

'I *am* pretty keen,' admitted the young man.

'I have only encountered one man whom I could describe as keener. I allude to Mortimer Sturgis.'

'The fellow who took up golf at thirty-eight and let the girl he was engaged to marry go off with someone else because he hadn't the time to combine golf with courtship? I remember. You were telling me about him the other day.'

'There is a sequel to that story, if you would care to hear it,' said the Oldest Member.

'You have the honour,' said the young man. 'Go ahead!'

Some people (began the Oldest Member) considered that Mortimer Sturgis was too wrapped up in golf, and blamed him for it. I could never seen eye to eye with them. In the days of King Arthur nobody thought the worse of a young knight if he suspended all his social and business engagements in favour of a search for the Holy Grail. In the Middle Ages a man could devote his whole life to the Crusades, and the public fawned upon him. Why, then, blame the man of today for a zealous attention to the modern equivalent, the Quest of Scratch! Mortimer Sturgis never became a scratch player, but he did eventually get his handicap down to nine, and I honour him for it.

The story which I am about to tell begins in what might be called the middle period of Sturgis's career. He had reached the stage when his handicap was a wobbly twelve; and, as you are no doubt aware, it is then that a man really begins to golf in the true sense of the word. Mortimer's fondness for the game until then had been merely tepid compared with what it became now. He had played a little before, but now he really buckled to and got down to it. It was at this point, too, that he began once more to entertain thoughts of marriage. A profound statistician in this one department, he had discovered that practically all the finest exponents of the art are married men, and the thought that there might be something in the holy state which improved a man's game, and that he was missing a good thing, troubled him a great deal. Moreover, the paternal instinct had awakened in him. As he justly pointed out, whether marriage improved your game or not, it was to Old Tom Morris's marriage that the existence of young Tommy Morris, winner of the British Open Championship four times in succession, could be directly traced. In fact, at the age of forty-two, Mortimer Sturgis was in just the frame of mind to take some nice girl aside and ask her to become a step-mother to his eleven drivers, his baffy, his twenty-eight putters, and the rest of the ninety-four clubs which he had accumulated in the course of his golfing career. The sole stipulation, of course, which he made when dreaming his day-dreams was that the future Mrs Sturgis must be a golfer. I can still recall the horror in his face when one girl, admirable in other respects, said that she had never heard of Harry Vardon, and didn't he mean Dolly Vardon? She has since proved an excellent wife and mother, but Mortimer Sturgis never spoke to her again.

With the coming of January, it was Mortimer's practice to leave England and go to the South of France, where there was sunshine and crisp dry turf. He pursued his usual custom this year. With his suit-case and his ninety-four clubs he went off to Saint Brûle, staying as he always did at the Hôtel Superbe, where they knew him, and treated with an amiable tolerance his habit of practising chip-shots in his bedroom. On the first evening, after breaking a statuette of the Infant Samuel in Prayer, he dressed and went down to dinner. And the first thing he saw was Her.

Mortimer Sturgis, as you know, had been engaged before, but Betty Weston had never inspired the tumultuous rush of emotion which the mere sight of this girl set loose in him. He told me later that just to watch her holing out her soup gave him a sort of feeling you get when your drive collides with a rock in the middle of a tangle of rough and kicks back into the middle of the fairway. If golf had come late in life to Mortimer Sturgis, love came later still, and just as the golf, attacking him in middle life, had been some golf, so was the love considerable love. Mortimer finished his dinner in a trance, which is the best way to do it at some hotels, and then scoured the place for someone who would introduce him. He found such a person eventually and the meeting took place.

She was a small and rather fragile-looking girl, with big blue eyes and a cloud of golden hair. She had a sweet expression, and her left wrist was in a sling. She looked up at Mortimer as if she had at last found something that amounted to something. I am inclined to think it was a case of love at first sight on both sides.

'Fine weather we're having,' said Mortimer, who was a capital conversationalist.

'Yes,' said the girl.

'I like fine weather.'

'So do I.'

'There's something about fine weather!'

'Yes.'

'It's – it's – well, fine weather's so much finer than weather that isn't fine,' said Mortimer.

He looked at the girl a little anxiously, fearing he might be taking her out of her depth, but she seemed to have followed his train of thought perfectly.

'Yes, isn't it?' she said. 'It's so – so fine.'

'That's just what I meant,' said Mortimer. 'So fine. You've just hit it.'

He was charmed. The combination of beauty with intelligence is so rare.

'I see you've hurt your wrist,' he went on, pointing to the sling.

'Yes. I strained it a little playing in the championship.'

'The championship?' Mortimer was interested. 'It's awfully rude of me,' he said, apologetically, 'but I didn't catch your name just now.'

'My name is Somerset.'

Mortimer had been bending forward solicitously. He overbalanced and nearly fell off his chair. The shock had been stunning. Even before he had met and spoken to her, he had told himself that he loved this girl with the stored-up love of a lifetime. And she was Mary Somerset! The hotel lobby danced before Mortimer's eyes.

The name will, of course, be familiar to you. In the early rounds of the Ladies' Open Golf Championship of that year nobody had paid much attention to Mary

Somerset. She had survived her first two matches, but her opponents had been nonentities like herself. And then, in the third round, she had met and defeated the champion. From that point on, her name was on everybody's lips. She became favourite. And she justified the public confidence by sailing into the final and winning easily. And here she was, talking to him like an ordinary person, and, if he could read the message in her eyes, not altogether indifferent to his charms, if you could call them that.

'Golly!' said Mortimer, awed.

Their friendship ripened rapidly, as friendships do in the South of France. In that favoured clime, you find the girl and Nature does the rest. On the second morning of their acquaintance Mortimer invited her to walk round the links with him and watch him play. He did it a little diffidently, for his golf was not of the calibre that would be likely to extort admiration from a champion. On the other hand, one should never let slip the opportunity of acquiring wrinkles on the game, and he thought that Miss Somerset, if she watched one or two of his shots, might tell him just what he ought to do. And sure enough, the opening arrived on the fourth hole, where Mortimer, after a drive which surprised even himself, found his ball in a nasty cuppy lie.

He turned to the girl.

'What ought I to do here?' he asked.

Miss Somerset looked at the ball. She seemed to be weighing the matter in her mind.

'Give it a good hard knock,' she said.

Mortimer knew what she meant. She was advocating a full iron. The only trouble was that, when he tried anything more ambitious than a half-swing, except off the tee, he almost invariably topped. However, he could not fail this wonderful girl, so he swung well back and took a chance. His enterprise was rewarded. The ball flew out of the indentation in the turf as cleanly as though John Henry Taylor had been behind it, and rolled, looking neither to left nor to right, straight for the pin. A few moments later Mortimer Sturgis had holed out one under bogey, and it was only the fear that, having known him for so short a time, she might be startled and refuse him that kept him from proposing then and there. This exhibition of golfing generalship on her part had removed his last doubts. He knew that, if he lived for ever, there could be no other girl in the world for him. With her at his side, what might he not do? He might get his handicap down to six – to three – to scratch – to plus something! Good heavens, why, even the Amateur Championship was not outside the range of possibility. Mortimer Sturgis shook his putter solemnly in the air, and vowed a silent vow that he would win this pearl among women.

Now, when a man feels like that, it is impossible to restrain him long. For a week Mortimer Sturgis's soul sizzled within him: then he could contain himself no longer. One night, at one of the informal dances at the hotel, he drew the girl out on to the moonlit terrace.

'Miss Somerset –' he began, stuttering with emotion like an imperfectly-corked bottle of ginger-beer. 'Miss Somerset – may I call you Mary?'

The girl looked at him with eyes that shone softly in the dim light.

'Mary?' she repeated. 'Why, of course, if you like –'

'If I like!' cried Mortimer. 'Don't you know that it is my dearest wish? Don't you know that I would rather be permitted to call you Mary than do the first hole at Muirfield in two? Oh, Mary, how I have longed for this moment! I love you! I love you! Ever since I met you I have known that you were the one girl in this vast world whom I would die to win! Mary, will you be mine? Shall we go round together? Will you fix up a match with me on the links of life which shall end only when the Grim Reaper lays us both a stymie?'

She drooped towards him.

'Mortimer!' she murmured.

He held out his arms, then drew back. His face had grown suddenly tense, and there were lines of pain about his mouth.

'Wait!' he said, in a strained voice. 'Mary, I love you dearly, and because I love you so dearly I cannot let you trust your sweet life to me blindly. I have a confession to make. I am not – I have not always been' – he paused – 'a good man,' he said, in a low voice.

She started indignantly.

'How can you say that? You are the best, the kindest, the bravest man I have ever met! Who but a good man would have risked his life to save me from drowning?'

'Drowning?' Mortimer's voice seemed perplexed. 'You? What do you mean?'

'Have you forgotten the time when I fell in the sea last week, and you jumped in with all your clothes on –'

'Of course, yes,' said Mortimer. 'I remember now. It was the day I did the long seventh in five. I got off a good tee-shot straight down the fairway, took a baffy for my second, and – But that is not the point. It is sweet and generous of you to think so highly of what was the merest commonplace act of ordinary politeness, but I must repeat, that judged by the standards of your snowy purity, I am not a good man. I do not come to you clean and spotless as a young girl should expect her husband to come to her. Once, playing in a foursome, my ball fell in some long grass. Nobody was near me. We had no caddies, and the others were on the fairway. God knows –' His voice shook. 'God knows I struggled against the temptation. But I fell. I kicked the ball on to a little bare mound, from which it was an easy task with a nice half-mashie to reach the green for a snappy seven. Mary, there have been times when, going round by myself, I have allowed myself ten-foot putts on three holes in succession, simply in order to be able to say I had done the course in under a hundred. Ah! you shrink from me! You are disgusted!'

'I'm not disgusted! And I don't shrink! I only shivered because it is rather cold.'

'Then you can love me in spite of my past?'

'Mortimer!'

She fell into his arms.

'My dearest,' he said presently, 'what a happy life ours will be. That is, if you do not find that you have made a mistake.'

'A mistake!' she cried, scornfully.

'Well, my handicap is twelve, you know, and not so darned twelve at that. There are days when I play my second from the fairway of the next hole but one, days when I couldn't putt into a coal-hole with "Welcome!" written over it. And you are a Ladies' Open Champion. Still, if you think it's all right – Oh, Mary, you little know how I have dreamed of some day marrying a really first-class golfer! Yes, that was my vision – of walking up the aisle with some sweet plus two girl on my arm. You shivered again. You are catching cold.'

'It is a little cold,' said the girl. She spoke in a small voice.

'Let me take you in, sweetheart,' said Mortimer. 'I'll just put you in a comfortable chair with a nice cup of coffee, and then I think I really must come out again and tramp about and think how perfectly splendid everything is.'

They were married a few weeks later, very quietly, in the little village church of Saint Brûle. The secretary of the local golf-club acted as best man for Mortimer, and a girl from the hotel was the only bridesmaid. The whole business was rather a disappointment to Mortimer, who had planned out a somewhat florid ceremony at St George's, Hanover Square, with the Vicar of Tooting (a scratch player excellent at short approach shots) officiating, and 'The Voice That Breathed O'er St Andrews' booming from the organ. He had even had the idea of copying the military wedding and escorting his bride out of the church under an arch of crossed cleeks. But she would have none of this pomp. She insisted on a quiet wedding, and for the honeymoon trip preferred a tour through Italy. Mortimer, who had wanted to go to Scotland to visit the birthplace of James Braid, yielded amiably, for he loved her dearly. But he did not think much of Italy. In Rome, the great monuments of the past left him cold. Of the Temples of Vespasian, all he thought was that it would be a devil of a place to be bunkered behind. The Colosseum aroused a faint spark of interest in him, as he speculated whether Abe Mitchell would use a full brassey to carry it. In Florence, the view over the Tuscan Hills from the Torre Rosa, Fiesole, over which his bride waxed enthusiastic, seemed to him merely a nasty bit of rough which would take a deal of getting out of.

And so, in the fullness of time, they came home to Mortimer's cosy little house adjoining the links.

Mortimer was so busy polishing his ninety-four clubs on the evening of their arrival that he failed to notice that his wife was preoccupied. A less busy man would have perceived at a glance that she was distinctly nervous. She started at sudden noises, and once, when he tried the newest of his mashie-niblicks and broke one of the drawing-room windows, she screamed sharply. In short her manner was strange, and, if Edgar Allan Poe had put her into 'The Fall of the House of Usher', she would have fitted it like the paper on the wall. She had the air of one waiting tensely for the approach of some imminent doom. Mortimer, humming gaily to himself as he sand-papered the blade of his twenty-second putter, observed nothing of this. He was thinking of the morrow's play.

'Your wrist's quite well again now, darling, isn't it?' he said.

'Yes. Yes, quite well.'

'Fine!' said Mortimer. 'We'll breakfast early – say at half-past seven – and then we'll be able to get in a couple of rounds before lunch. A couple more in the afternoon will about see us through. One doesn't want to over-golf oneself the first day.' He swung the putter joyfully. 'How had we better play do you think? We might start with you giving me a half.'

She did not speak. She was very pale. She clutched the arm of her chair tightly till the knuckles showed white under the skin.

To anybody but Mortimer her nervousness would have been even more obvious on the following morning, as they reached the first tee. Her eyes were dull and heavy, and she started when a grasshopper chirruped. But Mortimer was too occupied with thinking how jolly it was having the course to themselves to notice anything.

He scooped some sand out of the box, and took a ball out of her bag. His wedding present to her had been a brand-new golf-bag, six dozen balls, and a full set of the most expensive clubs, all born in Scotland.

'Do you like a high tee?' he asked.

'Oh, no,' she replied, coming with a start out of her thoughts. 'Doctors say it's indigestible.'

Mortimer laughed merrily.

'Deuced good!' he chuckled. 'Is that your own or did you read it in a comic paper? There you are!' He placed the ball on a little hill of sand, and got up. 'Now let's see some of that championship form of yours!'

She burst into tears.

'My darling!'

Mortimer ran to her and put his arms round her. She tried weakly to push him away.

'My angel! What is it?'

She sobbed brokenly. Then, with an effort, she spoke.

'Mortimer, I have deceived you!'

'Deceived me?'

'I have never played golf in my life! I don't even know how to hold the caddie!'

Mortimer's heart stood still. This sounded like the gibberings of an unbalanced mind, and no man likes his wife to begin gibbering immediately after the honey-moon.

'My precious! You are not yourself!'

'I am! That's the whole trouble! I'm myself and not the girl you thought I was!'

Mortimer stared at her, puzzled. He was thinking that it was a little difficult and that, to work it out properly, he would need a pencil and a bit of paper.

'My name is not Mary!'

'But you said it was.'

'I didn't. You asked if you could call me Mary, and I said you might, because I loved you too much to deny your smallest whim. I was going on to say that it wasn't my name, but you interrupted me.'

'Not Mary!' The horrid truth was coming home to Mortimer. 'You were not Mary Somerset?'

'Mary is my cousin. My name is Mabel.'

'But you said you had sprained your wrist playing in the championship.'

'So I had. The mallet slipped in my hand.'

'The mallet!' Mortimer clutched at his forehead. 'You didn't say "the mallet"?'

'Yes, Mortimer! The mallet!'

A faint blush of shame mantled her cheek, and into her blue eyes there came a look of pain, but she faced him bravely.

'I am the Ladies' Open Croquet Champion!' she whispered.

Mortimer Sturgis cried aloud, a cry that was like the shriek of some wounded animal.

'Croquet!' He gulped, and stared at her with unseeing eyes. He was no prude, but he had those decent prejudices of which no self-respecting man can wholly rid himself, however broad-minded he may try to be. 'Croquet!'

There was a long silence. The light breeze sang in the pines above them. The grasshoppers chirruped at their feet.

She began to speak again in a low, monotonous voice.

'I blame myself! I should have told you before, while there was yet time for you to withdraw. I should have confessed this to you that night on the terrace in the moonlight. But you swept me off my feet, and I was in your arms before I realized what you would think of me. It was only then that I understood what my supposed skill at golf meant to you, and then it was too late. I loved you too much to let you go! I could not bear the thought of you recoiling from me. Oh, I was mad – mad! I knew that I could not keep up the deception for ever, that you must find me out in time. But I had a wild hope that by then we should be so close to one another that you might find it in your heart to forgive. But I was wrong. I see it now. There are some things that no man can forgive. Some things,' she repeated, dully, 'which no man can forgive.'

She turned away. Mortimer awoke from his trance.

'Stop!' he cried. 'Don't go!'

'I must go.'

'I want to talk this over.'

She shook her head sadly and started to walk slowly across the sunlit grass. Mortimer watched her, his brain in a whirl of chaotic thoughts. She disappeared through the trees.

Mortimer sat down on the tee-box, and buried his face in his hands. For a time he could think of nothing but the cruel blow he had received. This was the end of those rainbow visions of himself and her going through life side by side, she lovingly criticizing his stance and his back-swing, he learning wisdom from her. A croquet-player! He was married to a woman who hit coloured balls through hoops. Mortimer Sturgis writhed in torment. A strong man's agony.

The mood passed. How long it had lasted, he did not know. But suddenly, as he sat there, he became once more aware of the glow of the sunshine and the singing of the birds. It was as if a shadow had lifted. Hope and optimism crept into his heart.

He loved her. He loved her still. She was part of him, and nothing that she could do had power to alter that. She had deceived him, yes. But why had she deceived him? Because she loved him so much that she could not bear to lose him. Dash it all, it was a bit of a compliment.

And, after all, poor girl, was it her fault? Was it not rather the fault of her upbringing? Probably she had been taught to play croquet when a mere child, hardly able to distinguish right from wrong. No steps had been taken to eradicate the virus from her system, and the thing had become chronic. Could she be blamed? Was she not more to be pitied than censured?

Mortimer rose to his feet, his heart swelling with generous forgiveness. The black horror had passed from him. The future seemed once more bright. It was not too late. She was still young, many years younger than he himself had been when he took up golf, and surely, if she put herself into the hands of a good specialist and practised every day, she might still hope to become a fair player. He reached the house and ran in, calling her name.

No answer came. He sped from room to room, but all were empty.

She had gone. The house was there. The furniture was there. The canary sang in its cage, the cook in the kitchen. The pictures still hung on the walls. But she had gone. Everything was at home except his wife.

Finally, propped up against the cup he had once won in a handicap competition, he saw a letter. With a sinking heart he tore open the envelope.

It was a pathetic, a tragic letter, the letter of a woman endeavouring to express all the anguish of a torn heart with one of those fountain-pens which suspend the flow of ink about twice in every three words. The gist of it was that she felt she had wronged him; that, though he might forgive, he could never forget; and that she was going away, away out into the world alone.

Mortimer sank into a chair, and stared blankly before him. She had scratched the match.

I am not a married man myself, so have had no experience of how it feels to have one's wife whiz off silently into the unknown; but I should imagine that it must be something like taking a full swing with a brassey and missing the ball. Something, I take it, of the same sense of mingled shock, chagrin, and the feeling that nobody loves one, which attacks a man in such circumstances, must come to the bereaved husband. And one can readily understand how terribly the incident must have shaken Mortimer Sturgis. I was away at the time, but I am told by those who saw him that his game went all to pieces.

He had never shown much indication of becoming anything in the nature of a first-class golfer, but he had managed to acquire one or two decent shots. His work with the light iron was not at all bad, and he was a fairly steady putter. But now, under the shadow of this tragedy, he dropped right back to the form of his earliest period. It was a pitiful sight to see this gaunt, haggard man with the look of dumb anguish behind his spectacles taking as many as three shots sometimes to get past the ladies' tee. His slice, of which he had almost cured himself, returned with such virulence that in the list of ordinary hazards he had now to include the tee-box. And, when he was not slicing, he was pulling. I have heard that he was known, when driving at the sixth, to get bunkered in his own caddie, who had taken up his position directly behind him. As for the deep sand-trap in front of the seventh green, he spent so much of his time in it that there was some informal talk among the members of the committee of charging him a small weekly rent.

A man of comfortable independent means, he lived during these days on next to nothing. Golf-balls cost him a certain amount, but the bulk of his income he spent in efforts to discover his wife's whereabouts. He advertised in all the papers. He employed private detectives. He even, much as it revolted his finer instincts, took to travelling about the country, watching croquet matches. But she was never among the players. I am not sure that he did not find a melancholy comfort in this, for it seemed to show that, whatever his wife might be and whatever she might be doing, she had not gone right under.

Summer passed. Autumn came and went. Winter arrived. The days grew bleak and chill, and an early fall of snow, heavier than had been known at that time of the year for a long while, put an end to golf. Mortimer spent his days indoors, staring gloomily through the window at the white mantle that covered the earth.

It was Christmas Eve.

The young man shifted uneasily on his seat. His face was long and sombre.

'All this is very depressing,' he said.

'These soul tragedies,' agreed the Oldest Member, 'are never very cheery.'

'Look here,' said the young man, firmly, 'tell me one thing frankly, as man to man. Did Mortimer find her dead in the snow, covered except for her face, on which still lingered that faint, sweet smile which he remembered so well? Because, if he did, I'm going home.'

'No, no,' protested the Oldest Member. 'Nothing of that kind.'

'You're sure? You aren't going to spring it on me suddenly?'

'No, no!'

The young man breathed a relieved sigh.

'It was your saying that about the white mantle covering the earth that made me suspicious.'

The Sage resumed.

It was Christmas Eve. All day the snow had been falling, and now it lay thick and deep over the countryside. Mortimer Sturgis, his frugal dinner concluded – what with losing his wife and not being able to get any golf, he had little appetite these days – was sitting in his drawing-room, moodily polishing the blade of his jigger. Soon wearying of this once congenial task, he laid down the club and went to the front door to see if there was any chance of a thaw. But no. It was freezing. The snow, as he tested it with his shoe, crackled crisply. The sky above was black and full of cold stars. It seemed to Mortimer that the sooner he packed up and went to the South of France, the better. He was just about to close the door, when suddenly he thought he heard his own name called.

'Mortimer!'

Had he been mistaken? The voice had sounded faint and far away.

'Mortimer!'

He thrilled from head to foot. This time there could be no mistake. It was the voice he knew so well, his wife's voice, and it had come from somewhere down near the garden-gate. It is difficult to judge distance where sounds are concerned, but Mortimer estimated that the voice had spoken about a short mashie-niblick and an easy putt from where he stood.

The next moment he was racing down the snow-covered path. And then his heart stood still. What was that dark something on the ground just inside the gate? He leaped towards it. He passed his hands over it. It was a human body. Quivering, he struck a match. It went out. He struck another. That went out, too. He struck a third, and it burnt with a steady flame; and, stooping, he saw that it was his wife who lay there, cold and stiff. Her eyes were closed, and on her face still lingered that faint, sweet smile which he remembered so well.

The young man rose with a set face. He reached for his golf-bag.

'I call that a dirty trick,' he said, 'after you promised –' The Sage waved him back to his seat.

'Have no fear!' She had only fainted.'

'You said she was cold.'

'Wouldn't you be cold if you were lying in the snow?'

'And stiff.'

'Mrs Sturgis was stiff because the train-service was bad, it being the holiday-season, and she had had to walk all the way from the junction, a distance of eight miles. Sit down and allow me to proceed.'

Tenderly, reverently, Mortimer Sturgis picked her up and began to bear her into the house. Half-way there, his foot slipped on a piece of ice and he fell heavily, barking his shin and shooting his lovely burden out on to the snow.

The fall brought her to. She opened her eyes.

'Mortimer, darling!' she said.

Mortimer had just been going to say something else, but he checked himself.

'Are you alive?' he asked.

'Yes,' she replied.

'Thank God!' said Mortimer, scooping some of the snow out of the back of his collar.

Together they went into the house, and into the drawing-room. Wife gazed at husband, husband at wife. There was a silence.

'Rotten weather!' said Mortimer.

'Yes, isn't it!'

The spell was broken. They fell into each other's arms. And presently they were sitting side by side on the sofa, holding hands, just as if that awful parting had been but a dream.

It was Mortimer who made the first reference to it.

'I say, you know,' he said, 'you oughtn't to have nipped away like that!'

'I thought you hated me!'

'Hated *you*! I love you better than life itself! I would sooner have smashed my pet driver than have had you leave me!'

She thrilled at the words.

'Darling!'

Mortimer fondled her hand.

'I was just coming back to tell you that I loved you still. I was going to suggest that you took lessons from some good professional. And I found you gone!'

'I wasn't worthy of you, Mortimer!'

'My angel!' He pressed his lips to her hair, and spoke solemnly. 'All this has taught me a lesson, dearest. I knew all along, and I know it more than ever now, that it is you – you that I want. Just you! I don't care if you don't play golf. I don't care –' He hesitated, then went on manfully. 'I don't care even if you play croquet, so long as you are with me!'

For a moment her face showed rapture that made it almost angelic. She uttered a low moan of ecstasy. She kissed him. Then she rose.

'Mortimer, look!'

'What at?'

'Me. Just look!'

The jigger which he had been polishing lay on a chair close by. She took it up. From the bowl of golf-balls on the mantelpiece she selected a brand new one. She placed it on the carpet. She addressed it. Then, with a merry cry of 'Fore!' she drove it hard and straight through the glass of the china-cupboard.

'Good God!' cried Mortimer, astounded. It had been a bird of a shot.

She turned to him, her whole face alight with that beautiful smile.

'When I left you, Mortie,' she said, 'I had but one aim in life, somehow to make myself worthy of you. I saw your advertisements in the papers, and I longed to answer them, but I was not ready. All this long, weary while I have been in the village of Auchtermuchtie, in Scotland, studying under Tamms McMickle.'

'Not the Tamms McMickle who finished fourth in the Open Championship of 1911, and had the best ball in the foursome in 1912 with Jock McHaggis, Andy McHeather, and Sandy McHoots!'

'Yes, Mortimer, the very same. Oh, it was difficult at first. I missed my mallet, and longed to steady the ball with my foot and use the toe of the club. Wherever there was a direction post I aimed at it automatically. But I conquered my weakness. I practised steadily. And now Mr McMickle says my handicap would be a good twenty-four on any links.' She smiled apologetically. 'Of course, that doesn't sound much to you! You were a twelve when I left you, and now I suppose you are down to eight or something.'

Mortimer shook his head.

'Alas, no!' he replied, gravely. 'My game went right off for some reason or other, and I'm twenty-four, too.'

'For some reason or other!' She uttered a cry. 'Oh, I know what the reason was! How can I ever forgive myself! I have ruined your game!'

The brightness came back to Mortimer's eyes. He embraced her fondly.

'Do not reproach yourself, dearest,' he murmured. 'It is the best thing that could have happened. From now on, we start level, two hearts that beat as one, two drivers that drive as one. I could not wish it otherwise. By George! It's just like that thing of Tennyson's.'

He recited the lines softly:

> *My bride,*
> *My wife, my life. Oh, we will walk the links*
> *Yoked in all exercise of noble end,*
> *And so thro' those dark bunkers off the course*
> *That no man knows. Indeed, I love thee: come,*
> *Yield thyself up: our handicaps are one;*
> *Accomplish thou my manhood and thyself;*
> *Lay thy sweet hands in mine and trust to me.*

She laid her hands in his.

'And now, Mortie, darling,' she said, 'I want to tell you all about how I did the long twelfth at Auchtermuchtie in one under bogey.'

From *The Golf Omnibus* by P. G. Wodehouse
(Barrie and Jenkins, London, 1973).

He overheard one guy say: 'I just got a new set of clubs for my wife.' The other replied: 'Now that's what I call a real good trade.'

Joe Chase, professional at Plantation Golf Club.

Golf Gamesmanship

Stephen Potter

The late Stephen Potter's *Gamesmanship* was one of the great humour books of the immediate post-war years. He then followed it up two decades later with the *Complete Golf Gamesmanship*, introducing yet more advanced psychological warfare techniques – the ploys and gambits which can sometimes displace skill with club and ball. Does gamesmanship exist at the top level of golf? Most certainly. There are some players who will murder your concentration with quips and chatter if you give them half a chance.

I.W.

The Swing

'Look out,' he said, just as Big Jim Dougan was about to drive. 'There's a fly on the ball. Stand back and start all over again.'

This ploy from an early gamesmanship school story may seem naïve yet it demonstrates well the truism that the first object of the gamesplay should be to break flow, and the second to introduce non-golf thoughts in the swing and the golfgame.

How many people realize that every part of the swing is associated with irrelevant and putting-off thoughts? It is these irrelevant thoughts, always latent, which the gamesman must try to bring to the surface, however buried and fleeting they may be.

Playing for Money

'What shall we play for?'
'You say.'

The man who says 'you say' is one up. It suggests that to play for half-a-crown would be amusing but that his ancestors, members of White's Club to a man, were equally prepared to stake an estate or a mistress on a game of shove-groat or 'Rock-i'-the-Ring'. Opponent is likely to suggest playing for something decidedly larger than is usual for him. May I tentatively suggest that for this occasion a new ploy I am provisionally calling 'To-him-that-hath-shall-be-givenmanship' may be tried? Let slip suggestions that there is wealth in your family. Say 'Have you got a car coming for you?' (suggesting chauffeur *milieu*) or 'Father has been asked to lend his Bernardino Taddi for next year's Quattrocento Italian exhibition at the R.A.' (picture worth £100,000). This will bring in the unbreakable rule of money play:

If stake is more than mother says
Ah then 'tis you it is who pays. *

The Drive

Of all the problems which face the golf gamesman, the problem of pure good play is the most difficult to fight. In particular, some of the best gamesmanship brains in America, many of them drained from England which drained them from Scotland, have been bent to the problem of how to be one-up on the man who hits the longer ball.

In normal circumstances it may be possible, for instance, to give advice to a man who is 2 or 3 up: but it is difficult indeed if he is outdriving you. A list of attempted ploys looks little better than a confession of failure. There is the driver from the head of which you unbutton a head cover marked with a large 'No. 4'. There is the remark, if your own drive of 150 yards happens just to have cleared the rough on the right, that 'position is the point here, not distance'.

Then there is the old ploy, first mentioned by me in 1947, of giving your Vast Distances man a caddy who never says 'good shot' but often points to a place, 30 yards ahead, which was reached by Byron Nelson when he played the course in 1946, or, better still, by J. H. Taylor, when he played there with a gutty in '98.

It is important to warn your female partner, in a foursome, especially if she is your wife, not to say 'Ooo' or give a little scream of female admiration. Tell her to say, 'Well, he got away with that one.'

The problem will be solved in time. Funds for our Long Ball Research Wing are welcome and needed. Meanwhile let me give one piece of general advice. Never, never comment on the fact that your opponent has got distance. Never say 'You certainly powdered that one'. Puzzled by your silence, long driver will try to outdistance himself until, inevitably, he ends up out of bounds.

But the important point to remember is that superiority in length is a myth, or is at any rate cancelled out by relativity. It depends on the standard of measurement. The man who is outdriven at Sandwich can always say 'when Sarazen won here he never used more than a 3 wood'. A following breeze may help you to make the 200 yard mark down wind at the 18th at St Andrew's. But if your opponent beats you by his usual fifteen yards it is usually safe to say:

'Amazing to think that in these conditions Nicklaus *reached the green* in all four rounds of the open.'

Safe unless you are up against a St Andrew's type gamesman who will probably say:

'Yes. I wonder what club he used from the tee. After all, two generations ago Blackwell reached the *steps leading up to the clubhouse* with a gutty.'

---

*My wife heard a celebrated version of this ploy when we were watching the pro–amateur at Seminole, Fla. There was a new young professional, Mike Souchak, under whose huge frame and footballer's feet the earth trembled. 1952 was a successful year for him on the circuit 'because he had learned to reduce the length of his drive'. We passed this on to Wiffley, J., (16) of our Club.

It might be added here that the inferior player should never, never in any way behave differently, let alone apologize, because he is inferior. In the days when I was genuinely young and had muscles like whipcord I used to drive nearly 210 yards on the downhill hole at Redhill. My father's best was 140 yards. As soon as he had struck one of these hundred-and-forty-yarders, he would stand back still gazing after the ball till it had stopped and then pace the distance, counting out loud, and ending in a crescendo 'a hundred and thirty-eight, *thirty-nine*, FORTY'.

It is worth noting here that if Long Handicap is playing Short – 14 playing 4, for instance – never must 14, if he wins, admit, recall, apologize, or refer in any way to the fact that he has received 8 strokes in the round; and it is most unusual to refer to this when telling the story to family, particularly wife.

Tickler, having won the Doverbridge Tea-tray playing off 16, used to like putting on the special Tea-tray tie, particularly when he was playing against men whom he had just beaten in this competition, men who had given him perhaps as much as nine strokes.

This situation and its handling shows yet once again the deep relationship between life and golf, of which life is so often the metaphor or mime.

Style

This is the place to say something not about the style of gamesmanship but the gamesmanship of style. A perfect, flowing, model style can be alarming to an opponent. The teaching of golf is not our domain: but the teaching of style comes very much into our orbit. An appearance of a strong effortless style, flowing yet built on a stable foundation, can be alarming to an opponent even if it has no effect on one's shots.

'Right, let's have a game then!' says Jeremy Cardew to comparative stranger after a dinner party.

'I haven't played for ages,' he goes on. Though in full evening dress, he may pluck a bamboo stick from a pot in the conservatory and begin to take a practice swing, left hand only.

'My, what a wide arc to that swing,' thinks Wiffley, who is already wondering if he, too, ought to have worn a white tie instead of a black. We recommend the suggestion of great width, on this back-swing, and long relaxed follow-through.

Above all we recommend practising a practice swing which ends with the body turned correctly square to the direction of the ball, the hands held high, an expression of easy confidence on the face, a touch of nobility, as if one were looking towards the setting sun. Students who find themselves unable even vaguely to simulate a graceful finish may do well by going to the opposite extreme. It is possible to let go of the club almost completely at the top of the swing, recover it, and by a sort of half-paralysed jerk come down again more or less normally. Opponent will find himself *forced to stare at you*, and may lose his rhythm.

Straight Left Arm: A Personal Confession

I am sometimes asked which, of all the gambits I have invented, do I personally find most useful. Here, exclusively and for the first time, let me reveal the answer to this question.

In *Lifemanship* it is either 'Yes, but not in the South' (when Man who has Actually Been There is holding forth as if he alone, therefore, had any right to speak about the subject). Or perhaps it is the use, in motoring, of 'Plaste's Placid Salutation' (recorded in *One-Upmanship*).

In golf I have no doubt. Described in *Gamesmanship*, it is for use against the man who is driving further and less erratically than yourself.

'I see how you're doing it,' you say, 'straight left arm at the moment of impact, isn't it? Do you mind if I stand just *here* and watch?'

In spite of the fact that the left arm is always straight at the moment of impact, this used to cause a pull in the old days. Now there is a well-developed counter. (Driver says, 'Do you mean like this?' and if drive is unsatisfactory takes out another ball and drives again as if first drive was for demonstration only. 'Now let's watch *your* arm,' he then says.) But I am still finding it useful.

Later History of the Frith-Morteroy

Long before gamesmanship was invented, competitors in any sport used to use game leg play – 'my leg is troubling me a little today'. Gamesmanship described its use in lawn tennis and produced the famous Frith-Morteroy counter – the pause, half-way through the second set, the grave smile, the reference to the 'ticker', and the 'I'm supposed not to hit the ball too hard'.

All this was almost immediately taken up by golfers, as we hoped it would be. Equally predictable was it that ripostes suitable for golf were found to the Morteroy counter. Indeed a splendid gamesfield was at once exposed and I was lucky enough to be within earshot of one match played between experts in this technique.

The venue was in the Isle of Mull, with its delicate colouring, dignified coast line, and views of Gaelic place names, superb fishing and a distant sight of nervy looking stags, for we always played golf in the stalking season.

The golf-course, at Tobermory, is 9 hole; it is typically Highland – i.e. equal in effort to the playing of 27 holes in Leeds Castle Park. Two or three holes involve driving across a vast valley or *druchaid*. In this foray I saw it was Seligmann against Saxe. So far as golf was concerned, Seligmann was better than Saxe, as one would expect from their handicaps, Seligmann being a clicketty-click 14 and Saxe a soft-centred 12.

Climbing up to the second tee to play up to the Hole o' Crest, Seligmann began to use his club as a stick. By the time he had reached the green he was limping. Saxe might at this point say:

'OK?'

'Yes – yes, perfect,' Seligmann replied: though a hundred yards further on he would give a curious sideways kick with his left leg.

'They tell me I've got to have this op,' Seligmann remarked to Saxe, who was taking no notice.

Thus was the scene set for the counter to Game Leg Play; and sure enough, at the top of the second hill Saxe said classically:

'Sorry, I've got to stand still for two seconds. Nothing to worry about.'

Seligmann kept his head.

'Yes, well,' he went on at once, 'as I was saying, the end of the hip bone fits into the socket or acetabulum. While we're waiting I'll draw it for you . . .'

At first Seligmann did well simply by taking no notice of Saxe's troubles – did well that is until yet another deer-stalking man joined our little party at Knock. This was Boyce, a red-hot 10, and it was he who, in our 4-ball, all against all, out Seligmanned Seligmann. Boyce had never held down a job for more than a year but Boyce had this remarkable pet subject, knowledge of medical terms. His study was full of pale blue piles of the *British Medical Journal*. He had Gray's *Anatomy* and the nineteenth-century edition of Stedman's *Medical Dictionary* which Tickler and Odoreida – both of them, rather surprisingly, part of Seligmann's circle – liked to look at because it was illustrated, rather thrilling if one was a layman, which speaking personally one wasn't.

I first noticed Boyce for his deft treatment of our (5) man Cardew, a bit of a hero at Old Soaking, who was having lessons from Campion, then the pro at Royal Hampton. 'How's it going?' Boyce asked him.

'Marvellous. Campion really gave me an *image*; for a bit I knew what hitting was all about.'

'Oo – I bet you did.'

'How do you mean?'

'I only mean that Campion plays every day and he's a man of *immense strength*. He can break your back, you know. That full professional swing puts a huge strain on the deep muscles of the back, especially the *transverso-spinalis* system with the – what's it called – *semispinalis capitis*?'

At Tobermory I remember that at the 4th, second time round, Seligmann, finding himself 3 down, was glad to get one back by holing a long putt.

'I say,' he said, 'somebody pick that ball out for me. Suddenly I can't stoop.'

He only vaguely knew Boyce, who was on to the situation like a knife. However Boyce said nothing.

On the next tee Seligmann reiterated his point by slowly sinking on to both knees to fix his peg into the hard ground.

'Afraid I shan't be getting any distance,' he said.

'You were always pretty short,' said Boyce.

'I can't turn my hip,' said Seligmann, smiling as if not complaining though in pain. He had never pivoted in his life. 'Maybe a slipped disc.'

'So *that's* turned up again, has it?' Boyce said. 'Probably it's just O.A.'

Seligmann didn't get it.

'Forgive me; it's just a technical term for Old Age. Anybody over the age of 45 suffers a slight disintegration of the bone structure and the joint mechanism. Splendid view.'

Round the corner below there was a huge chunk of sea, which was just beginning to roughen up.

'The wrinkled sea beneath him crawls,' said Saxe, always a bit of a quotesman.

'And there's a slight diminution of the intervertebral spaces,' Boyce continued as they walked to their respective drives. 'Staggering isn't it?' he went on, gazing out to sea. 'In the distance you can see McCoutinglass's Mouse-trap.'

'Criminy,' said Seligmann with his smile, but he was being out-gambited and he knew it. Boyce was well ahead, on the other side of the fairway.

'Your spine begins to SHUT UP LIKE A TELESCOPE,' Boyce called out in a high, cheerful, carrying voice, rather throaty. 'They call it the CONCERTINA EFFECT.' Seligmann looked round to see if anyone was listening. Boyce was pointing to an uninteresting rock which he said was called Coolie McCoulin's Collar-stud.

'No, actually,' Boyce went on quietly when they had to wait on the next tee. 'You're rather a marvel. Let me look at your spine. Very little kyphosis. Think of Lionel – on two sticks now.'

'Hooray,' said Seligmann: but he never played with Boyce again.

Boyce certainly did well with his medical knowledge. Three or four members of his Club – we all know who – began to suffer from hypochondria. It was said that Wiggs, now, never touched spirits before 10.30 a.m.

'Have you noticed?' Boyce would begin. 'Strang is developing quite a tremor of the right hand.'

'How do you mean?'

'I simply just mean it trembles slightly. Watch it when he's bending down to put his ball on the peg, first thing.'

Boyce went through six members of the Club in the same way. 'Look at that walk,' he would say. In the end he was bound to describe some hitherto unsuspected weakness of his opponent, or better still, create an imaginary one.

In the twenties the average age at Mid Surrey was high, and they knew it. There was said to be a Death Expectancy Chart above the Secretary's desk. I do know that in the doorway, only half hidden, was a hand ambulance in wickerwork for collecting coronaries in the summer months.

As our techniques get nearer to the ultimate margins of human character, as the psychologies merge with the psychoses, we may have to pass forwards towards, or perhaps we should say fall backwards on, one of the most questionable questions in Gamesmanship.

It is this: 'Do you yip?'

Readers are reminded that the word 'yip' was invented by T. D. Armour the great teacher of golf and a fine teacherman as well. I once watched him working his way through what I hope and believe was a very profitable morning's instruction near Palm Beach. Comfortably seated in a shady arbour, with a large glass at his elbow, he sat relaxed while pupil after pupil twisted and turned in the heat of the Florida sun.

Armour defines 'yips' as a 'brain spasm which impairs the short game.' 'Impairs' is a euphemism. Since Hogan has stepped down from the throne, thousands of spectators have suffered with him as he stands motionless over his putter unable to move it. The disease seems to affect men of highly strung and subtle temper who have practised an art too long or with too dedicated a concentration. There is our own Peter Alliss, with his putts; Dave Thomas with his short chips. Control of that complex joint, the elbow, seems to be lost. A great snooker player has been a victim, and a famous violinist.

No need to point out to the gamesman the uses to which these facts may be put, nor which of them to choose. No need – and on my part small desire. This is for a last resort only. There is even a possibility that during play any mention of yips, however indirect, may be banned at the next meeting of WOGG (World Organisation of Golfing Gamesmen). The necessity of some such law was made clear when H. Longhurst reported the case of the gamesman (if indeed the man deserves such a title) who revealed before a match that he did not suffer from yips himself but 'was a carrier'.

Complete Golf Gamesmanship by Stephen Potter
(William Heinemann, London, 1968).

It is a law of nature that everybody plays a hole badly when going through.

Bernard Darwin, *Playing the Like*
(Chapman and Hall, London, 1934).

Golf in a Dinner Jacket

Walter Hagen

Walter Hagen not only ended the American inferiority complex about golf by winning the British Open four times, starting in 1922, he also did a lot to create the British inferiority complex – only now coming to an end. More than that, Hagen was the playboy hero with style. Who else could turn up on the first tee after a night's revelling still dressed in his dinner jacket? Have tux – will drive.

I.W.

My tendency to stay up late at night was another little bit of business that bothered a few of my fellow golfers. I usually managed to get eight hours sleep, but there were a few times when I stepped up to tee off with an hour or less spent on my cool white pillow. Every athlete needs plenty of sleep and rest during strenuous competition. But few actually get it. This is particularly true of golfers in a championship tournament. I was able to get what I required because I knew I was going to need steady nerves and good physical co-ordination the next day. I never hurried. This goes for both on and off the golf course. People have written that I've no regard for time. I respect time highly and I try to make the most of it. There is just as much in saving time as there is in spending it properly. It fits the old Army gag about 'Hurry up and wait'. That's pretty much my idea. I don't hurry, therefore I'm not bothered with waiting.

From the minute I rose in the morning, I kept on an even keel until I reached the first tee. I got up in plenty of time to dress and breakfast leisurely and to arrive at the golf course just when I was due to play. There's a certain sort of rhythm in such a smoothed-out routine that carried over to my game . . . a rhythm that helped me avoid the jerky, gear-shifting movements which characterised the game of many easily upset or nervous golfers.

There were a few times when I stepped up to tee off with not even one hour of sleep. One such occasion has been narrated incorrectly so often that I'm going to set it straight. When I was president of the Pasadena Golf and Country Club at St Petersburg, Florida, we made it a point to have exhibition matches over every week-end and on holidays to interest the public in the home site possibilities of the place.

These exhibitions were bread-and-butter promotions for us and the main reason for building the course. This particular exhibition was scheduled for New Year's Day, at ten in the morning. My wife and I had been on a round-robin party on New

Year's Eve and had ended up at the home of Gene Elliott for breakfast. Gene's place was a good half-hour drive from the club. My chauffeur, James Randall, came in and reminded me of the exhibition match.

The sun had been up so long I'd no idea of the correct time. Checking my watch I found I had slightly less than thirty minutes to motor across to Pasadena. I arrived at the first tee wearing my dinner clothes and patent leather pumps. The few hundred people in the gallery thought that was great fun. I was sliding in all directions trying to tee off in those slippery-soled shoes and after several attempts I got my drive away. I gave the gallery the impression that I intended playing the entire match in those clothes. Then, after taking my second shot, I made my excuses and explained that I'd go into the clubhouse and dress for the game. Looking over the gallery I remarked that I thought a number of them hadn't been up too long, either. They laughed and agreed I had a lot of company.

In the clubhouse I changed to regular golf clothes and spiked shoes. Even then, for the next several holes, I noticed that the fairway was much more slippery than it had ever seemed the dozens of times I'd played it. I managed to keep my footing and balance and went on to win my match with a 68.

From *The Walter Hagen Story* by Walter Hagen
(William Heinemann, London, 1955).

The Wit and Wisdom of Sam Snead

Talk to the ball: 'This isn't going to hurt a bit.' I tell the ball under my breath: 'Sambo is just going to give you a nice little ride.'

Is that right? How long are decades nowadays?
(When told he had won tournaments in six different decades.)

The valleys are so narrow that the dogs just have to wag their tails up and down.
(On his Virginia birthplace in the mountains.)

Many a golf course and many a gambler would have eaten me up if I hadn't eaten them first by having a mean frame of mind.

No matter what happens, *never give up a hole*. In tossing in your cards after a bad beginning you also undermine your whole game, because to quit between tee and green is more habit-forming than drinking a high-ball before breakfast.
From *The Education of a Golfer*
(Cassell and Co., London, 1962).

Lay off for three weeks and then quit for good. (Advice to a pupil.)

You've got one problem. You stand too close to the ball – after you've hit it.
(Advice to a pupil.)

I'm only scared of three things – lightning, a side-hill putt, and Ben Hogan.

You're Supposed to Enjoy Golf – Even with a Pain

Peter Dobereiner

Whatever your handicap, whether it's 28 or plus 5 like mine, golf is what you make it. And yes, Peter Dobereiner, whose golf reports in the *Observer* give me a lot of amusement, is right – a pain or an ailment, real or imaginary, can aid your concentration because it can divert your mind from self-doubt and needless worries. When I won the world's first million-dollar cheque at Sun City in 1987, I had the most fearful stomach cramps – and they weren't imaginary!

I.W.

People take up golf for a variety of reasons, all of them more or less harmless. Ambitious business types sometimes turn to golf as another professional skill, like doing a fast-reading course or computer studies, and very useful it can be too, now that so many deals are negotiated on the course and birdie talk has become the *lingua franca* of the commercial world.

Doctors frequently prescribe golf for patients who are running to fat in sedentary occupations although the medical profession is by no means unanimous on the value of once-a-week golf. At least one medical report has branded golf as a killer in certain conditions and certainly for people of uncontrollably volatile temperament it is, as they say, contra-indicated. Tournament players are prone to backache and a lifetime of intensive golf sometimes results in a rounding of the shoulders, a natural consequence of a crouching posture and as much an occupational disease as the elongated arm of a fast bowler. The main condition associated with golfers, however, is chronic hypochondria. Many of them play better when they are suffering from some slight ailment and if they don't have one they invent it. It is an interesting delusion, arising I suppose from the need to have a ready-made excuse to hand in case of failure, although there is a school of thought which holds that an ailment makes a golfer swing more slowly and therefore better. Or perhaps a nagging pain, real or imaginary, prevents the mind from wandering into distracting areas of speculation about the prize money or how they are swinging the club. Whatever the reason, the history of famous golfing victories reads like a medical dictionary – Ben Hogan, limping heavily from the car crash which nearly ended his golf career, as he won the US Open in 1950; Ken Venturi in the last stages of exhaustion and supported by a doctor as he took the 1964 US Open; Doug Sanders with his foot gashed open after stepping barefoot on a piece of broken glass and yet spreadeagling the field in the Peniscola Open in 1962.

Bruce Devlin won the biggest prize of his or anyone else's career by lifting the record Carling first prize of 35,000 dollars when he was convalescing from a varicose vein operation. Many players do not sleep, or eat, properly during big events but neither fatigue nor hunger prevents them from winning. There are many more examples of invalid supermen; Billy Casper, the most successful golfer of them all, suffers from allergies so obscure that at one time he had to live on a diet of rattlesnake and buffalo steaks.

The favourite standby is bursitis, a condition related to housemaid's knee. When all else fails, and a golfer is enjoying apparently perfect health, he can usually rely on a few psychosomatic twinges of bursitis to boost his confidence. Golf must be the only sport in which the discerning punter is encouraged by the sight of his selection receiving a pain-killing injection or bandaging an inflamed wrist. For most of us the pressures of golf will never bear heavily enough to force us into the esoteric realms of beneficial disabilities. We can enjoy the game and good health at the same time. And I suppose that the commonest reason for taking up golf is not to make a fortune or to clinch deals, but simply because of its intrinsic appeal.

It looks like a pleasant game, specially for those who have grown too old for more athletic sports. And it looks easy. The ball is not moving; it sits there waiting to be hit and you can take as much time as you like over the hitting. The novice takes club in hand, addresses the ball and takes a swing at it. Nine times out of ten he misses by about a foot. Now is the chance, if he wants to escape an obsession which may well transform his whole life, for him to say 'What a bloody silly way of spending your weekend', cast the club aside and dismiss the subject of golf from his mind for ever.

Human nature, however, is a ruthless slave-driver. The would-be-golfer undergoes a bewildering sequence of emotions. Astonishment, embarrassment and frustration are submerged by determination. He tries again. And again. And again. By now the challenge is overpowering; he *must* hit that ball, his self-esteem is seriously threatened. It is absurd that a perfectly normal human being should be unable to hit a stationary ball which is fast turning into an enemy with an insolent sneer and hypnotic powers.

The novices' attitude, which started as faintly amused contempt and turned to blind anger, now changes again. He realizes that he is getting nowhere and if he is to keep his sanity he must approach the problem in a coldly rational manner. The ball is a doughty adversary, the trick is to match cunning with cunning. He takes the club back slowly, with as much care as approaching a sitting bluebottle with upraised fly-swot. The club descends, not very fast but with intense deliberation. There is a click, not unlike the sound which Hollywood would have us believe is made by John Wayne's clenched fist on a villain's jaw. The shock wave being absorbed by the shaft of the club is transmitted to the player as a sensuous tingle in the hands and forearms. And the ball, as it is picked up in flight by the wide-eyed gaze of the striker, is soaring straight and true into the far distance. At that moment a golfer is born. The memory of his first accidental good shot may have to sustain him through a tiresome period of learning. The pro makes him hold the club in a manner which is uncomfortable, unnatural and clearly ill-suited to the purpose. He hits a thousand shots that go scooting off along the ground to the left, or curl feebly into the right rough, or miss altogether with the head of the club burying itself into the ground behind the ball.

He learns the most complex set of rules known to sport, spends a small fortune on equipment and gives assurances about the religious persuasion of his ancestors in applying for membership of a club. All the while the memory of that one golden shot fortifies his ambition. And, in due course, there are other shots, raking drives, chips from 100 yards that run into the hole, miraculous recoveries from bush or bunker. There are plenty of bad ones as well but the glory of golf is that they are forgettable and forgotten.

It would be nice to be able to say of this type of novice that he takes up golf and lives happily ever after. Unfortunately, happiness is by no means automatic. Once a golfer is established in the game he should take stock of himself and decide exactly what it is about the game which he enjoys. There are several satisfactions from which to choose. The deepest joy is to improve and with sensible application and good instruction everyone can enjoy reducing his handicap. After a certain point, however, the graph of improvement which has been rising like a well-struck nine iron flattens out and the player must accept that unless he is prepared to devote an inordinate amount of time and energy to the game, his future progress will be considerably slower. We may live in hope that next time we shall find the secret: it is a harmless and indeed healthy delusion but most people have to work or raise families. Golf can claim only a small proportion of time; enough perhaps for a couple of games at weekends. If so, it is only sensible to take a rational view, spend the available time in playing for enjoyment and accepting improvements, if any, as extra bonuses.

In that case, with pleasure as the main aim, a distinction should be made. Some people like to wallop the ball. Fine. Let them wallop it. There are players who take four strokes at a short hole while their opponents take three but nevertheless enjoy the smug satisfaction of a moral victory at having got up with an eight iron while the lower-handicap opposition took a six iron. To such people three-putting is an irrelevance; length is all and golf is a trial of strength.

Another type of player gets his kicks from stylish golf. He is a perfectionist, more concerned with hitting good shots than effective ones. This attitude is normally a symptom of ambition, commonest among younger players who are working hard to improve. I must say I find it slightly tiresome when an opponent lays his ball stiff, three feet from the hole, with a full seven and slams his club down in anger because he hit the shot a bit thin.

But if scoring is what you enjoy then it is necessary to recognize the fact and adjust your attitude to this end. A correspondent, a retired engineer, who suffered a serious disability as the result of a car accident, wrote to me with details of his personal system which I consider is worthy of general application. He objectively assessed his own capacity with each club, on the modest basis of what he was confident of achieving rather than blue-moon exceptions. With this information he translated the card of his home course and set himself a new set of par figures.

As he put it, a beneficent committee had given him a number of handicap strokes to use as wisely as he could. The long par-fours, the most difficult holes to score in regulation figures, he made par-fives. On such a hole he could just about reach the green if he hit his best drive followed by his best fairway wood. The odds against hitting two such wonder shots in succession were fantastic. However, by making the hole a par five he could take an easy four wood off the tee and then an easy five iron. That left him with seventy yards to cover in three more strokes, a push-over. And he only needed to hit one of those shots better than usual, pitching close or sinking a good putt, and he had a personal birdie.

The psychological advantage of picking up shots on par instead of dropping them was considerable. Obviously you cannot use this system of setting yourself a target and playing to a plan and at the same time indulge in heroics of enormous hitting. The two approaches are not compatible.

When I received this letter I indulged in an orgy of self-criticism and analysed my motives on the course. I decided that what I had been trying to do was not only to birdie every hole but with technically perfect strokes. No one in the history of the game has ever come within a mile of achieving that sort of standard. I felt thoroughly absurd at my own vainglorious fantasies. Since then, however, I like to think that my ambitions have been trimmed to something nearer my capabilities and certainly I have enjoyed my golf more.

And that, after all, is what golf is all about. It may be a banality but it is all too often forgotten. Golf should not be a battle in the lifemanship war, or a virility test, or a social asset or an excuse in gambling, or a character-building hobby, or an excuse for not taking the family out on Sundays, although it may contain elements of all of them. Essentially it is for amusement only. If it is played in that spirit it can be the most rewarding and satisfying game of them all and its fascination will endure for a lifetime.

From *The Game with the Hole in it* by Peter Dobereiner
(Faber & Faber, London, 1970).

Celebrity Quips

I have always found it to be the hole in one.

> Groucho Marx, asked what he thought was the most difficult shot in golf.

Give me golf clubs, the fresh air and a beautiful partner and you can keep my golf clubs and the fresh air.   Jack Benny.

Golf is a funny game. It's done much for health, and at the same time has ruined people by robbing them of their peace of mind. Look at me: I'm the healthiest idiot in the world.   Bob Hope.

And the name that is synonymous with Ford – Fore!   Bob Hope.

I know I'm getting better at golf because I'm hitting fewer spectators.

    Gerald Ford, 1984.

Jack Lemmon has been in more bunkers than Eva Braun.   Phil Harris.

I would rather play Hamlet with no rehearsal than play golf on television.

    Jack Lemmon.

3

THE GREAT TRIUMVIRATE

Bernard Darwin

At the turn of the century people talked about the Great Triumvirate of golf – Vardon, J. H. Taylor and Braid – who from the mid-1890s till the outbreak of the First World War dominated golf as surely as the Big Three of Nicklaus, Palmer and Player did in the 1960s. Between the three of them they won sixteen British Opens.

I.W.

Harry Vardon

The greatest member of the Triumvirate – for a period in a class by himself – was Jersey-born Harry Vardon (1890–1937), one of seven sons of a gardener. Harry's brother Tom was also a pro. Like many great golfers of that (and this) era, he started as a caddie, only seven years old at the time. Vardon won the British Open a record six times, in 1896, 1898, 1899, 1903, 1911 and 1914. He won the US Open in 1900 when he also went on a 20,000-mile tour of the USA playing exhibition matches to popularize the game there. In those pre-aviation days the strain of all that travel helped contribute to his breakdown in health from TB, causing him to spend many months in a sanatorium. He came back to go on winning and only lost the US Open in 1913 after a tie with the then unknown American amateur Francis Ouimet.

He is credited with the invention of the Vardon overlapping grip, now almost universal. Here is the first of three pieces on the Big Three of yesteryear by Bernard Darwin, grandson of the great Charles Darwin of Evolution fame; he was, as the anonymous golf correspondent of *The Times* for many years, still just about the most famous golf writer of his day.

I.W.

In the case of each of the other heroes of the past of whom I have tried to write it is easy to say in effect that he was in his day a great golfer and to leave it at that. In the case of Harry Vardon it is not easy to resist comparisons.

When he was in his prime, the question was constantly debated whether or not he was better than the now almost mythical young Tommy Morris had been. To-day people will insist on wondering how he compares with Bobby Jones. Such comparisons are tempting, but essentially futile, and I am going resolutely to resist them. But this much I will say: I cannot believe that anyone ever had or ever will have a greater genius for hitting a golf ball than Harry Vardon.

Courses and clubs and balls change; it is of no use to compare his scores with those either of his predecessors or his successors. But with anyone who ever saw him at the zenith of his game that impression of supreme genius will abide.

What is, in a few words, the general belief to-day about Vardon? I should say it was this, that he was a grand player up to the green and a very bad one when he got there. That belief is, I venture to say as regards the second part of it, false.

Until his illness, now thirty years ago or more, Vardon was not a bad putter. He was not in the class of great putters such as Hagen or Bobby Jones. He lost on the green something of that air of supreme grace which distinguished the rest of his game.

He did not make putting look absurdly or hopelessly easy, but he was a really good approach putter and at least a perfectly competent holer-out.

He gave himself probably less putting to do than any other man, and he did it something more than adequately. As one very small illustration, I remember going to Ganton and seeing Vardon play for the first time, soon after he had won his first championship. I talked to a good local amateur, who played with him constantly, and the point that he emphasized then was not Vardon's wonderful wooden club play up to the pin nor his mastery of all irons, but his relentlessly good putting.

Possibly the amateur had suffered from some particularly long putts and exaggerated a little, but I am quite sure I have not invented what he said.

After his serious breakdown in health, Vardon admittedly became a misser of short putts. He remained a sound approach putter, but there used to attack him some curious 'jump' in hand or wrist which made him stab at the short ones more quickly than he meant. It not unnaturally got on his nerves, and he became capable of putting very badly indeed, but this had not been so in his prime. Indeed, how could a man have beaten the heads off everybody in the way that Vardon did and yet have been the deplorable putter than he has been painted? The supposition refutes itself.

Vardon's greatest golf was undoubtedly played with the gutty ball – the ball he has never ceased to regret. He was a magnificent wooden club player with a unique power – due in some degree to his upright swing – of hitting the ball high and clean from almost any sort of lie. The brassy was not almost atrophied as it is to-day, in the times of the gutty, and it was Vardon's brassy shots that broke the hearts and backs of his competitors.

He was very long, so that he could reach in two wooden club shots holes at which most other people needed two and a chip. He was so accurate with those high-floating, quick-stopping brassy shots that he would put the ball as near the hole in two as his toiling, sweating adversaries would put theirs with their third, the chip. What hope was there against such a man? In truth, in his great years, nobody had any real hope.

'I played my game, sir, I played my game,' said Taylor after a memorable match at Newcastle in Ireland, and so no doubt he had, but Vardon had beaten him 13 up and 12 to play.

Vardon was certainly as good an iron player as any other of his contemporaries, and I do not exclude J. H. Taylor. At one time he was hideously long with a driving mashie and could use it at anyone else's brassy range, but it was not the length of his iron but its accuracy that was so devastating. He was as good with a short mashie pitch as he was with his famous push-shot with the cleek, and no man ever played iron shots more prettily. He merely shaved the turf and did not take cruel divots out of it.

Everybody has agreed from his first appearance as to the beauty of his iron play, but it is odd to remember now that by no means everybody admired his style with wooden clubs. It was so exceedingly unlike the big, sweeping St Andrews swing which had been deemed almost necessary to salvation; it had such a perceptible 'lift' in it, the club went up so straight, that at first there were cavilling critics.

It certainly seemed to me very strange and heterodox when I saw it. Perhaps it was something of an acquired taste, in that, at first, one looked at the things that did not matter and so did not perceive the perfectly beautiful rhythm which was so much more important.

The more triumphant Vardon became, the more utterly he routed his rivals, the more his style became admired. The overlapping grip was not exclusively his own, for Taylor had found it out for himself at Westward Ho, and Mr Laidlay had used it years before either of them. But it was Vardon that made it popular, and, when he was making victorious progresses up and down the country, 'Have you tried the Vardon grip?' was almost as common a greeting amongst golfers as 'Good morning.'

In the end, Vardon won our Open Championship six times, as compared with the five apiece of Braid and Taylor, but it is not unfair to the others to suggest that but for his illness, his total would have been considerably higher. People to-day are apt to forget how completely for a time he dominated the golfing world. Perhaps I had better very briefly set out his record.

He was born in Jersey in 1870, and when he was about twenty-five he became professional at a good inland course at Ganton in Yorkshire. In 1895 some of the leading professionals were bidden to play in a tournament at Pau in France. Somebody knew something and Vardon was included in the party. He did well and the golfing world began to say, 'Who is this Vardon? He seems a good player.'

In 1896 he came into his kingdom. Taylor was then king of the castle, having won the championship two years running. He went to play Vardon at Ganton and came away heavily beaten, declaring that this conqueror was a great player. The Open Championship at Muirfield proved it. Taylor and Vardon tied, and on the play-off Vardon won by four strokes. He was now, of course, one of the elect, but his most dominating time had not yet come.

In 1897 he did nothing very notable in the championship which was won by Harold Hilton. Then came the overwhelming years. In 1898 he won again, just beating Willie Park at Prestwick. Park challenged him to their historic seventy-two-hole match – North Berwick and Ganton – and Vardon made mincemeat of him. In 1899 at Sandwich nobody so much as dreamed of anyone else being champion, and he won, easing up, almost as he liked.

And during all those two years, he was winning nearly all the other tournaments there were to win and murdering his enemies in exhibition matches. He made a triumphant tour through Scotland, and that dour country had to admit that England had the best of it. His play was as Andrew Kirkaldy said, 'Enough to break the heart of an iron horse.' The only way in which Vardon could be beaten was by the better ball of two of the very best amateurs, Mr Laidlay and Mr Balfour-Melville at St Andrews, and St Andrews was never Vardon's course.

Next came his first triumphal tour through America and his winning of the Open Championship there. It was an amazing programme alike in the hard work it involved and the almost unbroken success of his play. There is, I take it, no doubt that he gave a wonderful stimulus to golf throughout the United States, and there is very little doubt that he left just a little of the fine edge of his game behind him there. Great as he was for years afterwards, he was never again – and this is, I think, his own opinion – quite the same player, never again quite so conquering and untiring and confident.

There were splendid things, of course, yet to come. In 1903 he won the Open

Championship at Prestwick and won it easily, although he was so 'done' in the last round that he several times thought he would be unable to finish. In 1905, with Taylor as his partner, he administered a fearful drubbing to Braid and Herd in a foursome match over fast greens. He played superbly, but he was wholly unfit for such a strain. Serious illness had him in its grip and soon he was in a sanatorium. He recovered, but it was some time before his golf recovered.

It was not till 1911 that he came back to something very like his greatest game, when he won the championship again after a tie with Massy. Finer wooden club play has never been seen than his on the play-off of that tie, and he played Massy to a standstill; the Frenchman gave up on the thirty-fifth green.

In 1913 there was another historic play-off and Mr Ouimet's victory at The Country Club, and then in 1914 Vardon won his sixth and last British championship at Prestwick. He and Taylor were leading the field with the last day to come and they were drawn together. Never was there so near an approach to pandemonium on a golf-course, and it was truly astonishing that the two men could play as they did. After that came the war years, and, when they were over, Vardon's championships were over too. He remained for a long time, and remains now, a model for all golfers, a true aesthetic joy to watch, the old master of old masters, but as far as championships go, time has won the match.

Harry Vardon has kept not all his old untiring energy, but all his old enthusiasm for golf. He loves playing it and teaching it and watching it. He is not given to saying very much, but very little escapes his eye and he is an acute and stern critic. While he is always ready to help young players, he is essentially a praiser of the time that is gone. He has never ceased to regret the coming of the rubber core and the passing of the gutty. He liked the old ball, which required clean and perfect hitting; he dislikes the new one, which he thinks enables many an imperfect hitter 'to get away with it.'

Neither is he in favour of some modern doctrines. He says he is constantly having to cure patients who have been ruined by the 'stiff left arm.' Who shall blame him if he is inclined to look back at the end of the nineteenth century as the golden age of golf? At any rate golf was a great game then, and how he could play it with the gutty!

From *Playing the Like* by Bernard Darwin
(Chapman and Hall, London, 1934).

J. H. Taylor

John Henry Taylor (1871–1963) won the British Open five times, in 1894, 1895, 1900, 1909 and 1913. He was also runner-up six times. A leading light in the founding of the PGA in 1901, he did much to boost the professionals' lot. He was renowned for his play with the mid-iron – the mashie, or what is now the 5 iron – a club which he virtually invented. He was professional at Burnham and Winchester but his name will forever be associated with Royal Mid Surrey from 1899 until his retirement.

I.W.

No greater or more characteristic figure has ever appeared in the ranks of professional golf than John Henry Taylor.

He was a very great golfer indeed; he won five Open Championships and was second so often that his record for consistency is unique. He is still a very, very good golfer, but he is first of all a man of character. Whatever walk of life he had chosen, it is safe to say that he would have made his mark in it, for he possesses in a remarkable degree enthusiasm, imagination, resolution.

When he had emerged from the caddie stage to that of working on the greens at Westward Ho! he wanted, I believe, to be, in turn, first a soldier and then a sailor, and by a curious irony was rejected for some defect of eyesight. What he would have done in either of those professions it is impossible to say, since peace-time in his young days gave no great opportunity of rising from the ranks, but it is certain that everyone who served him would have remembered him.

He is, as far as I know, a conservative in politics; if his life had been cast in other ways, he might have been a trade union leader who swayed crowds by his fierce oratory, for he is a natural speaker. I have often heard him speak and always well, but there is one little speech of his in particular that I recall. It was when his eldest son, J. H., junior, was on the Oxford Golf Team and he, together with some other fathers, came to the dinner after the university match. He spoke very shortly and simply and I do not remember exactly what he said, except that he thanked people for being kind to his boy, but it will always stick in my head as one of the best and most moving speeches I ever heard.

Because he was born by a famous golf-course and had a natural genius for the game, J. H. became a professional golfer and, being so, he has now inevitably become the leader of his profession, respected by everybody, *the* man who instantly comes to mind when there is needed someone to represent professional golf, to express its views or to negotiate on its behalf.

He has not only played hard but worked hard. He has for many years been the professional (he is now an honorary member) at the Royal Mid Surrey Club at Richmond, where there are probably more rounds played in the year than on any other course except St Andrews. He has in addition a flourishing club-making factory unconnected with that club, and he has done a good deal of work as a golf architect. Yet he has found time to take interest in many things and to read many books, and, I believe, his favourite book is Boswell's *Life of Johnson*.

It strikes me as eminently characteristic of J. H. that of the illustrious four – Vardon, Braid, Taylor and Herd – he has been the first to give up playing in championships. No one of the four was keener or perhaps so keen as he was; no one of them took the game so much to heart. I am sure that he hated giving up, and as long as he played he played with all his fiery might, because he was incapable of doing anything else.

Yet, once he made up his mind that the years had become too much for him, he would have no lagging superfluous on the stage, no playing 'just for fun'; he stopped there and then and he had his reward in that the game no longer tortures him, and he is as happy as can be looking on and encouraging the younger ones. When at last he saw a Briton win our Open Championship again, I thought he would explode with happiness.

I use the words 'tortures' and 'explode' deliberately, because they are appropriate to Taylor's temperament. I do not believe that anyone, not even the great Bobby himself, suffered more over championships than he did. Like Bobby, he had great control and might appear outwardly cold, but the flames leaped up within. Vardon had a naturally gay courage, Braid a dour and stoical calm. J. H. was a man on wires, having to choke down his temper and often suffering agonies.

Now and again perhaps he could not wholly master himself. Then he would say with that shake of his head which everyone knows so well, 'He didn't beat me, sir, I beat myself, I beat myself.' On the other hand, if he had a bad time and got over it, he was neither to hold nor to bind, there was no stopping him then.

I remember one championship at Deal in 1909. He had been playing superbly in practice, but for the first nine holes or so everything went wrong. The score was piling up horribly, he was palpably at the boiling point, and I felt in watching him that not for a hundred pounds would I dare speak to him. Then on about the ninth or tenth green he holed a good putt for a three and from that moment his cares dropped from him; he came home in one long-drawn-out burst of inspiration, and remained inspired for the rest of the championship, which we won easily. It is a maxim of his that the only way to win a championship is to win it easily, and he has lived up to it, for at least three times out of his five he won by large margins.

There can hardly be a doubt that his best win of all was his fifth and last at Hoylake in 1913, and it had an even more touch-and-go start than did the one I have just mentioned at Deal. He made terribly hard work of it in the qualifying rounds and was in the gravest danger. At long last he seemed in the haven of safety, for he had only to do a five at the last hole to qualify; he had hit a fine drive and had a straightforward iron shot for the green. He half hit it, was caught in the cross-bunker, got out too far and finally had to hole a putt of fully six feet to save his neck. Down it went and those who knew him exclaimed in chorus, 'It would be just like J. H. to win the whole thing now.'

'Win' proved a most inadequate word, for he ended eight strokes ahead of Ray, who was second, and his total of 304 in sheets of rain and a tearing wind will always remain one of the outstanding feats in our championship. How he did stick his chin out and pull his cap down over his nose and bang that ball right through the gale! It was the greatest of all golfing victories of man over nature.

Taylor was always at his best on such a day of tempest as that was, not merely on account of his pugnacious turn of mind, but because of his methods. 'Flat-footed golf, sir, flat-footed golf.' Thus I have heard him several times proclaim his faith, and no man ever lived up to it better. He was as firm as a rock, as if his feet were positively entrenched, and his swing was a marvel of compactness with his elbows close in to his body throughout. It needed a strong man to play in this style and he was and is a very strong man.

No doubt he could have hit the ball farther with something more of freedom – his club never came through very far after the ball and he seemed to punch it away with a little grunt rather than swing it away with lazy grace as did Harry Vardon. It was, however, his natural method, and, if he lost something in power, he was a miracle of accuracy. The old joke that the only hazards for him were the guide-flags was well justified.

Taylor's reputation has always been that of a supreme mashie player up to the pin. He was, to be sure, extraordinarily good and accurate, and was a master of the low flying shot with backspin when the art of backspin was not perhaps so generally understood as it is now. Yet he was no better a player of this shot than was Harry Vardon; indeed, I incline to think Vardon was the better of the two.

To my mind his undeviating accuracy in full shots, whether from the tee or up to the pin, has been every bit as big an asset to him as his pitching. In the days of the gutty, when there was far more brassy play than to-day, his wooden club shots, played right up to the flag, came as something of a revelation. He was likewise a magnificent player with the cleek, and, once he is within reach of the green, he is almost as accurate now though not quite so long, as ever he was.

As a putter he was eminently sound without being brilliant. He was not in the class of great putters with, let us say, Bobby Jones or Hagen; he did not hole a great many long putts, but he could be relied on to lay the ball dead and he did not miss it when it was dead. Vardon and Braid had their bad days on the green; Taylor was always there or thereabouts.

Finally, in J. H. and his illustrious contemporaries we have to salute men who raised the whole status of their profession in their own country. When they first made their appearance, the professional golfer here was apt to be a rather shiftless, feckless person – a pleasant enough fellow, but living from hand to mouth and not always to be relied upon. That he is to-day a respected and self-respecting, prosperous member of society is largely due to the generation of professionals which arose in the early nineties with J. H. as their natural born leader.

From *Playing the Like* by Bernard Darwin
(Chapman and Hall, London, 1934).

James Braid

James Braid (1870–1950) won the British Open five times, in 1901, 1905, 1906, 1908 and 1910. Renowned for the 'divine fury' of his drives, he was not always a long-hitter. 'It was as if I went to bed a short-driver one night and got up a long-driver in the morning . . . the greatest golfing mystery I have ever come across,' he once recalled. Professional at Walton Heath for forty-five years, he was also a golf architect of repute, designing or restyling Gleneagles, Carnoustie, Royal Blackheath and Forfar among other courses.

I.W.

It has been said of some celebrated person – perhaps of several of them – that nobody could be so wise as So-and-so looks. As regards golfers, I feel inclined to transpose the aphorism and say that nobody could look so wise as James Braid is. There is nobody whose every word and action is so redolent of sagacity. He has a great twinkle of humour, too, humour such as the Scots call 'pawky,' and many other admirable qualities, but one thinks of him first and foremost as a man of extraordinarily cool, wise judgment.

Certainly no man ever played golf with a cooler head, though I have heard him say that he liked to feel just a wee bit nervous before starting. Oddly enough, he combined with this quality a power of hitting at the ball with an almost reckless abandon as if he meant to kill it. He would march along the course with a long, slow, almost sleepy stride, and then, when he came to the ball, he would lash at it with what Mr Horace Hutchinson well called a 'divine fury'; and indeed, though one must write of his triumphs in the past tense, he can still do so.

He was a superb iron player, famous especially with the now departed cleek, a master of every kind of running shot, and though not naturally a good putter, he made himself for one period of his career almost a great one. A better player out of difficulties I am sure was never seen, for not only could he by pure strength remove tons of sand and acres of heather, but he was as skilful and resourceful as he was strong. In fact at his best, he was almost impregnably armed at all points, but it was his driving that delighted people when he first appeared, and it is still his driving, more especially against the wind, that they remember best. It was at once so appalling in its ferocity, so rhythmical in its majesty.

Braid may almost be said to have inherited long-driving, since he was a cousin of Douglas Rolland who came, like him, from Elie in Fife, and was the legendary long-driver of the eighties and early nineties. He himself has given to the world the mysterious piece of natural history that he went to bed one night a short-driver and woke up next morning a long one. We must take his word for it, but I never heard of anyone who remembered him as a short-driver, and he assuredly was a long one, when, with something of the suddenness of a meteor, he flashed upon the golfing world about 1895.

Everybody thinks of him now as one of the famous three – Braid, Vardon and Taylor, who were known as the 'triumvirate' and for years almost monopolized the Open Championship. But we are apt to forget that in point of fame though not of age (he was born in 1870), he began a little later than they did. He started life as a joiner, first at Elie, then at St Andrews and at Edinburgh, and was working at his trade while Vardon and Taylor were already budding professionals. Braid's own desire was always for golf, but his family thought nothing of it as a career and so he worked away as a joiner and played his golf when he had time as an amateur, and a very good amateur, too, at St Andrews or on the Braid Hills course, near Edinburgh.

It was almost at the end of 1893, the year before Taylor won his first championship, that Braid crossed the Rubicon and became a club-maker. The manner of his doing so was rather odd. A friend of his, C. R. Smith, was a club-maker at the Army and Navy Stores in London. He wanted help and offered Braid the job, and Braid accepted it, though he had never in all his life made a club. His trade had taught him, however, all about the use of tools, and he had golf in his blood, so all was well.

Even so, he had very little time for playing, and I well remember, when I was an undergraduate at Cambridge, hearing rumours that there was a wonderful golfer (name to me unknown) at the Stores, who would do terrific things if he could only get the chance.

The chance was bound to come and it actually came in 1895, in the form of an exhibition match which somebody got up between Braid and Taylor, then reigning champion, on a suburban course. After a great struggle the match was halved, the newcomer's fame was established straightway, and he became not only a regular professional, but one of those at the top of the tree.

Braid was second in the championship of 1897, beaten by Mr Hilton by a single stroke, but he did not win till 1901 (at Muirfield), the last year before the coming of the rubber-cored ball. It always seemed strange that of his five championships, Braid won only one with the gutty ball, for there was surely no one better calculated to fog that comparatively unresponsive and stony-hearted ball. I remember that a good many years after the coming of the Haskell there was staged an exhibition between Vardon, Taylor, Braid and Duncan in which one side played with the gutty and one with the rubber core. Braid's play with the gutty that day was something to remember, and one had the impression that if that ball could be restored, there would never be any other champion but he.

How, then, was it that he did not really come into his kingdom till the rubber core was established? I think the answer can be given in a single word – putting. Braid's putting was for several years almost the despair of his supporters. I recollect that the first time I ever saw him was in the late nineties, when I went down with a friend to Romford to match our best ball against his. Up to the green he was overpowering, but I am almost sure we won one round because of those putts, and Braid remarked, more in sorrow than in anger, that he had putted 'like an auld sweetie wife.'

In those days he putted with a cleek and had a great deal of that 'knuckling' movement of the knees, as it was called, which then marked the caddie-bred putter. It tended to a movement of the body and a pushing out of the ball and had nothing whatever to recommend it. Braid toiled away at his putting with but varying success, and I think it was when he got to Walton Heath and played with that fine putter, Mr Herbert Fowler, that he really improved. He took to an aluminium club, he curbed that 'knuckling' and developed a smooth movement with a noticeably slow take-back of the club.

Putting never looked as if it came quite naturally and easily to him, but – artificial or no – he undoubtedly became a highly effective putter and, if he remained just a little vulnerable over the short ones, he holed the most inordinate number of middle length and downright long ones. The putts won championships for him, and once he started he did win them with a vengeance.

I said he won in 1901. In 1904, for the third time in his career, he had a putt to tie and did not hole it. Then at St Andrews in 1905 he won for the second time, despite some desperate adventures at both the fifteenth and sixteenth holes, where he put his ball on the railway line (not then out of bounds) and had to batter it back to the course from amongst metals and sleepers. Now that he was fairly started he won again in 1906, 1908 and 1910.

At the same time he made a not infrequent practice of winning the *News of the World*, the unofficial match-play championship, and it may be said that from 1905 to 1910 he ruled the roost. Of all his wins that in 1908 at Prestwick was the most impressive. Not only did he hole the four rounds in 291 – magnificent scoring – and win by eight clear strokes, but in the third round he took eight to the third hole, the dreaded Cardinal.

Never shall I forget the ghastly silence that reigned as he tried to get out of the big bunker with his mashie and twice in succession the ball glanced off the boarded face and went out of bounds into the burn. Neither shall I forget, when at last he got clear, the utter impassivity alike of countenance and of gait with which he advanced towards the green. Those that awaited him there had not a guess that anything untoward had happened.

It was much argued at the time whether first of all Braid ought to have played short of the big bunker, and second whether he ought to have been content to get out and no more with his niblick. Perhaps he ought, but despite all his coolness and dourness Braid was always a bold player and went out unhesitatingly for the big shot. Sometimes he got into trouble, for he had not quite the machine-like accuracy of Vardon and Taylor and could at rare intervals hit a devastating hook. In a sense one of the greatest compliments I ever heard paid him was by an illustrious contemporary, who said that he ought to have won more than he did and that the hook was responsible.

Well, he won a very great deal and, moreover, there never was such a recoverer. A friend of mine once took a charming lady to Walton Heath to play a foursome with Braid as her partner. At hole after hole she toppled the ball off the tee into heather and Braid with terrific blows of the niblick put her ball far down the course. At last came a lie too much even for him. He removed the greater part of a young tree, but the ball moved only a few yards – nobody else could have moved it at all. Then said the lady with a sweet smile, 'Oh, Mr Braid, I am glad to see that even you can make a mistake sometimes!'

After 1910 Braid won no more championships, partly, I think, because his eyesight troubled him, but he remained a great player not only up to the war but after it. He reached the final of the *News of the World* Tournament when well on in his fifties, and even to-day, when he accepts the inevitable gliding of the years with entire placidity, he is perfectly capable of a sixty-nine or so in a friendly round at Walton Heath. At that noble course he has now been the professional for some thirty years, and reigns there an undisturbed monarch.

If all monarchs had been as sage and suave, as imperturbable and as far-seeing as he is, what a lot of crowned heads there would be in the world to-day! He has done much work as a golfing architect, and, though the kindliest of men, is rather ruthless in the matter of bunkers. His old friend, J. H. Taylor, once got into one of Braid's creations at Prestwick and remarked that the man who made that bunker ought to be buried in it with a niblick through his heart.

Alone of our great professionals, Braid has never visited the United States, having, I believe, a well-grounded apprehension of sea voyages. I am afraid he never will now, and if it is his loss it is also America's. Every American golfer who comes here should make a pilgrimage to Walton Heath to see this monument of a man.

From *Playing the Like* by Bernard Darwin
(Chapman and Hall, London, 1934).

Sam Snead's legendary career spanned five decades. Here he gets in some practice at Wentworth for the 1956 Canadian Cup watched by 12-year-old son Jackie. (*Keystone Collection*)

Harry Vardon did not believe in the straight left arm, and with the cumbersome jackets worn in those days it must have been difficult to achieve. But his results spoke for themselves. (*Keystone Collection*)

James Braid is well-jacketed, as was the custom of the day. Braid drives off at Walton Heath in the professional golfers' tournament in 1927. (*The Photo Source*)

At 86, J. H. Taylor had lost none of his appetite for demonstrating the game. On the extreme left, George Duncan, and next to him, the Open Champion Alf Padgham. (*Keystone Collection*)

Walter Hagen, otherwise known as 'the Haig', four times winner of the British Open, twice winner of the US Open and five times winner of the USPGA. The flamboyant Haig dominated professional golf after the First World War. (*Topham Picture Library*)

Bobby Jones, majestic, graceful, the true amateur, here drives off in the Walker Cup at Sandwich. (*The Photo Source*)

Ben Hogan survived a near-fatal car crash and came back greater than ever to win his only British Open at Carnoustie where he is pictured driving at the second tee. (*The Photo Source*)

Henry Cotton in 1985.
(*Peter Dazeley*)

Cotton in his younger years
(this is a 1938 picture) was
ruggedly handsome. Ian
Fleming said he was the
physical prototype for James
Bond. (*Popperfoto*)

Henry Longhurst as commentator. 'He looks like W.C. Fields in drag. But he happens to be the best in the business,' said a CBS producer. *Below:* The tricky 16th at Augusta. The hole that Henry made his own as a commentator. (*Peter Dazeley*)

4

THE IMMORTAL BOBBY AND THE INDOMITABLE BEN

Bobby Jones

Bernard Darwin

Nerves are an inseparable part of golf at the top level. Without them you are nothing and with them you are nothing until you learn to play through them. Nobody had a more nervous temperament than Bobby Jones, one of the truly heroic figures of the game from the Golden Age of golf in the 1920s – four times winner of the US Open and three times winner of the British Open, the last in 1930. That was his greatest year when he brought off what was then called the Grand Slam or Impregnable Quadrilateral, winning the American and British Open and Amateur Championships. He was still only twenty-eight but found the strain so great that he gave up competitive golf. He played big-time golf only once again, in 1934, the opening year of the Augusta National Invitation Meeting, later, of course, to be known as the Masters. He returned a respectable 294. The Augusta Club was the brainchild of Bobby and his friend Clifford Roberts. Stricken by a disease that confined him to a wheelchair, Bobby died in 1971. Here a master writer, Bernard Darwin, who elevated golf writing to the level of literature (as well as being good enough to win in the Walker Cup of 1922), looks at the nervous tribulations of a master golfer who learned to tame his wilder habits like club-throwing but who could still lose a stone in weight during a championship.

I.W.

As far as the United States is concerned the Bobby Jones era began, I suppose, in 1916 when at the age of fourteen-and-a-half he reached the third round of the American National Championship at Merion and went down after a hard match before an ex-champion, Robert Gardner. From this time onward till he retired full of honours if not of years, he was a great figure in American golf. For us, however, his era began somewhat later, since he came here first in 1922 and did not show us his full

powers till 1926 when he had reached the immense age of twenty-four. He then won
our Open Championship for the first time and perhaps this is the best place to set out
his record in the barest and briefest outline. In his own country he won the Open
Championship four times (he also tied for it twice and lost the play-off) and the
Amateur Championship five times. Here he won one Amateur and three Open
Championships. In 1930 he established what has been picturesquely called 'the
impregnable quadrilateral' by winning the Open and Amateur Championships of
both countries in a single summer. He played against Britain in six International
Matches, five of them for the Walker Cup; he won his single every time, sometimes
by immense margins, and he won his foursome five times and lost once by a single
hole.

Bobby's first appearance here was in the International Match preceding the
Amateur Championship at Hoylake in 1921. He won both his single and his foursome
handsomely, and impressed everybody, as he could not fail to do. Then came anti-
climax. His career in the Amateur Championship was short and rather chequered.
He began well enough against a good Scottish player, Mr Manford, and there
followed that rather farcical encounter with Mr Hamlet of Wrexham. Whatever he
might be at Wrexham it is pardonable to say that Mr Hamlet was not of the stature to
face Hoylake, even though it was made less formidably long than usual by the hard
ground. Yet with the match all square going to the Royal, which is the seventeenth, it
really seemed as if he were going to beat Bobby, which, as Euclid might remark,
would have been absurd. This was not due to any great golf of his but to a sort of
general futility and paralysis on the greens on Bobby's part. However, the crisis
passed, Bobby scrambled through with a score nearer ninety than eighty and
proceeded to play devastatingly well in his next match against Mr Robert Harris. He
had got his bad round over, he was going to win – and then he relapsed again and was
beaten by many holes by Mr Allan Graham. There was a chance of redeeming
himself in the Open at St Andrews but all went ill; he felt a puzzled hatred for the
links which he came afterwards to love and at the eleventh hole in the third round he
picked up his ball. Legend declares that he relieved his feelings by teeing it up and
driving it far out into the Eden. If he did it was a gesture deserving of sympathy, and if
he did not I am very sure he wanted to.

In 1921, at the age of nineteen, Bobby was already a magnificent golfer, as great a
hitter of the ball though not as great a player of matches or medal rounds as he ever
was. Several years before Mr Walter Travis had said he could never improve his
strokes, and that was true enough; there was, humanly speaking, no room for
improvement; it was simply a matter of stringing them together more successfully.
There could be no more fascinating player to watch not only for the free and rhythmic
character of his swing but for the swiftness with which he played. He had as brief a
preliminary address as Duncan himself, but there was nothing hurried or slapdash
about it and the swing itself, if not positively slow, had a certain drowsy beauty which
gave the feeling of slowness. There was nothing that could conceivably be called a
weak spot. The utmost that could be said – and this may be a purely personal
impression – was that he did not seem quite so supremely happy with a mashie-niblick
as when playing approaches with longer irons.

People liked Bobby at once, and that not only for his natural pleasantness of manner; they discerned in him a very human quality; he was no cold machine but took his game very much to heart as did humbler people. In his almost infantile days he had been inclined to throw his clubs about. This we were told since the American Press had once emphasised it rather unkindly; otherwise we should never have guessed it, for he had already tamed his naturally fiery temperament into betraying no outward signs. Those indeed how knew him well professed to know the symptoms which showed the flames leaping up within. I remember once watching him at an Open Championship, it may have been at St Anne's, in company with that fine American golfer, the late Mr J. G. Anderson; Bobby missed a shortish putt and 'Now, he's mad,' said my companion. I could detect nothing, but doubtless Mr Anderson knew his man and Bobby did hate missing a shot. Perhaps that was why he missed so few, for in the end that highly-strung nervous temperament, if it had never been his master, became his invaluable servant. In his most youthful and tempestuous days he had never been angry with his opponent and not often, I think, with Fate, but he had been furiously angry with himself. He set himself an almost impossibly high standard; he thought it an act of incredible folly if not a positive crime to make a stroke that was not exactly as it ought to be made and as he knew he could make it. If he ever derogated from that standard he may even in his most mature days have been 'mad' in the recesses of his heart, but he became outwardly a man of ice, with the very best of golfing manners.

How much other people have suffered over their golf we do not always know; the light of fame has not beaten on them so fiercely. Of Bobby we do know that he suffered greatly. How he could scarcely eat anything till the day's play was over; how on occasion he felt that he could not even button his shirt collar for fear of the direst consequences; how he could lose a stone in weight during a championship; how he was capable of breaking down to the point of tears not from any distress but from pure emotional overstrain – these things are now well known and may be found in Mr O. B. Keeler's admirable and Boswellian pages. No doubt his capacity for an emotional outlet was at that time a relief and a help to him, but there must be a limit. I was in his company soon after he had finished his fourth round when he won the last of his three Open Championships here in 1930, and seeing him nearly past speech I thought that the time had come for him to call a halt and that his game could not much longer be worth such an agonising candle. He had great courage and ambition, and these not only pulled him through but probably made him a more successful player than he would have been had he been gifted with a more placid temperament. There is much to be said for the stolid, phlegmatic player, but the great golfers have never had what I once heard Jack White call a dead nerve. It is worth remembering that James Braid, most rock-like and apparently impassive of men, has said that he 'liked to be a wee bit nervous' before a big game. The steady-going and unimaginative will often beat the more eager champion and they will get very near the top, but there, I think, they will stop. The prose labourer must yield to the poet and Bobby as a golfer had a strain of poetry in him. He stands for ever as the greatest encourager of the highly-strung player who is bent on conquering himself.

In 1926 we saw Bobby on his second visit. Four years had passed since he had been here before and he had now, as the Americans called it, 'broken through'; the lean years were over. In 1923 he had won the American Open after a tie with Cruikshank, thus emulating Mr Hilton here in winning the Open before the Amateur. In the following year he had put this to rights by winning the Amateur with triumphant ease and had been runner-up in the Open. In 1925 he had won the Amateur again and had tied in the Open, to lose rather surprisingly after a protracted play-off with Willie Macfarlane. He was in the plenitude of his powers and who should stand before him? And yet there was a moment when it seemed as if his second visit, like his first, would end in disappointment. All went swimmingly in the Amateur Championship at Muirfield till he reached the fifth round and then out he went and that with a resounding crash, for he was well and truly beaten by Mr Andrew Jamieson who was then hardly known outside Scotland. I believe that Bobby woke with a stiff neck that morning though he was most anxious to conceal it. Certainly he seemed to lack something of his usual ease, but Jamieson, a very neat, unobtrusive, efficient golfer, did play uncommonly well, well enough to beat anybody if anybody gave him, as Bobby did, the very slightest opening. What was more, having got away with a lead he never grew frightened of it but played with victorious confidence. I saw only odd holes of the match but I remember one vividly. This was the short thirteenth called 'The Postage Stamp', though whether it or the hole at Troon has the prior right to the title I do not know. The hole as it then was, had a long narrow green with a drop to perdition on the right, and on the left a high rough bank. Jamieson, with victory firmly in his grasp, if he could keep steady, had the honour and he made a slip; he hooked his tee-shot and the ball lighted on the top of the left-hand bank. Would it stay there? It hovered for a moment and then, audibly encouraged by the crowd, began to topple downward by stages, almost coming to rest and then moving on again till at last it ended its rather nefarious career on the green. That was the final blow and Jamieson, having had his little bit of luck, went on to win calmly and easily by 4 and 3.

Mrs Gamp has remarked how little we know 'what lays before us'. If Bobby had won that championship he has said that he would have sailed straight for home after the Walker Cup match. As it was he decided to give himself another chance in the Open at St Anne's. So, after duly doing his deadly stuff at St Andrews in the Walker Cup – he beat Cyril Tolley by 12 and 11 – he went to Sunningdale for the qualifying rounds of the Open and proceeded to play there what was by common consent as nearly flawless a round as ever had been played. He went round in 66 and he may be said to have holed only one putt worthy of mention, one of eight yards or so for a three on the fifth. Otherwise if he missed nothing short – and there were one or two putts missed to be called shortish – he holed nothing that could conceivably be called long. He simply went on and on with exact perfection. There was indeed one slip, an iron shot pushed out into a bunker at the short thirteenth, but it cost the player nothing since he chipped the ball out dead. It probably brought relief to him as it did to the spectators, who had been feeling that they must scream if perfection endured much longer. It was Mr Keeler, I think, who once wrote, 'They wound up the mechanical man of golf yesterday and set him clicking round the East Lake course.' All great golfers at their best are more or less mechanical, for they do the same thing over and over again, but I doubt if any of them save perhaps one has given quite such an impression of well-oiled, impeccable machinery as Bobby did from tee to green. The notions of beauty and machinery do not go well together; the word 'clicking' may suggest something done 'by numbers' and so far it is inappropriate; but Mr Keeler's was nevertheless an apt and memorable phrase. Harry Vardon and Bobby Jones combined exquisiteness of art with utterly relentless precision in a way not quite given to any other golfers.

Few joys in this world are unalloyed, and though Bobby was naturally and humanly pleased with that 66 he was a trifle worried because he had 'reached the peak' rather too soon before going to St Anne's. His second round of 68, with, if I remember, one innocuous misunderstanding with a tree, did nothing to reassure him on this point and he was so far right that, though he won at St Anne's, his play there was not quite of the same unrippled smoothness as at Sunningdale. The game was by contrast 'aye fechtin'' against him and he had to work hard for his scores. That was as exciting a championship as any between the wars, save only for this, that from the very start it seemed that no Briton was likely to win it. Mitchell ended fifth but he only accomplished so much by two very fine rounds on the last day; as far as winning was concerned he had put himself out of court by beginning with two 78s. So to the narrowly patriotic this championship was merely a brilliant, alien exhibition contest.

The invaders went off with a bang: Hagen had a 68 and the powerful, broad-backed, rough-hewn Mehlhorn, said to have graduated as hod-carrier to the champion bricklayer of America, had a 70. Then came McLeod, an expatriated Scot, and Al Watrous with 71 and then Bobby in the position he liked, lying well up but not prematurely leading, with a 72. It was a good round but he had to fight for it, since at each one of the last four holes he made some sort of a slip and had, in Mr Laidlay's phrase, to 'trust to a pitch and a putt' to get his four. In the second round Hagen had a compensating and disastrous 77 and at the end of it Mehlhorn with 70 and 74 and Bobby with two 72s led the field. Watrous, 71 and 75, was two shots behind them.

On the last day Bobby and Watrous were drawn together, and as it turned out this chance involved just such a strain on them and just such a terrific duel for first place as Vardon and Taylor had endured at Prestwick ten years earlier. Watrous was a very good player who had left no very distinct image on my mind; he had no tremendous power, but he had all the American virtue of smoothness and rhythm and he was a very fine putter, bang on his putting. Bobby was two strokes ahead when they set out and he had a 73 in a good fresh wind, but Watrous playing perfectly had a 69 and so – again this brought back memories of Vardon and Taylor – turned the deficit of two into a lead of two. Hagen took 74 and Mehlhorn began to fade. So the battle was to be fought out between these two and they were fully conscious of it as they went back to their hotel together, lunched together and even lay down to rest in the same room – a pleasant picture of friendly rivalry.

When it was all over and Mr Topping, who had been in charge of this couple, gave away the prizes he declared that Bobby had made but one remark to him in the course of the last round, 'My golf is terrible.' In fact it was terribly good except in one important respect; he was taking too many putts. By his own account he took thirty-nine of them and what he gained on Watrous in length he certainly threw away on the greens. The short ninth which had consistently bothered him beat him again and he was still two down with five to play; in what was in effect a match the language of match play may be used. Then at last the strokes came back one at a time and the pair were all square with three to play. At the seventeenth came Bobby's historic second, which I must presently describe yet again, but before that on the sixteenth came an incident of which a friend has lately reminded me; it gives force to the ruthless doctrine that someone ought to murder a photographer *pour encourager les autres*. Watrous had played his second to the green and Bobby had got half-way up with some pitching club when a fiend with a camera stepped out and tried to snap him. Bobby stopped and began again, and again the photographer tried. This time he was metaphorically lynched; he was shooed out of the way, and Bobby, by a considerable display of control, pitched safely to the green and the hole was halved in four.

Now for the seventeenth, a hole a little over 400 yards in length. The course of the hole bends to the left and the line is well out to the right, in order to get a clear view of the hole and avoid the sandhills guarding the left-hand side of the green. Nor is that the only reason for keeping to the right, for on the left of the fairway is a wilderness of sandy, scrubby country dotted here and there with bunkers. Bobby with the honour, drew his tee-shot, not badly but badly enough to be obviously in some form of trouble; Watrous went straight and playing the odd reached the green; he was some way from the hole but he was on the green and that looked good enough. Bobby's ball lay in a shallow bunker and it lay clean, but he was 170 yards or more from the flag and between him and it were the sandhills. He took what I think he called his mashie-iron (it now reposes a sacred relic in the St Anne's Club) and hit the ball perfectly clean, playing it somewhat out into the wind so that it came in to finish on the green and nearer the hole than his opponent. Admittedly the ball lay as clean as clean could be and this was the kind of shot that he might very well have played in a practice game, but in the circumstances, when a teaspoonful too much sand might have meant irretrievable ruin, it was a staggering shot, and it staggered poor Al Watrous. He took three putts, Bobby got down in two and everybody felt that that shot had settled it. Watrous was bunkered at the home hole, Bobby nearly bunkered but not quite; he got a four against a five and finished in 74 against 78, 291 against 293.

There still remained Hagen and George Von Elm, both of whom were rumoured to be doing well. Hagen arrived on the last tee wanting a four for 74 and a two to tie. He could doubtless have tied for second place with Watrous but Hagen was never interested in second prizes. After a fine drive, he walked some way forward and then with a characteristic gesture had the flag taken out. His ball very nearly pitched into the hole and ran on into the bunker behind the green. *Aut Caesar*, etc. His effort had failed and he took four more to get down, so that Von Elm coming with a wet sheet and a 72 tied with him for third place. Let me add as a postscript that the Council of the Royal Lytham and St Anne's Club have now decided to mark, as far as it can exactly be done, the spot at the seventeenth from which Bobby played his shot. This is a precedent that could not often be followed, but here the geographical conditions are favourable and if now and then someone has to lift a drop from behind the monument he will do so in a reverent rather than an exasperated spirit.

I have written at perhaps excessive length about the St Anne's Championship both because it was Bobby's first and because it was so dramatic. When he came back next year to defend his title at St Andrews, having in the meanwhile won the American Open at Scioto, he played unquestionably better; he enjoyed the greatest single triumph he ever had here, but there seems much less to say about it, for the reason that it was 'his' championship, he was winning all the while. By this time St Andrews had taken a thorough hold on him. He was amused by its problems; he knew whereabouts were its hidden bunkers and was not annoyed by them, as some people never cease to be, because they are hidden; he has devised some three different ways of playing the Long Hole In according to the wind; he had realised that for a player of his parts the Road Hole need hold no excessive terrors, unless he is over-ambitious. In short he had proved the truth of Mrs Malaprop's saying that, ''Tis safest in matrimony to begin with a little aversion,' for he was now thoroughly in love with the Old Course and played it as if he loved it.

Bobby's four rounds were 68, 72, 73 and 72 and he led from the start. I do not know that he played any better for his 68 than in any of the other three rounds; it was simply that everything came off for him, as for example a putt holed for three at the Hole o' Cross going out. It is by far the biggest green in the world and if this was not the longest putt ever holed it must have been very nearly so. Mr Keeler's brow was a little knitted, for he was not sure how his man would like to be 'in the lead' straight away instead of lying a stroke or two behind, but the general impression was that there would be no holding Bobby. After two rounds he only led Hodson by two strokes, but good player as Hodson was he could scarcely hope to give the leader two strokes; in fact the third round destroyed him as far as winning was concerned and those who were more likely to hold on were several shots further behind. At the end of the third round Bobby led Fred Robson, who had just done a splendid 69, by four shots and Aubrey Boomer by six, and it was for him to set the pace.

Only at the beginning of the last round was there a moment's doubt, for Bobby frittered away a couple of shots in the first four holes, and so with an orthodox five at the fifth his score was three over fours – a definitely vulnerable start. At that point I left him to look at other people, meaning to pick him up again at the thirteenth on the way home. Some bursts of clapping from the neighbourhood of the 'loop' suggested that he was doing well, but how well no one of us waiting on the big double green knew. The advance guard of his crowd came towards us, in the van one who trotted briskly, as if big with news to impart. I have a well-grounded distrust of spectators' tales but this one looked a man of good counsel, sober and unimaginative; so I button-holed him and asked his tidings. When he said that Bobby was now two under fours I thought he was only the usual liar, but what he said was true, for Bobby had done the holes from the sixth to the twelfth in twenty-four shots. After that the round was a triumphal procession. His second to the last hole was a little cautious and ended in the Valley of Sin. Thence he ran it up dead and as he scaled the bank the crowd stormed up after him and lined the edge of the green, barely restraining themselves. He holed his short one and the next instant there was no green visible, only a dark seething mass, in the midst of which was Bobby hoisted on fervent shoulders and holding his putter, 'Calamity Jane', at arm's length over his head lest she be crushed to death. Calamity Jane had two pieces of whipping bound round her shaft where she had been broken, not we may trust in anger but by some mischance. When some years later the market was flooded with exact models of her, each of them duly bore two superfluous black bands. Did ever imitation pay sincerer flattery than that?

Only once more, in 1930, were we destined to see Bobby here in battle array, though he has returned once since his retirement and in playing a friendly round of the Old Course took the major part of St Andrews round with him. It was at St Andrews in 1930, the year of the 'impregnable quadrilateral', that he realised almost his last unachieved ambition and won our Amateur Championship. He did not win it without his bad moments, for he had never concealed his dislike of eighteen-hole matches. In the American Championship the first two rounds, which were of eighteen holes only, had at least once brought him to grief and he had had, in the words of old Beldham the cricketer, 'many an all but'. Once safely through them and in the haven of thirty-six holes, where he felt that he had space to manoeuvre, he had crushed his men one after the other by murderous margins. Thus in our championship he could never feel really at ease until in the final and he had never yet reached the final. He set out on the enterprise strung up to a high pitch and no one who saw the beginning of his match against a good Nottinghamshire golfer, Mr Roper, will forget it. On the first green he holed a long putt for a three, the ball going in with an almost suspicious rattle against the back of the tin. Bobby looked a little apologetic and made several little practice movements of his club. I remember Mr Hilton whispering to me that he was trying to get the swing of his putter smooth; that first putt, successful as it was, had shown signs of tension. After a four at the second he holed another and shorter putt for a three at the Cartgate and then at the fourth hit a very long tee-shot rather to the left into the Cottage bunker. Thence, a culminating atrocity, he holed out, a full shot of 150 yards or so, with some sort of iron, for a two.

After this astonishing display Bobby became comparatively quiescent and had to struggle as hard to get through as many less gifted players have done. Two of his most close-run things were against compatriots, Mr Harrison Johnston and Mr George Voigt. Mr Johnston, after being several holes down, chased him to the last gasp and Mr Voigt, if I may permit myself an 'if', ought to have beaten him. Bobby was obviously struggling and when Mr Voigt, very cool and steady and putting beautifully, stood two up with five to go, he looked like a winner. And then he committed what the onlooker, who has nothing to do but criticise, felt inclined to call a gratuitous folly. With the broad space of the Elysian Fields to drive into he cut his tee-shot over the wall and out of bounds. It was a heaven-sent reprieve; Bobby took it and fought his way home to win by a hole.

Yet even this paled before his battle with Cyril Tolley. Every man, woman and child in St Andrews went out to watch it, and Mr Gerard Fairlie was quite right to set the scene of the murder in one of his stories on the afternoon of that match. There would have been ample opportunity to commit several murders and escape un-detected through the lonely streets, though stained with the marks of crime. Never was there more perceptible the silence of expectation, that lull before the storm in which men speak instinctively in whispers, and Cyril gave it, if possible, a more thrilling emphasis, since he began with a full-blooded top from the first tee. It was ominous but it was no presage of disaster for he played finely afterwards and a dog-fight on a magnificent scale ensued, which delighted everyone save other poor wretches who were trying to play their own insignificant matches. Each man seeing the mighty flood approach him must needs crouch over his ball guarding it as best he might and pick himself up again when the torrent has swept over him. The most discussed shot in the match was Bobby's second to the Road Hole, as to which hundreds are prepared to take their oath that the ball would have been on the road if it had not hit a spectator and an equal number of witnesses are quite certain that it would not. I was there but was running for my life with my head well down at the moment and can offer no opinion. The hole was halved; so was the last and Bobby won at the nineteenth, where his adversary played a rather loose second and was punished by a stymie. Exactly how good the golf was I cannot now remember for there are occasions when that is of secondary importance. It was the devil of a match.

At last Bobby was in the final – against Mr Wethered; his chance had come and he did not mean to waste it; he was on his favourite long trail of thirty-six holes. At the very first hole a shudder of surprise went through the crowd as he entirely missed his pitch and stayed short of the burn, but from there he chipped dead and got his four; nor did he ever exceed that figure till he put his second into the Road bunker at the seventeenth. I can see him very clearly now, as the stewards are moving away the crowd at the back of the green. He is gently smiling a protest to the effect that he does not mean to go on to the road. In fact his explosion shot gave him quite a good chance of a four but the putt did not drop; there was to be no fiveless round for him. His opponent fought manfully but without avail and Bobby won by 7 and 6.

Now for the last lap, the Open at Hoylake, which was won in the end as had been that at St Anne's by sheer, hard fighting. As at St Andrews Bobby jumped away with the lead with a 70 which was equalled by Macdonald Smith. He added a 72 while Mac Smith took 77 and his nearest pursuer was now Fred Robson with 143. The third round was sound enough, 74, but meanwhile another British hope had arisen. Compston, who had begun with 74 and 73, added to these a tremendous 68 and led Bobby by a stroke. Diegel was not far behind with a 71, giving him a total of 228; but Diegel, though having an astonishing game in him, has been in championships one of those unfortunates who can never quite do it. He has said bitterly himself that however hard the other fellows try to give it him he will not take it. This may be partly due to his highly artificial method of putting, 'contorted almost to anguish', as was written of a fine putter of a much older generation.

Such styles are always apt to break down under strain, and apart from this Diegel was cursed with a temperament the most highly strung possible. Walter Hagen, once sitting up cheerfully late before a final against Diegel, was told in a tone of mild reproach that his adversary had been in bed for hours. 'Ah,' said Hagen, 'but he's not asleep.' I have seen Diegel, as 'crazy' as ever was Duncan, and as brilliant as anyone I ever did see, but somehow he did not quite seem the man to stop Bobby, and in any case it was with Compston that were all British hearts.

I went out to see him play the first hole in the last round. His drive was perfect; his iron shot inadequate, to the edge of the green, and he took three putts. One five meant nothing to be sure but there came other fives and the final 82 was heart-breaking. So out again in search of Bobby. All went if not perfectly according to plan at least reasonably well until he came to the eighth or Far Hole, which measures according to the books 527 yards, two shots and a pitch for Bobby in ordinary conditions with the ground fairly fast. The two shots were entirely satisfactory but the pitch was weak and the ball rolled back from the plateau; the next was nothing to boast of and at the last he missed a shortish putt; result, a horrid seven without touching a bunker. As Ben Sayers might have said, 'It was no possible but it was a fact.' The news of that seven quickly spread all over the links bringing consternation or encouragement. To Bobby himself it must have been a cruel blow but he pulled himself together and fought his way home, much, I imagine, in the frame of mind of a runner running himself blind, not seeing the tape but determined to get there. He was round in 75 and now we knew what had to be done. Compston was dead and buried; Diegel did a 75, good but not quite good enough for he had started two strokes behind. Those of us who were with him in one of the smaller rooms of the clubhouse united in assuring Bobby that all was well, as he wandered restlessly about holding a glass in two hands. And then there came a suggestion that all might not be well since Mac Smith was doing great things. To be sure he had to do a 69 to tie and that to an impartial judgment seemed very unlikely, but at such moments judgments can scarcely be impartial.

I remember very well going out to meet him. I could not go far for I had to broadcast and time was getting hideously short, but I *must* know. He holed out at the Dun taking to my jaundiced eye a very long time over it, and then we knew; two threes to tie. It was almost but not quite impossible. I saw him play the Royal – I was to broadcast from a house not far off – and his putt for three did not go in. Two to tie and that was surely impossible, but with an obstinate fidelity to duty I waited till his second had pitched on the home green and had palpably not holed out. Then I ran and ran and arrived just in time to announce in breathless tones to an expectant world that Bobby had won again.

I will not follow him home to America. He won the Open at Interlaken and the Amateur at Merion where he had played in his first championship at fourteen and won his first Amateur Championship at twenty-two. But as far as this country is concerned he departed in a blaze of glory from Hoylake.

He retired at the right time and could say with Charles Lamb, 'I have worked task work and have the rest of the day to myself.' After Tom Cribb had beaten Molineaux for the second time in the great battle of Thistleton Gap it was decided that he need never fight again but should bear the title of Champion to the end of his days. I think that most golfers in their hearts grant the same privilege to Bobby Jones.

From *Golf Between Two Wars* by Bernard Darwin
(Chatto and Windus, London, 1944).

Ben Hogan

Geoffrey Cousins and Tom Scott

I'll always admire a gutsy fighter. Ben Hogan overcame a near-fatal car crash in 1949 to win six more majors (out of a career total of nine). He won the Masters twice (in 1951 and 1953), the US Open four times (in 1948, 1950, 1951 and 1953) and the US PGA twice (in 1946 and 1948). But perhaps his greatest achievement was to win the British Open at Carnoustie at the first attempt in 1953. He believed that no golfer could regard himself as one of the all-time greats unless he could master a British links course. The Scots christened him 'the Wee Ice Man'. He was a perfectionist who once shot a round with half a dozen birdies – and promptly went out on to the practice ground. His friend Jimmy Demaret said: 'For Christ's sake, Ben, nobody ever played better than you today. You can't birdie every hole.' 'Why not?' demanded Hogan. He once had a dream in which he played 17 holes in one and woke up angry to have missed on the other one. At almost 5 feet 9 inches, the tough Texan was no midget, but it's proof nonetheless that size is not vital in golf – thank goodness. Here's an account of that memorable Carnoustie triumph.

I.W.

This chapter – and the 1953 Championship at Carnoustie is well worth a chapter all to itself – is not so much about the competition as about the man who won it, Ben W. Hogan from Fort Worth, Texas.

On February 2nd, 1949, Hogan was driving with his wife Valerie back home to Fort Worth when a huge bus loomed out of the fog into the path of the Hogan car. A collision was certain and Hogan threw himself in front of his wife in order to save her from the inevitable impact. In doing so, he saved her life and also his own, for in a flash his car was a heap of twisted metal and the steering wheel had been forced back into the seat he had occupied a split second before.

But his injuries were severe: a broken collarbone, a fractured ankle, a smashed rib and a broken pelvis. He was taken to hospital at El Paso, where doctors struggled for hours to save his life. Thrombosis developed, and his life was despaired of. In the end the doctors and Ben Hogan won. He lived, but the general opinion among medical men and laymen alike was that he would never play golf again. Hogan had different ideas on the subject. He did play again, and so became a legend.

The road back was long and hard. For before his accident Hogan had been a 'loner', a man not easy to understand, a man with whom even his closest friends found it hard to communicate and who liked to work out his own problems. After his accident he mellowed to some extent, but even then he kept himself to himself. There was no change in his outlook on golf; his dedication to the game became, if possible, greater than ever. His recovery from the accident was slow, very slow; there were some who thought he would lose the uphill fight, and more who thought his dream of playing golf again would never come true. Then came the electrifying news that he had entered the 1950 Los Angeles Open. In his first round he scored a 73. Then he tacked on a 69 and then another 69, and in the last round it was another 69 to tie with Snead. True, he lost the play-off, but the 'little man', the 'hawk', the 'ice man', was back in business.

His next test was the US Open. He still required treatment for his legs, but his courage and ability triumphed. He tied with George Fazio and Lloyd Mangrum, then romped home in the replay to prove to himself and to the world in general that he had regained his place as the top man in golf.

In 1951 he won the Masters and also his third US Open. The following year was not so good for him, but in 1953 he surged back and again won the Masters with a tournament record of 274, including a never-to-be-forgotten round of 66. He followed that with a sweeping win in the US Open, beating off all the opposition with apparent ease and winning by six strokes from Snead, the man who despite all his greatness was to find the national title beyond his reach.

There was only one world for Hogan to conquer – the British Open. To some of the old-timers in American golf, men like Sarazen and the great amateur Chick Evans, the British title still meant a great deal and it was such men who let it be known that if Hogan was to be the King he would have to win the British Championship. Hogan succumbed to the persuasion and decided to go to the great golf centre at Carnoustie in Angus to try to win the British crown.

As with everything that Hogan did, his preparation for the event was meticulous. He came over early, settled himself into a suite in an hotel and spent hours and hours practising on a nearby course. The only onlooker was his caddie, Cecil Timms. When Hogan did appear on the course at Carnoustie it was mostly by himself. He was closely watched by the knowing locals, who after they had seen him in action declared that there was no way he could lose the Championship – and that, from the dour Scots, was praise indeed. Seldom had they been so much impressed by a visiting golfer, and not even the fact that few men had ever succeeded in winning the title at the first time of asking deterred the Carnoustie experts from plumping for the little Texan. To them he was the epitome of golfing perfection, not because he was the best stylist they had ever seen – Hogan was no Snead in that respect – but because of the amazing accuracy of his shots. Even on the long, testing links and in the wind which blows there so often, Hogan showed a complete mastery in placing the ball. And that, thought the locals, would be the decisive factor in the Championship. How right they were. The question was whether Hogan would rise to the occasion and win what was for him 'The little slam' – the US Open, the US Masters and the British Open.

But Fate stepped in and attempted to halt the great bid that thousands of golf enthusiasts had gathered to see, for just before the event Hogan developed a feverish cold and the opening day of the Championship was wet and miserable, so the American set out swathed in sweaters. His long shots were as they had always been, as fired from a rifle, but his putting on the slow greens was no more than ordinary. A

73 went down on the card, and the man who stole the limelight was the amateur Frank Stranahan who had so nearly won at Hoylake six years before. Stranahan returned a 70. Eric Brown, much to the delight of his fellow-Scots, was only one stroke more than Stranahan and there were other strong contenders like Thomson, Rees, Locke and de Vicenzo. If Hogan was going to win it was going to be by the hard way, or so it seemed.

A second round of 74 put Stranahan out of the way, but Rees, whose favourite course is Carnoustie, produced a brilliant 70 and Brown repeated his 71 of the first round to share the lead. Hogan's round was 71 as well, so at the halfway stage he was two strokes behind.

We can forget now about Brown, who, to the great misery of his many admirers, scored 75, a figure he was to repeat in his last round. Rees had 73 third time out and de Vicenzo, the tall Argentinian, who in the last two or three years had been building up a formidable record in the Championship, moved up with a 71 to challenge Hogan who had 70. That meant de Vicenzo and Hogan were level with one round to play.

Things were shaping well for the Texan after his modest start and there wasn't a man or woman in Carnoustie that night who would not have staked their all on a Hogan victory. The others had had their chances, and thrown them away.

Hogan's cold had got no worse, but after that first round in the wet his back had been giving him some concern. And so had his putting. True, in the first round it was patchy, but after that almost any golfer would have been pleased enough with it. Not so Hogan. But in the end it was not his putting which was to play a vital part in the proceedings. It was his woods and long irons. Time and again he placed his wooden shots exactly where they should be placed, and those shots made up for any deficiency with his putter, and such deficiencies, may it be said, were few. So on he went relentlessly. He was still out on the course while those who were his challengers were finishing. They were Dai Rees, who had won the Match-Play title at Carnoustie, and who was desperately anxious to win the Open there; Peter Thomson, still chasing his first British title; the incredible Stranahan who finished with a 69, and Tony Cerda who had followed Faulkner home at Portrush. And all were on the same aggregate, 286.

It seemed too high a total to cause Hogan any grave concern for now one of the biggest-ever crowds in the history of the Championship was seeing Hogan at his thrilling best. True, on the outward journey he had twice been over par, but to counter that he had made three birdies. Only at one hole did he fail: the seventeenth, where he cut a No. 4 wood into sand. Then he three-putted and a six went down on the card. By then, however, he could afford the luxury of a six and still win by two strokes. But as it happened he finished with a flourish worthy of the occasion, a birdie 4 at the long last hole which had been the graveyard of hopes on more than one occasion at Carnoustie. His round was a 68 for a total of 282, four strokes ahead. The quality of his golf throughout can be judged from the fact that his aggregate was eight strokes better than Cotton's total in 1937 and fourteen strokes better than Armour's in 1931. In fairness to Cotton, however, it must be said that in his Championship on the great links the weather conditions were deplorable.

Still, Hogan's feat in winning at the first time of asking was something for every golf enthusiast who saw it to cherish for the rest of his days. He had won as he had set out to do, and the only regret was that he was not to play in the Open again. British spectators were, however, to see him show his brilliance once more, when along with Snead he won the Canada Cup for the United States at Wentworth in 1956.

On returning to the United States after his victory at Carnoustie Hogan was accorded, just as Bob Jones had been accorded, a hero's welcome in New York, when the ticker tape showered down on to his car. And after, as he stood on the steps of New York's City Hall, the man of iron all but broke down with emotion. 'I owe it all,' he said, 'to God and my wife, Valerie.'

Carnoustie was the climax of his greatest year. He was still to be in the limelight in several big events, and he so nearly won the US Open and the US Masters once again. He narrowly failed, but what did it matter? He had been acknowledged to be the greatest golfer of all time in the eyes of many. A film, *Follow the Sun*, had been made of his life, honours were showered on him, and he continued to make appearances in Championships and leading events for a long time afterwards. Wherever he appeared the crowds flocked to see him, and to enjoy some of the magic that was still his.

The legend of Hogan still lives on. There will always be arguments as to whether he was greater than Vardon or Nelson or Palmer, but the American golf writers at least had no doubt as to his stature in the game. In 1965 they voted him the greatest professional golfer of all time.

One thing is certain – Hogan in his era was the undisputed king of the links.

From *A Century of Opens* by Geoffrey Cousins and
Tom Scott
(Frederick Muller, London, 1971).

The answer to Hogan is, I fancy, that if Hogan means to win, you lose.

Henry Longhurst in 1953.

Hogan came as near to dehumanising golf as anyone ever has done.

Pat Ward-Thomas.

5

HENRY THE GREAT
Banned from Cricket – So I Take Up Golf
Henry Cotton

Many successful golfers will acknowledge the debt they owe to their father – I know I do; not for bequeathing me his swing (though it isn't a bad one) but because he gave me encouragement and that essential competitive edge. You can have all the natural talent in the world but without the overwhelming urge to win it will come to nothing great. In *This Game of Golf* Henry Cotton describes how his father started him on the road to golfing fame. Like me, Henry had a keen golfing brother, Leslie, who (like my own brother Gareth) didn't have quite the dedication to reach the top. Like me, Henry, as a young man, was torn between two sports, in his case golf and cricket. It was a disciplinary offence at Dulwich School and his refusal to be caned for it which led to his being banned from cricket. So he filled in the time playing golf instead. With me it was my father's fear that I would do my limbs a permanent injury at soccer, because of my whole-hearted 'get stuck in' attitude, that switched me over to golf. Like me, Henry developed a competitive spirit as a teenager by playing with older golfers and going all out to beat them . . .

I.W.

How did I come to be a professional golfer? Although I can claim to have chosen this profession for myself, I suppose I must have been guided in some way to pick one in which I could succeed, if my achievements entitle me to use such a word.

My father was a keen golfer of the week-end type, with a very ugly style which, as I realised later, was caused because he had a 'gammy' left knee and had to do a sort of hop in his downswing to prevent too much strain going on to the delicate joint.

He encouraged my brother and me by every means in his power and to the limit of his financial ability, and was very proud of his 'little boys.' One of my proudest days was when I beat him on level terms for the first time. I was about eleven or twelve years old at the time and he was about 59 years old and had a 16 handicap, but allowing for this, he was very good in his own way. He was an enthusiastic member of the Honor Oak and Forest Hill Golf Club, and then of the Dulwich and Sydenham Hill Golf Club, and on this particular day I insisted on playing him level. He had been giving me a gradually diminishing number of strokes for some months previously and I had been beating him regularly and, parent-like, he hesitated to let me play him with no handicap. I beat him, and he later recalled my telling him very seriously at the time, 'Father, you will never beat me again.' He never did.

My brother and I were made full members of the Aquarius Golf Club, a nine-hole course belonging to the Metropolitan Water Board, and this privilege we enjoyed until we both became professionals, I at 16 and my elder brother at 17. I think the encouragement I got from the golfers at this little nine-hole golf course did much to build up the competitive spirit which I expect it will be conceded I possess.

It almost goes without saying that I love golf, and long before I had really set my mind on being as good as the professionals I saw playing in the various tournaments around London, which could be seen in the holiday periods, I used to spend every moment I could chipping a golf ball about in the garden.

My brother and I both played cricket well and got our colours at Alleyn's School, and we used to take it in turns to 'bowl' to one another with a golf ball played with a golf club, the batsman playing cricket strokes back with a cricket bat. We thought this a good way to practise two games at once! Original, anyhow.

Although I have had a better golfing temperament than my brother Leslie and perhaps more ambition, I have been a more accurate striker all along. When we only had one ball left between us, we used to practise hitting the ball to and fro, one to the other, with all sorts of clubs up and down a fairway, and it was always I who had to do all the running about at my end. I used to grow annoyed at some of my brother's wild shots and so, brother-like, to get even with him, I would hit some of my shots off the line on purpose to make him run too!

When my father played regularly at Dulwich and Sydenham, we were allowed to be schoolboy members there. During our summer holidays we used to go to the club early in the morning, play 27 holes before lunch, eat the lunch we had taken with us, have a short rest, play 27 holes again after lunch and then feel we were all ready to take on my father and his partner, whoever it was, in his evening round. These four rounds a day carrying our own clubs seemed to be no bother at all in those days, but just good practice.

When my brother, who was not as good at the three 'Rs' as I was, left school, he decided to become a professional golfer. At this moment he was almost as good a player as I was, within a stroke or two anyhow, but had less power of concentration. He went to George Oke, professional at the Fulwell Golf Club, as assistant. In his younger days before going to Fulwell, George had been professional to the Honor Oak and Forest Hill Golf Club, so we knew him well.

I was determined to stay on at school and pass my Matriculation examination, and then decide whether or not to try for a University scholarship, and go then for Civil Engineering, which I always had in mind to do. However, an incident in what turned out to be my last term at school, the summer term of 1923, decided my future.

I was in the school first eleven, having worked my way up as 'under 14' Captain, and a good first-wicket bat and was definitely a better cricketer than golfer. We went to play at Marlow, and the match finishing early, the six prefects left the five non-prefects, of whom I was one, all the cricket gear to take back to the school that same night. So with four other boys I dragged the three large school cricket bags and two private cricket bags all the way to Dulwich by train and bus. We arrived late and very tired, and wrote a very pointed note to our prefect team-mates telling them it was a bit hot to expect us to do all the dirty work.

A lot of fuss was made over this note by the prefects, and the headmaster ordered the prefects to cane us. I refused to be caned by other boys for an offence against them and said an apology, which I would give, should cover our bad taste. This case developed into quite a serious affair, and I was banned from further cricket until I had had my caning. When the headmaster told me this, I suppose my seemingly innocent answer to his question as to what would I do with myself when the other boys were playing cricket, must have sounded very insolent. I said: 'I'll play golf, sir.'

That is just what happened; I played golf whenever I could, and from that moment decided I would become a champion.

When J. H. Taylor, whom I succeeded as professional at the Royal Mid Surrey Golf Club in 1946, was presented with a testimonial and the honorary life membership of the club after 46 years' service, he recalled, in his speech after the presentation, a day when my father took my brother and me to play with him many years before. I was 13, I suppose, at the time, and J. H. was asked to give a written report on his impression of us both. He said he remembered writing to my father, who died in 1941, aged 81, that he thought I would be the better player ultimately as I apparently had much more determination than my brother and more power of concentration.

After matriculating, my mind was made up to become a professional and my taregt was the 'stars.' I do not quite know what influenced me finally to become a professional, the incident at school, my brother being already a professional, or just the love of the game. But, having taken this decision, I tried hard with all I had got. A golf net built in the garage adjoining our house was pounded far into the night by my brother and me till we were exhausted, in an endeavour to perfect our swings.

I feel that it was the love of the game that kept me at it, and the competitive spirit.

From *This Game of Golf* by Henry Cotton
(Country Life, London, 1948).

My Three British Opens
Henry Cotton

It comes to only the very great in modern times to win the British Open three times. Henry Cotton was one of those. Henry died at the end of 1987, just days before the news was announced that he was to have been knighted. But he knew about the accolade just before his death and this is my salute to Sir Henry. Though I never really saw him in action – just in the odd clip on TV – I'd love to inherit his mantle as 'the finest British golfer of modern times'. I may have inherited some of his swing – one of my early tutors was Cyril Hughes, who was a disciple of Henry's.

When he was forty-one, Henry wrote the story behind his three Open triumphs of 1934, 1937 and 1948, from which I quote below. He did much to revive the lowly fortunes of British golf after years of American dominance (a very similar state of affairs to that in 1985 when Sandy Lyle broke a sixteen-year largely American monopoly of the Open).

One big difference between Henry's time and mine was in the professionals' pay. He says that in his early days the caddies sometimes earned as much as the players. Part of Henry's achievement in golf was vastly to improve the status of the British professional.

I.W.

Golf is a wonderful game. It is more than a game to me; it is a life's work, a career, a profession. Whether it is a science or an art I do not know – it is probably half and half – but it is a noble occupation all the same.

Nobody can pick a profession and make good at it without having some flair for it – at least that is as I see it. I came into golf fully aware that it was a hard game, but with the maximum amount of enthusiasm, which led me to burn up more energy than I possessed; and this is where I nearly failed. As the years have passed I have learned to place a greater value than ever on my health, which in general has been below the average, but I am grateful in every way for my earthly state today.

To say I have fought ill health is to some extent an exaggeration, but I might have had a stronger stomach. On the other hand I have only myself to blame for some of its weakness, as I did not for some years count meals as of sufficient importance to warrant the waste of an hour on them, and so ruined my digestion. Now I am very French in my outlook, and vote for a two-hours break for the world at midday. I feel I am getting the proportions right – perhaps values is a better word.

I owe everything to golf. This is a fact I cannot or would not deny, and I only hope that as far as it has been in my power, I have been able to put something back into the game to help others. Many of my actions have been wrong, I know, and many must have been right, though sometimes misunderstood. I may sum it all up by saying that while trying to please everyone, I have finally learned that a parady of Lincoln's famous saying might finish, 'You can't please all the people all the time.' So I said I would please myself as a start – that must be mostly right, surely!

I have always received, or rather patiently listened to, much unsolicited advice on how to run my career. This topic has interested many people – in fact, so many people that at times I have forgotten my rule to be polite to everyone, and let go. This gratuitous advice extends often to the golf course, and even on occasion to the final round of a major competition, when surely one can be excused for being cutting, for the same person would never walk in on, say, a most important conference or interrupt a private conversation; he would be too polite.

Naturally, the big slice taken by the war out of the best part of my golfing life has caused me to revise my plans, for from one with much future and little past, I became, as it seems now almost overnight, one with much past and a little future, in the tournament sense at least. This I know applies to nearly everyone in our Islands, but I am here putting my own case.

I have enjoyed my life as a professional golfer and still do, for it is a great life. To travel, to meet the world and his wife, and to live in the open air, what more can one ask?

Teaching golf is great work. It means helping people to enjoy themselves more, and with my temperament, it means suffering with them when they are tortured by failure and sharing their elation when they touch their high levels. Many people, often those who do not know me at all, think I enjoy teaching and playing only with scratch players. How wrong they are! I spend more time with the good players because they feel they can get the best value from my lessons, but I get much pleasure from enlightening the golfer who is doing everything wrong. 'Oh! I am not good enough to play with you.' I get tired of hearing this remark, and of explaining that I do not mind whom I play with so long as he is a decent fellow and enjoys his golf.

The person I cannot bear on the links is the grumbler, the person who is never satisfied and thinks he is only getting 25 per cent value for the money he is spending, and who never plays his real game. If he only knew it, his real game is his ordinary rotten stuff. He could remember with advantage the story of the old golfer at St Andrews, who after a round was sitting with his partner in the famous bay-window looking down the course, when a friend approached and asked him how he had played.

'I played rotten stuff,' he said. 'Nothing like my real game.' Then, after taking another sip at the glass of whisky at his elbow, he added very slowly, 'Come to think of it, I have never played my real game.'

I have, like many other players, done only two holes in one. I have had many very 'near ones,' but there were nearly 20 years between these flukes of flukes. I have had disappointments by the score, but they have taught me lessons; some I have learned, I suppose, and of course these disappointments have made success all the sweeter and more appreciated.

I have always tried to better myself, and as soon as I was old enough to appreciate the difference between the good and the shoddy, I went for the good all the time, for I think it is not a bad thing to hold that 'the best is just good enough.'

I have had a go at nearly every thing in golf, from shoes with running spikes to 47-inch long drivers with deep faces, in order to try to do something a bit better than before. There is still much more I want to do in golf for myself, and the game, and I hope I shall be forgiven for trying to do it my own way.

My attempt to win the Open always started from the moment the preceding one was over, and I kept setting my target 12 months ahead to achieve a certain result on a certain course. I suppose this obsession to win the greatest title of them all made it all the more difficult for me, but it was foremost in my mind for years. I do not pretend I am not ambitious now, but the same burning desire has cooled off with the passing years and three successful attempts to my credit.

I was taken by Cyril Tolley to Prestwick for the 1925 Open when an assistant at Rye, and I played badly, or rather putted badly. The next year when regional qualifying was tried out I failed to qualify at Sunningdale. I was partnered by George Gadd, who was a really extraordinary putter at that time. George did 70 and 71 and I did 80 and 81, and I, childlike, worked out afterwards that if I had putted as he did and not taken any three-putt greens, I would even have beaten his score.

The following year, 1927, at St Andrews, I was well up after two rounds with 145, but slipped up on the greens again, on the final day especially.

In 1928 I qualified well but did not do anything to remember.

In 1929 I reached the last day after having the interesting experience of playing the first two rounds with Walter Hagen, who played beautiful golf to win, for the fourth and last time, his most esteemed title.

In 1930 at Hoylake, I did well in a way, for after the first round Bobby Jones and I were on the 70 mark with Macdonald Smith. On the morning of the second day I woke up and found my right wrist was set so stiffly that I could not bend it either way without great pain. I remembered jarring it badly against a tuft on the fairway playing to the old 12th hole the previous day. I was in a panic, and I chased around trying to find someone to help me; I finally got an early appointment with a famous Liverpool bone specialist who for my three guineas told me to get it massaged. I then chased off to find a masseur, had 30 minutes' massage and then chased to the station to get the train, for the road tunnel was not yet open, barely arriving on the first tee in time to drive off. Naturally I was upset by all this and with my wrist still worrying me I played the first nine holes badly; 43 out. I was back in 36, however, when I got the feel of the club again, though 79 was too many. I could have cried when I read, 'Cotton blows up' for it was no use telling the world my wrist was not normal *after* 79. Before, yes! – one might get some sympathy; but after all it was not sympathy I wanted but results, at least that is what the public wanted. So it meant cutting out the squealing and getting on with the practice.

At Carnoustie, in 1931, I did well again, better in fact than before. I was leading the field with Jurado after two rounds at 147. Looking back on this Open I am not sure that I was really good enough to win it, but I think that 'my adviser' did not understand me well enough, or he would have left me alone. Eliot Cockell, who ran *Golf Illustrated* for many years until his death just before the war, arrived at Carnoustie, having travelled overnight from London, to help me win the Open.

His plan was, 'Take no risks this morning, then get the "whip out" in the afternoon and go for everything.' So he walked around as my bodyguard and saw me endeavour to carry out his schedule. In so doing I took 79 strokes, which ruined my chances for this Open, though I lost by only six strokes.

In golf there is no playing safe; the ball can still run against you wherever you hit it, as I realised, and there is no whip to take out, unless to beat yourself after the round for making a mess of things.

In 1932 I had a sharp dose of 'flu' after the qualifying rounds and played the first round on half a bottle of champagne, because I was so weak after a night's perspiration in pulling down my temperature that I could scarcely walk at all. It did seem as though I would never win this event, and to take champagne, which I had very rarely tasted, though I had been ordered red Bordeaux wine by a French specialist, was considered my last chance of being able to play at all.

I did the first nine at Prince's in 32, and then on the longer homeward half, with the effect of the champagne already worn off, I did 42 back. I have often wondered whether another half-bottle would have 'done the trick' or put me out of action altogether. Sarazen won with 283, which stood as the lowest total ever put up in the Open. I always thought the Prince's course of 1932 just about as perfect a links as I ever played on.

This same year I did my usual summer trip to the Continent, where I have always felt at home; it might be because of some distant link with the French in me, because my sweet mother was Alice Le Poidevin, from Guernsey in the Channel Islands. Anyhow, whilst I was playing in Belgium, I was asked by Major J. C. Symonds, secretary of the Waterloo Golf Club, near Brussels, if I knew of any well-known English professional who spoke French and would like to come to his club.

Some six weeks later I had a sudden impulse one morning to send him a telegram offering to go to the Waterloo Golf Club myself. Not that I was unhappy at Langley Park, but I felt that it was, at the moment, necessary to be a visitor to our shores to receive any appreciation from both the Press and the public.

I suppose the long years of American domination had made everyone lose confidence in our golf. Anyway, that was how I felt about it.

Also, I could not see the way to get better fees for playing and teaching where precedents existed for caddies to receive as much for carrying the clubs of a golfer as the professional received for teaching and playing – and he might be Open Champion or an International player. I thought I was worth more than this poorly paid tariff, but it seemed that no one else did.

I made this decision alone, and it turned out to be a complete surprise to the golfing world and to my friends, but I went to a club where I felt very much at home, and where I spent four very happy years; it turned out to be a very good decision, one of the best I have made in my life. I had for a year or two now been suffering from gastric trouble. I expect the continual tournament strain was telling on me, and I was paying the price of trying to subdue an excitable temperament.

I found it much easier to follow a diet on the Continent for one thing, and for another, I think the variety of life appealed to me. As I have already mentioned, I had been ordered red wine by a famous French specialist. In Belgium I could afford to enjoy my wine, as it was well within my pocket.

During the first two years in Brussels, where I lived for the best part of each year, my health improved greatly, and I began to get fitter and stronger, and this led up to my winning the Open, which I did in the middle of my second year as professional at Waterloo.

One of the letters I treasure and which is stuck in one of my many scrap-books is from 'Sandy' Herd, a great friend of mine until he died. It is dated in December, 1932, when I was being criticised for going away from England. Sandy wrote as an old man to a young one, telling me to keep my chin up. I have never forgotten Sandy's words, and I was delighted to receive and acknowledge his congratulations in 1934, and on many a later occasion, too!

In 1933 I paid another visit to St Andrews. Like all golfers who keep going back to this old grey city, I found that it grew on me. The Old Course, which I hope is never altered any more, is always wrongly and severely criticised because it is – well, just different and *difficult*.

This particular year it was presented to us dry and fast, and, although it is just as playable and just as good a test under these conditions, it is trying to players used to hitting them up to the pin to have to 'bumble' them along. Yet two American members of the Ryder Cup team tied with 292, Densmore Shute beating Craig Wood on the play-off.

I was sharing the lead on this occasion after three rounds with several other players and yet, although I started well enough on my final round with my four, I said to a friend on the second tee, 'I cannot win. I have just had a feeling it is not my year again.' I did my best, but without inspiration, and although I was well in it till the 13th, where I played safely on to the 6th fairway and got an impossible stance and took a stupid six, I felt I was pulling against the collar all the way. I finished only three shots out, but that was another Open gone. This year was Walter Hagen's last big try for the Open. He led the field after two rounds and then just faded out.

In 1934 I won. I led all the way and played really good golf during the whole week, including the qualifying rounds. Yet, curiously enough, after again beginning my training right after St Andrews the previous year, and working at my golf as never before, I arrived on the eve of the Championship week at Royal St George's, Sandwich, not knowing which of four sets of clubs I had with me to use, and I almost felt like scratching, for I had practised till I was dizzy, tried all the swings I knew and still could not get the ball to go properly. So, with a sort of feeling 'I might as well play now I am here, but I ought to quit,' I put my clubs in my bags on Saturday afternoon and threw them in behind the seat of my red Mercedes cabriolet and decided to forget golf, if I could, till Monday morning, when I was due to play my first qualifying round at Royal St George's.

I was out very early on the Monday and, accompanied by a marker and a couple of friends, I played 18 of the most perfect holes I have ever played and holed the course without a long putt going in, in 66. I did a 75 at Deal the next day, on a course I did not know very well, and then came back to play on the Championship course on the Wednesday. I did 67 for my first round, then finished my second round with three threes and did a 65 this time, and I knew this virtually gave me the Championship if I could hang on, as I had a seven-stroke lead. On the final day – I remember it well, it was a lovely day at the seaside, bright sun and with a nice breeze – I did a 72 for my third round, which gave me a further two strokes lead. So here I was with my life's ambition within my grasp, having only to finish the 18 holes in decent figures to win by a 'street.'

People, meaning to be kind, kept congratulating me prematurely, and although I was feeling like the 'King' but uncrowned, I kept asking them to wait till afterwards, saying, 'one never knows' with my lips, when my heart was telling me 'It can't be otherwise, unless you are too stupid for it to be believable.'

I had a light lunch. It would be not telling the truth to say I was not excited, but I did eat enough to sustain me, and I judged I had timed my arrival on the first tee just right when I got there five minutes before I was down to drive off. The starter, however, to my disappointment, informed me that my time had been delayed fifteen minutes to help the stewards to control the crowds better. I did not know what to do with myself; I was unprepared for this and, not wishing to talk to anyone, I went and sat alone in an empty tent by the first tee, whilst my closer friends stayed outside talking to my well-wishers, keeping them away from me. Those fifteen minutes dragged by; here I was waiting to see my life's ambition realised and I was powerless to get on with it.

I cannot remember all the things that flashed through my mind. All my dreams had come true in one instant, then in another instant I had gone all cold with the thought of what would happen if I slipped up. This anxiety proved more than my delicate stomach could stand and I had a terrible stomach cramp. I could hardly stand up. I must have looked pretty ill, for I could hear the comments of the crowd on my 'green' colour as I teed up. There was nothing to do but play and get on with it. I knew how little any excuses would help me: the crowd expected results. My long game was dreadful. I was all limp and perspiration was cold on my forehead. I seemed powerless to pull myself together whilst this stomach cramp continued. Luckily, I putted well, otherwise I dread to think what would have happened.

I had not eaten too much ice-cream or spaghetti, as has been suggested, for I was on a diet and had been for a long time. Anyone who has followed a strict diet for a time and who knows what it means in the way of self-control regarding food, will realise that at such an important moment I would be most unlikely to break my rules of diet. I got out in 40, and with three short holes in this half, too! I continued to struggle and looked like taking yet another five at the long 13th (which would have been the fourth in succession on the homeward nine) when I holed a ten-foot putt for a four. This seemed to cheer me up and I relaxed a little for the first time for over two hours, and from that moment I played as I had done all the week, and came back in par figures to finish the round in 79 and a 283 total, equal to Sarazen's record at Prince's in 1932. When the time came to step forward and get this most coveted of all golf trophies from the Hon. Michael Scott, Captain of the Club, I had no jacket with me, so I borrowed Henry Longhurst's camel-hair overcoat to wear over my pullover for the big occasion.

I saw quite a lot of Harry Vardon during that week, for he was also staying at the Guildford Hotel, Sandwich. On the final day, Harry was ill in bed and so could only follow the play from reports. When I took up to his bedroom the old Cup he had so gloriously won on six occasions, tears came into his eyes, and he could not say a word;

nor could I, for I was crying, too! Harry was always most encouraging to me, and on the rare occasions that I got talking golf with him in a serious way I was most impressed with his knowledge of the game. I learnt a lot from the old master; more, in fact, than I ever learned in America.

That year, the year of the first British win for eleven successive years, I had the friendly encouragement of all the 'Old Brigade' who wanted once again to see our golf on top. James Braid, J. H. Taylor, and Ted Ray were always on hand to give me a word of encouragement.

The 65 I did stands as the lowest score ever done in the Open, and what was unusual was to do 66 and 67 as well, during the same week on this great golf course. I look back on this week at the Royal St George's Golf Club as one of the highlights in my career.

There was no relaxing after this, for it was just as necessary to keep practising to hold the crown as to win it, and as I was only 27 I was now set on winning it again.

In 1935 we went to Scotland again, this time to Muirfield. I was favourite and did, I think, 141 in the qualifying rounds and was either first or second. This means nothing, though to read some reports of the play it might be considered almost a junior title. I then led the first round with a 68, a course record for the altered course. I never know why they keep altering these classic courses. They are still doing it, for they altered Hoylake in 1946 even.

My 68 left me very unhappy. I will tell you why! I was playing beautiful golf, as can be imagined by my scoring, but in this round I wanted a four for a 66. It was a drive and a No. 4 iron only, that day, for me, and things were going so well that I was even looking for a three to do another 65. I hit a long drive which curled dangerously towards one of the bunkers on the left, and although I could not see if the ball had dropped in I felt very uneasy about it. As I left the tee, a well-wisher, whom I could have slain on the spot without turning a hair, came up to me and began talking about my brother, whom he had not seen for a while, and enquired about his health, etc. My look did not deter him, nor could a hastened step shake him off. He clung like a leech, pouring out light stupid conversation into my ear, all the way to the bunker.

When I arrived there I was quite angry with myself for getting into the sand. I stupidly decided to go for the green, to get a No. 4 length shot with my number 7, which meant pressing like the dickens! I hit the top of the bunker with a powerful shot, and the ball fell down, and there I lay nearer the face than before, for two! This time shaken out of my anger by this other blow, my brain began to work coolly. I must cut my losses now. So I played out safely but a little too well, and my ball plugged into soft sand in another bunker 50 yards from the green. The ball was so deep down that I could not reach the putting surface even though I hit the ball with all my strength. So, out in four and still well short of the green. I got down in two more for a six. Sixty-eight was a fine round, but I was very uneasy. I felt the championship had already gone, although I was the holder and in the lead after the first round.

I played the rest of this championship with my tail down somehow, and finished poorly; Alfred Perry who won, also took my record with a 67.

Hoylake again, 1936. I have always liked this course despite the old-fashioned, very formal air about the club itself. I did 68 in the first qualifying round and then 67 at Wallasey, both course records, but rain washed out the second day's play and it meant another round that week. I played beautifully every day and yet could not score. My putts refused to drop and yet I was only two strokes out in the end, in spite of having two penalty strokes in my final round of 74. I hit the ball better and straighter all the time there than I had done before in my life.

Raymond Oppenheimer, a life-long friend of mine, who was my head gallery-steward during several rounds that week, was asked by a newly arrived spectator to the gallery, how Cotton was playing; he was overheard to remark in a way that only he can, 'Sir, he is driving so straight, it is impossible to tell whether his ball is on the left or right half of the fairway.' It was quite near the truth as well!

At the end of 1936 I decided to come back to England, and Lord Rosebery, the president of the Ashridge Golf Club near Berkhamsted, asked me if I would like to help the Ashridge Club get ahead. We got to terms and I joined the club in January, 1937.

I built a house in the beautiful Ashridge Park on a spur of the Chiltern hills, and called it 'Shangri-la' after the valley of that name, which plays a big part in the James Hilton book *Lost Horizon* – a valley in which 'no one grows old and happiness reigns.' The film of that name, in which Ronald Colman played the lead, I can still remember most vividly. I saw it several times as I enjoyed it so much.

From Ashridge I entered for the 1937 Open at Carnoustie, and with America's strongest Ryder Cup team also in the field, I won for the second time this treasured trophy.

I was playing well that year, and spent a week at Carnoustie in May, when I found the course in a very rough condition – as most of these public links usually are to be found, out of championship time – but I got a good idea of the layout as I did not know the course prior to this visit.

I did not play outstandingly better than other players in the field during the week, though I was in the running all the time, but on setting out for the final round in one of the most consistent downpours I remember, I told an intimate friend of mine, as we left the first tee, I had a feeling I could win.

I played one of the best rounds of my career, 71, one over the course record, and won by two strokes. I putted very well on the water-sodden greens and when I came to the last hole, which crosses two burns, with a four for a 70, I did not play safe, short of the burn, as I might have done, but concentrated on hitting the ball hard and as far from the 'out-of-bounds' on the left as I could. My No. 2 iron shot finished in a sand bunker, hole-high to the right of the green. Then I took my ordinary niblick, for, from the hard, wet sand, I figured 'one a bit thin with my blaster could go over the fence,' and I played out safely, short of the pin, got down in two putts and felt that unless something unusual happened I was 'home' – as the crowd also considered, judging from the reception I received.

The unusual nearly did happen, for the rain continued steadily and pools of water lay everywhere. If any holes had got under water things would have been awkward, but as it turned out, all was well, and my name went on the cup a second time.

One of my best friends, Leonard Crawley, later golf correspondent of the *Daily Telegraph* and a great supporter and demonstrator of the 'Cotton system,' was staying with us in our boarding house at the time, but after a week's practice with the American players he was of the firm opinion that we had 'had it.' He had seen our play at Southport, where we lost the Ryder Cup for the first time at home.

Leonard, for some unaccountable reason, failed to qualify and returned to London feeling very disappointed and anxious to get away from the sight of the inevitable American victory.

However, when I won and R. A. Whitcombe was second, I received one of the most appreciated telegrams, for Leonard was big enough to be humble over his mistake. This win is considered my best performance.

In 1938 the Open went to Royal St George's again, and, after two rounds, I was seven strokes behind the leader with 147. I seemed to have no chance, but the weather decided otherwise.

During the early hours of the morning of the final day, it started to blow a gale, and the gale increased as day dawned; the exhibition tents were blown down, and when we arrived the clubhouse surrounds looked like a battlefield. Naturally the scoring went up sky-high; my rounds of 77 and 74 gave me the best total of the day, and my round of 74 after lunch, which was three strokes better than any other, was nearly the best of my life, for I was level fours on the 16th tee.

The wind was so strong that afternoon that I drove the 2nd green, 370 yards, and holed my putt for a two. I drove also the 384 yards 11th hole, and got a three.

This was Reggie Whitcombe's 'year,' and his two rounds on the final day, 75 and 78, represented wonderful golf. He always is at his best when the going is tough.

My third championship visit to St Andrews was in 1939 and, while I appeared to play soundly, I was not, in fact, striking particularly well, though I was confident with a card and pencil.

I did a 69 in the qualifying rounds on the Old Course, the only time I broke 70 there until 1947 in the Spalding Tournament, when I had a similar score. Then after a 74 to open with, played during a foul thunderstorm, for a third part of the round I fell behind gradually. 'Dick' Burton won with 290 that year.

In my second round I stood on the 14th tee for 25 minutes waiting for the huge crowd (I was nearly last on the Thursday afternoon, and so picked up everybody's crowd) to cross from the 13th green to beyond the wall. This long wait ruined my round, for I was five under fours at this point and the strain of watching and thinking of that 'out-of-bounds' on one side, and the 'Beardies' on the other, was too much for me, and I finished weakly in 72.

It was from that moment that I really saw the necessity for making St Andrews a golfing arena completely, and my suggestion, carried out as far as possible under existing conditions in the 1946 Open, has proved to be the solution.

Then came the war, which completely stopped British golf of all sorts, and, except for the charity games and some weekend play, the British Isles thought little about the small white ball.

After the second World War the first Open Championship was at St Andrews in 1946, and the golfing public thought that this was a sign that at last the world was on the way to normality. So it was, but very slowly indeed as it turned out.

'Slamming' Sam Snead from USA flew over to Scotland a few days before the

Open and took the old Trophy back with him. My part in this event was a conspicuous one, for I led after two rounds with two 70s, but on the last day I gradually faded away. In the final round I could hardly walk the distance and realised how far from 100 per cent fit I was, for the strain of holding on in the last holes was too much for me and I finished absolutely exhausted. My long period of ill health in the RAF, which caused my discharge from the service and finished with a serious abdominal operation, plus the one year's convalesence during which period I was not allowed to hit a shot, and the absence of adequate rebuilding food, prevented me from making a complete recovery.

Then came 1947 at Hoylake. A great course in perfect condition; no Snead to defend his title, but Stranahan, Ghezzi and Bulla came to collect the cup. I led with a 69 with Laurie Ayton, but fell to second place on the next day with a thoroughly bad 78; then I recovered to a decent position, for with nine holes left to play I found myself in the lead again, but on the home stretch, battling against a gale of wind which had suddenly sprung up, I failed and finished tamely in 76. Fortunately for Britain, Fred Daly won, and a worthy champion he proved to be, for he won the *News of the World* PGA Championship the same year.

I realised that it was no good training hard for 1948 unless I could get really fit, and the only way to get proper food was to go abroad. My sincere American friends, R. A. Hudson, William Danforth and Ed. Lowery, were most encouraging and felt sure that even after our Ryder Cup failure another trip to America would set me up physically, so after a brief visit to Monte Carlo, I returned in the Spring of 1948 to USA, where I played better and returned fitter and more confident.

At Muirfield I found that the course for the Open was my course – narrow fairways and lots of rough. I played well all the week, scored 69 + 69 to lead the qualifying rounds by 2 strokes, and then won the Title for the third time with 284, to lead Fred Daly by 5 strokes.

My 66 in the second round, played in part before His Majesty the King, who followed the play keenly, was a course record and paved my way to success.

From *This Game of Golf* by Henry Cotton
(Country Life, London, 1948).

The Master and a Modest Case of Forgery·

Henry Longhurst

Though Henry Cotton had won the British Open in 1934 (and had been presented with the trophy wearing my overcoat – which I still possess), this year, 1937, really represented his prime. There had been no Americans when he won at Sandwich in 1934. In 1937 at Carnoustie there had been the whole American Ryder Cup team and with a stupendous final 71 in driving rain, almost the best individual round I ever saw, he beat them all. We all tend to inflate the heroes of our early days but I have seen them all since that time and cannot believe that any of them, Hogan included, hit the ball better than Cotton. Nor do I know anybody who did not himself automatically hit the ball better when playing with him, though this is no place in which to be tempted into the technicalities of golf. It was a great advantage in my own line of life, however, to be his contemporary and to be good enough to play occasionally in his company, albeit not on level terms. He won his third Open after the war, fourteen years after his first, and, when King George VI came to Muirfield to watch, he put on a 66 for his benefit.

I myself have basked in Cotton's reflected glory and still do. On coming off the last green at St Andrews not long after the war I was surrounded by autograph-hunting children and, making the elementary mistake of thinking they knew who I was – whereas all they do is to rush up to all and sundry, thrust their books under his nose and then see who they have got – I signed a good many books. I was cut down to size by hearing a freckled, fang-toothed, ginger-headed boy round at the back exclaiming, on seeing my signature, 'Och, he's no' anyone!' All right, I thought, but he bloody well will be in future. Since that day I must have signed *Henry Cotton* in at least a couple of hundred books, thereby giving much innocent satisfaction to both parties. Furthermore, I still produce the most excellent specimens, whereas the Maestro himself has been getting a little slack in latter years.

From *My Life and Soft Times* by Henry Longhurst
(Cassell and Co., London, 1971).

6

HENRY THE COMMENTATOR

Augusta in April

Henry Longhurst

Nothing to date has equalled the thrill of my first invitation to the Masters at Augusta – though having been disappointed the year before, I still didn't believe that it was really going to happen (despite several journalists' confident predictions) till I'd actually got the written invitation in my hand. Augusta has so many memories for so many people. For Gene Sarazen it's that incredible albatross which virtually won him the Masters at the fifteenth hole of the fourth round. For Gary Player it's that amazing fight back in 1978 when he came from nowhere in the last nine holes to clinch the title. For Henry Longhurst of the sonorous voice and wry wit, it was being made the best-known TV commentator on both sides of the Atlantic. As he relates here, he got on to American TV pretty much by accident and unwittingly caused a sensation just by being himself.

Our Henry was good enough to win the German Amateur Open in 1936. His post-war golf column in the *Sunday Times* was a must for every keen golfer of whatever ability. His rubicund nose was testimony to his robust drinking, though never to the detriment of his performance, not even when it came to climbing to perilous heights up what ABC TV christened the 'Longhurst ladders'. For all his fame in other directions, to the American in the street he was 'the guy that does the sixteenth in the Masters'.

I.W.

CBS (the Columbia Broadcasting System), who were televising the 1965 Carling Tournament at a course called Pleasant Valley outside Boston, wondered if it would interest me to go up one of their towers, it being their rehearsal day, and 'see how they did it'. I was naturally intrigued and did so, joining one of their announcers, as they call the commentators, John Derr. So far as I remember I only said a few words into their microphone, but to my astonishment I got a note from the producer, Frank

Chirkinian, inviting me to do the 16th hole next day. This turned out to be a long short-hole of some 210-odd yards, where the players drove from an elevated tee down between two bunkers and onto a huge green, behind which we sat under a big parasol on a tower no more than twenty feet high.

I did all I was called upon to do, which heaven knows did not seem very much, naming the players and their scores correctly as they came up to the tee, which one could hardly fail to do in view of the fact that a very efficient young fellow had already put a piece of paper in front of one's nose containing the information, and occasionally adding some commonplace comment before being told to 'throw it to 15'. It transpired, however, that completely unwittingly I had managed to cause two minor sensations in our limited little world. One was when towards the end a young Mexican called Homero Blancas came to the 16th hole with the prospect looming before him of picking up, if everything went right, the equivalent of some £12,000. It proved to be a little much for him, and taking a 2-iron, he hit the shot that a good many of us would have done in the circumstances; in other words he hit it right off the sole, half topped, and it must have stung like the devil. 'Oh, that's a terrible one,' I said instinctively. 'Right off the bottom of the club.' In fact, it scuttled down the hill and finished on the green, but that wasn't the point. I had said it was a bad shot – which of course it was – but no one, it transpired, had ever said such a thing before, at any rate in such downright terms. This, though it took some time for the penny to drop and I can sometimes scarcely believe it still, was the first 'sensation'. The second took even longer to dawn on me. Golf being, like billards, a 'silent' game, that is to say that silence is expected while a man is making his stroke – unlike, say, the Cup Final, when both viewer and commentator are conscious of being one of a vast vociferous crowd (though even so, compare the silence that comes over them when a man is to take a penalty and therefore to make a single individual stroke) – it had never occurred to me from the very beginning that one should do other than remain silent while the golfer was actually playing his shot, so that 'talking on the stroke' had always seemed to be one of the cardinal sins of golf commentating, even though, heaven knows, I have found myself often guilty of committing it. This had not been, up to that time, the accepted principle in America which it has since become and the 'brilliant flashes of silence' turned out to be the second 'sensation'.

Also, of course, the most commonplace little expressions in one man's country may seem strange and catch the attention in another's. Towards the end of this (for me) momentous day, for instance, I announced that the eventual winner, Tony Lema, later so tragically killed in a private plane accident, had a very 'missable' put. This, I was told, was greeted with much applause by the crowd watching in the locker room. 'You hear what the old guy said? He said, "He's got a *missable putt!*" ' For some extraordinary reason this commonplace and self-explanatory expression seemed never to have become part of golfing language in America.

Anyway, it was all good for trade and not only was I invited again by CBS, this time to the Masters at Augusta, but also by ABC (the American Broadcasting Company), who handle such 'prestigious' events as the US Open and the US PGA cham-pionships.

In a modest way, too, my name has gone into the language of television, for by the time we all met in America I had already grown portly enough to wonder what I was doing, climbing these ladders at my weight and age, and made so bold as to wonder whether it would not be possible to somewhat civilize this mode of ascent. From that time onwards a form of staircase, complete with handrail, has been the order of the day, for which I and all my successors may be truly thankful. What I am really proud about, though, is the fact that, in the directions to the scaffolders who erect the towers, these staircases are ordered by ABC under the name of 'Longhurst Ladders'.

Such is immortality!

As a result of the pleasant episode at Pleasant Valley CBS, as I have said, invited me the following April to cover a hole at the Masters at Augusta, Georgia, and for the past five or six years I have had the honour, to say nothing of the aesthetic pleasure, of sitting on a little tower at the back of the 16th there too, once again a short hole and clearly, I should have thought, among the first half-dozen in American golf.

Augusta in April is heaven. The course itself was a nursery and many of the original trees and shrubs were left to grow on when in 1930 Clifford Roberts, a New York investment broker, persuaded the one and only Bobby Jones, who had completed his Grand Slam (the Open and Amateur Championships on both sides of the Atlantic in the same year) and was himself from Atlanta, to join him in creating a national golf course – 'a retreat of such nature and such excellence that men of some means and devoted to the game of golf might find the club an extra luxury where they might visit and play with kindred spirits from other parts of the nation'. This they certainly succeeded in doing.

I shall never forget my first visit to the property [*Jones later recorded*]. The long lane of magnolias through which we approached was beautiful. The old manor house with its cupola and walls of masonry two feet thick was charming. The rare trees and shrubs of the old nursery were enchanting. But when I walked out on the grass terrace under the big trees behind the house and looked down over the property, the experience was unforgettable. It seemed that this land had been lying here for years just waiting for someone to lay a golf course upon it. Indeed, it even looked as thought it were already a golf course, and I am sure that one standing today where I stood on this first visit, on the terrace overlooking the practice putting green, sees the property almost exactly as I saw it then.

Year by year I myself have sat in the same chair on the same little balcony, upstairs, looking through the wisteria down at the same scene, while the same coloured waiter comes out and says, 'You like the same as last year, sah? Beefeater on the rocks?' Everything indeed, is the same and it is only by looking down at the huge scoreboard that you can tell which year it is – a Palmer year or a Nicklaus year or whatever it may be. The same people come, decked out in every colour of the rainbow – ridiculous under the grey skies of Britain but exactly right for the spring sunshine of Georgia. They bring the same folding chairs, take them to the same places as last year, and, many of them, sit there all day every day each year. One year we had a three-way play-off starting at one o'clock. This made it inconceivable that the game should reach the 16th hole before five, yet when I went down there to be 'taped' at about mid-day, many of the regulars, whom I had come to know by sight over the years, were already in their places, with no prospect of a shot being played before them for five hours.

The Masters, though it may have envious critics, is something special. A strong sense of traditional decorum is preserved, and woe betide the man or woman who did not observe it when Clifford Roberts's eye happened to be upon them. The spectators never run – would you mind! – but they do love to shout, and from time to time a colossal yell reverberates between the pines as someone holes a putt which, from the roar that greets it, might have been the winning goal in a Cup Final.

It all started in 1934 when the select gentlemen who had formed the Augusta National club, in a part of the world where the climate hardly permitted tournaments in the heat of summer, conceived the idea of inviting some of the leading players of the day to a tournament in the spring, when it was perfect in Georgia and the players were not engaged elsewhere. This was a great success and at once became an annual event. Who christened it 'the Masters' no one seems quite to know, nor is it certain that the pious founders would ever have started it at all if they had known what eventually they would be letting themselves in for. However that may be, the tournament they created remains unique. No advertisements are allowed to disfigure the scene either inside or outside the grounds – except when some supporter of Arnold Palmer (not, we may be sure, the great man himself) hired an aeroplane to fly noisily over the scene all day trailing a banner with the words GO ARNIE GO – nor is any mention of filthy lucre permitted, and this really is something when you consider that the 'leading money-winner' seems to be the chief focus of interest in American golf. All the television directors and commentators have to submit to a solemn lecture forbidding mention of any tournaments other than the US and British Open and Amateur championships and the American PGA (other tournaments on the professional tour simply do not exist) and especially forbidding them to mention money in any form. No prize money is announced beforehand and none presented at the time, it being held sufficient for the winner to have won the Masters and to have been invested with the traditional green blazer which thenceforward, even though he be a millionaire, he wears with justifiable pride. Only later is it revealed that the first prize this year came to $25,000 or whatever it may be.

From the side of the town on which I am usually billeted, one drives to the course through avenues of elegant houses whose gardens – open to the road, as always in America, not hedged in – are ablaze with azalea, rhododendron and dogwood. On the course itself two holes stand out and on a sunny afternoon they really take your breath away: the 13th and 'my' hole, the 16th, of which I will let the picture tell the story, except to add that on the 13th you may imagine the great Georgia pines a hundred feet high and the bank at the foot of them a solid mass of vivid scarlet, orange and yellow azaleas. At both holes the water is liable to remain an equally vivid blue, even on a cloudy day, due possibly to the fact that, if you get there early enough, you will see a gang of dusky workers, each with a watering-can full of blue dye! It was in this that I once said that Doug Sanders's ball had 'found a watery grave'. This appears to have given much innocent pleasure, since I am still reminded of it.

Augusta National, rare among the more prosperous clubs in America, is a golf club pure and simple, like Pine Valley and Cypress Point, with no swimming-pool nor gigantic locker room complete with barber, masseurs and the rest – an old porticoed plantation-style house with an unspoilt air of elegance and peace. Among the pines on the left are a number of white cottages, or 'cabins', as they call them, in the same style, one of them a gift from the members to President Eisenhower, and behind these, discreetly secluded by a hedge, is what is probably the best 9-hole, par-3 course in the world, again enclosed by a background of spectacular colour. Here they hold a tournament on the day before the Masters, the record for which is held by Art Wall, who, believe it or not, had two 3s and seven 2s for a 20. So altogether, as you may gather, the Augusta National is not a bad place for us scribes and commentators to earn our living in, especially those of us who arrive, in April, fresh from an English winter.

Perhaps I may add one final comment on my own modest operations in television, namely that, whatever you may say, it is nice to be recognized, even if only by one's voice. This is not vanity. It adds much to the pleasure of a taxi ride, for instance (as well as to the tip!), if the driver says, 'I'd know your voice anywhere,' and starts talking about golf. Only the other day, hailing a cab opposite the American Embassy in Grosvenor Square, I said, 'I wonder if you could take me to Cricklewood Broadway?' to which the man at once replied, 'I'd take *you* anywhere.' Like so many London taxi-drivers he was an avid golfer – they have a golfing society of their own – and actually had a golf magazine beside him in the cab, open at a picture of Arnold Palmer, who once, he said, the biggest day of his golfing life, he had driven in this very cab. All this is not, however, the irrelevance of the subject of the Masters that it may seem, for my peak was reached, and you can hardly blame me for relating it, when, on handing in my baggage at Cape Town airport in South Africa, I had had time to say only, 'I wonder if you could check in this shooting-stick as well as the suitcase?' when a transatlantic voice behind me said, 'Hey! Aren't you the guy that does the 16th at the Masters?'

From *My Life and Soft Times* by Henry Longhurst
(Cassell and Co., London, 1971).

I just don't know about the guy. He looks like W. C. Fields in drag. But he happens to be the best in the business.

CBS TV producer Frank Chirkinian on
Henry Longhurst as commentator.

On Augusta National Golf Club, Georgia

The only difference is at Augusta the divots tear loose on dotted lines.
John Updike, 1980.

The greens *are* the course. . . . They are faster than a fart in a hot skillet.
David Mill, 1977.

7

THE BIG THREE

The Million-dollar Shot – How Arnie Palmer Made Boldness His Friend

Arnold Palmer

Of the Big Three of golf in the 1960s – Player, Palmer and Nicklaus – it was Arnie who commanded the biggest following because of his spectacular 'go for broke' style. Many top-class golfers play the percentage game and handicap golfers always should. But that has never been Palmer's style. He says: 'You must play boldly to win. My whole philosophy has been based on winning tournaments, not on finishing a careful fifth or seventh or tenth.' Here he explains how he turned that philosophy into a glorious winning streak, starting with his victory in the US Open in 1960. In a way it all began with his first shot at what he called 'that maddening first hole'. International golf is so competitive now that it isn't enough to 'keep shooting par and the other guy will crack', as Bobby Jones used to say. Now the winner of a major needs an Arnie-type charge in at least one of the four rounds.

I.W.

There was a sharp bite and sparkle in the mountain air. The Rockies loomed clearly in the distance – immense, clear, barren. I remember on the first hole at Denver, the sun was so bright that it hurt your eyes to look down the fairway. Standing on the tee, it was difficult to see the green without a pair of dark glasses. It took me four rounds to find it – but when I did, the whole thrust of my life was altered.

The time was 1960. The place was Cherry Hills Country Club. The event was the US Open.

On the fourth round of that tournament, I tried a shot that I'd missed three times in three rounds. I tried it again not because I'd failed – or because I like failure – but because I was convinced that it was the shot necessary to win the tournament.

A bold shot?

Yes.

But you must play boldly to win. My whole philosophy has been based on winning golf tournaments, not on finishing a careful fifth, or seventh, or tenth.

A reckless shot?

No.

In eighteen years of tournament golf I feel that I've never tried a shot that I couldn't make.

On that summer day in 1960, I was young in what the world calls fame, but I was ripe in golfing experience. I'd been a professional golfer for five years, and up to then I'd won twenty tournaments. In those years, I'd learned something about the strategy of the game and its psychology and rewards. If there was any reward I treasured most, it was the way that the game responded to my inner drives, to the feeling we all have that – in those moments that are so profoundly a challenge to man himself – he has done his best. That – win or lose – nothing more could have been done.

My own needs were deeply driven ones: I could not retreat from a challenge. If the chance was there and if – no matter how difficult it appeared – it meant winning, I was going to take it. It was the 'sweetness' of risk that I remembered, and not its dangers.

In looking back, I feel that in these years I was learning something of the subtle dimensions of all this – I was learning the *meaning* of boldness as well as its feeling.

For boldness does not mean 'recklessness' to me. Rather it involves a considered confidence: I *know* I'm going to make the shot that seems reckless to others. I also know the value of the risk involved: A bold shot has to have its own rewards – winning or losing the match, winning or losing the tournament.

But perhaps it was not until the US Open at Cherry Hills that I put it all together, philosophically as well as physically. For not until that summer day in 1960 did it become apparent to me how boldness might influence not just a hole but an entire round, an entire tournament, and even an entire golfing career.

It began, really, on the first tee of the last round at Cherry Hills. On the face of it, there was nothing terribly subtle about this hole: You could see every mistake you made. It was downhill to the green; the tee was elevated perhaps 150 feet above the green. It was only 346 yards long, not a terribly long par 4 – and a terribly tempting birdie 3 . . . to me. It was guarded on the left by an irregular line of poplars and pines and on the right by a ditch that the membership had practically paved with golf balls. A nice direct hole for the strong driver, somebody who could – in that thin, mile-high air – get the ball out there 300 yards or so.

But there *was* one nasty little afterthought that had been provided for the US Open: The grass was allowed to grow very long and become a 'rough' right in the fairway, about 50 or 60 yards in front of the green. Moreover, the hazard was heightened by a treacherous bunker guarding the gateway to the green. It had grass in it that looked like it was three feet deep. If you got in there, you might never be found again. I mean it was the kind of place where you hunted buffalo – not par.

The idea, of course, was to penalize the strong driver, to threaten him with capture by the rough – and a difficult second shot – if he played to his own best game (a powerful drive) on his first shot.

The safe way to play that hole, for most golfers, was not to invite trouble – not to challenge the rough or the bunker in the first place. In that sense, the first hole was an authentic mirror of the entire course. For Cherry Hills was long in yardage (7004) but not in reality: The thin air gave most tee shots a much longer carry than on a sea-level course. But its greens were small and well guarded by bunkers and water hazards; there was an added danger that under the hot, direct sun and the afternoon winds they would become so dried out that it would be all but impossible to get the ball to stop on them. If you hit those greens with power, the ball would roll right over and off them on the far side. So it was a course that took accuracy, touch, and an unflagging concentration. It *looked* to many like a course whose yardage beckoned to power – Mike Souchak, a powerful golfer, led at the halfway mark of the 1960 Open with a remarkable 68–67 for a thirty-six-hole score of 135. But it was, in reality, a course that catered to placement more than to power – in that opening round of 68, Souchak had only twenty-six putts, nine or ten short of normal for an eighteen-hole round. So he wasn't up there scattering power shots; he was getting good placement with everything he did.

To focus on the first hole: It was the kind of hole that shaped your entire approach to the course in that it could reward you for power or for placement.

To the pretty good amateur golfer, it was an opportunity for a par 4. He might put the ball out in the fairway pretty much where he could – far short of the rough – and then hope to get close to, or onto, the green with his second shot.

To the venturesome pro, it was an opportunity for a birdie. He'd use an iron to hit his shot off the tee, expecting to get enough accuracy from it (which he would less likely get from a driver) to drop the ball precisely in the fairway, where he'd have the ideal second shot. In short, he intended to place his first shot so that he could hit his second shot precisely to the cup – not just any old place on the green but *specifically* to the cup. For this was the kind of shot where the pro prefers – where he *intends* – to get his second shot so close to the cup that he'll need only one putt to 'get down.' So if he emphasized placement over power, he hoped to wind up with a birdie 3, not a par 4.

From my angle of vision – somewhat singular, I'll admit – this was an eagle hole, not a birdie hole. I figured that, with boldness, I could get down in two strokes, not three or four.

That meant being on the green in one shot, not two.

That meant getting into the cup in one putt, not two.

That meant emphasizing power over placement.

That meant using my driver, not my iron.

My intention was simply to drive the ball hard enough and far enough so that it would bound through the rough in front of the green and run up on the putting surface to a good position near the cup. To get a ball to stop precisely on a green, you must give it backspin, so that it bites into the grass when it hits and then stops short, or even hops backward. That's fairly easy to do when you're using an iron from the fairway that is fairly close to the green; you merely strike straight downward at the ball, taking a divot after making contact with the ball, and take a normal follow-through. But it is difficult to do while driving off the tee and ramming the ball through the rough. For one thing, on tee shots you may be hitting the ground a microsecond before you make contact with the ball. At least that's what I was doing with my driver back in 1960 (though since then I've changed my style somewhat). Then you normally give the ball a considerable overspin when you hit the ball dead centre (or thereabouts) and make the big follow-through. Normally you want to give the ball some overspin when hitting off the tee with a driver. Overspin will cause the ball to roll a little farther after it hits the ground. So my tee shot would, I expected, be hitting those small greens without backspin. And if the greens were dry and hard, as I expected, the ball might never stop rolling this side of the Continental Divide.

So I was proposing to use a power club – the driver – rather than a placement club – the iron – on a hole that demanded placement as well as power. And I was accepting overspin, not backspin, on a green that threatened to be faster than the Indianapolis Speedway on Memorial Day.

'Boldness' is what my friends called it. 'Insanity' is what they meant.

But I figured to have two things going for me when the ball hit the green:

If the ball went through the rough, not over it, the thick grass would cut down significantly on the ball's momentum, and very likely on how far it would roll, once it hit the green. Also, I'd be playing this hole relatively early in the morning on the first three rounds. (On the fourth and last round – because of the way the US Open was run in those days – I'd be playing it in the early afternoon.) I knew that every green was being heavily watered at night, simply because the tournament officials were afraid that otherwise the greens would be hard and dry by the afternoon. So in the morning, the first green – obviously the first to be played – would likely be heavily laden with the water from the all-night sprinkling, and the water residue would slow down any ball hit onto it. That's another reason why the roll of the ball would be reduced.

(You didn't *really* think that I just went out there and hit the ball hard, without giving any thought to what would happen to it once it came down – now did you?)

The way I looked at it, all I had to do was pound the ball bouncingly through the rough and onto the heavily watered green. Then I'd one-putt and have an eagle. I'd have that course by the throat, and – as my fellow pro, Jerry Barber, once said – 'shake it to death.'

Only it didn't happen. Not on the first three rounds. That green was tough to reach with a rifle, much less a driver. In my first round I sent my tee shot into the ditch on the right. I didn't get an eagle or a birdie or a par on the hole. I didn't even get a bogey, for that matter. I got a double-bogey 6 – two over par, instead of the two under par that I'd aimed for. After that, things got better – but not much. I got a bogey 5 on the second round and a par 4 on the third round. So in the first three rounds, I'd taken fifteen strokes on that hole, instead of the twelve strokes that playing it safe might have given me. And instead of the six strokes that – in wild flights of genius – my boldness might have given me.

More than that, starting off every round with a deep disappointment damaged my whole pattern of play. After three rounds, I had a total of thirteen birdies in the tournament, but they were so scattered that I'd never gotten any momentum out of them – no 'charge,' so to speak. The result was that I was in fifteenth place with a 215 after three rounds.

Just before lunch, and the start of my last round, I paused outside the vast white scoreboard outside the rambling, neo-Tudor clubhouse at Cherry Hills. There in the elaborate black and red numerals of golf, written in a manner as highly stylized as medieval script, I saw how the field lay. I was seven strokes behind the leader, Mike Souchak. But Mike wasn't the only hurdle. Between me and the leadership lay such great golfers as Ben Hogan and Sam Snead, Julius Boros and Dow Finsterwald, Dave Marr and Bob Goalby, and a twenty-one-year-old amateur named Jack Nicklaus.

By the time I sat down to a sandwich in the clubhouse, my mood was about as black as a witch's heart. Ken Venturi and Bob Rosburg, who also seemed to be out of contention, joined me, and a couple of newsmen stopped by our table to offer solace to the newly bereaved.

One of them was an old friend, Bob Drum, then of the Pittsburgh *Press*. He knew of my tribulations with that first hole and of my conviction that it was an eagle hole that would unlock the entire course to the player bold enough to attack it. He also knew that my failure in a daring power approach had – in an era of golf when meticulous precision was most admired – given a certain satisfaction to a few older hands around professional golf. 'There are some guys out there who think you're just an upstart, a flash-in-the-pan,' he'd told me. So when he began to console me, and hint that maybe it was time to play it safe and try to pick up some good also-ran money in the US Open – since it was obvious I couldn't go from fifteenth place to first place in one round – the chemistry began working in me. Explosively.

'What would happen if I shot a 65 on this last round?' I asked, perhaps more aggressively than in the thirst for pure knowledge.

'Nothing,' said Bob. 'You're out of it.' He was an old friend but a realistic one. Only one man had *ever* shot a 65 in the final round of the US Open: Walter Burkema in 1957.

But that got to me. And to my pride. Realism – and pessimism – I did not need.

'Well,' I said, my voice lowering into my don't-tread-on-me tone, 'the way I read it is that a 65 would give me 280 for the tournament. And 280 is the kind of score that usually wins the US Open.'

Bob gave me a startled look, as if he just noticed I had two heads.

'Sure,' he said, 'but you won't do it by taking another double-bogey on the first hole.'

So there it was: I still looked at the first hole as a chance for triumph; Bob – and a great many others – looked at it as a place for patent disaster. I suppose they were right. If I'd played it safe on the first hole and teed off with my iron, instead of the driver, and gone for placement and par, I'd be three shots closer to the leaders after the first three rounds. If I'd picked up a birdie or two along with it, I might even be right on their necks. So the thing to do now was admit that the first hole had me beaten and go back to playing it like the other pros did – with an iron off the tee – and figure that by placing the ball and playing it safe, I might pick up enough strokes in the standing to avoid further shame.

But that's not the way I saw it. I wasn't playing golf to avoid shame. I was playing it to win championships. And the last round of a National Open is no place to start changing your whole style and philosophy of golf.

The way I looked at it, being fifteenth made it more *imperative* that I play boldly. It couldn't cost me much: The difference between being fifteenth or twenty-fifth or fifty-fifth is not terribly meaningful – at least to me. It's the difference between first and second that has meaning. And a considered boldness might – I was sure – still win me the tournament.

So when I got to the first tee, I reached for my driver. Even though it was now one-forty-five in the afternoon and the green figured to be dried out and it would take incredible accuracy to hit the green and hold it. One of my luncheon companions (not Bob Drum) had come along, and he looked as if there were nothing wrong with me that brain surgery couldn't cure. I addressed the ball as if it were my enemy – or my slave – and hit it with everything I could get into it. The ball went up and hung in the sharp, clear air as if it had been painted there. When it came down – with overspin – it leaped forward and ran through the rough and right onto the middle of the green.

Twenty feet from the hole.

Three hundred and forty-six yards and I'd not only driven the green but drilled it right in the heart!

Just like I'd been planning it all along.

Right? Right!

Okay – two putts. A birdie, not an eagle. But that didn't much depress me. For I'd shown that my idea *did* work – that boldness could conquer this hole. And that if it made the first hole yield, then the whole course could be conquered with boldness.

Suddenly my whole spirit, my entire attitude changed.

I charged onto the second hole – a 410-yard par 4 with an elevated green and trees right in the fairway. In two shots I was not quite on the green. But I chipped the ball from off the green right into the cup for another birdie 3. I charged onto the 348-yard third hole and birdied it. I charged onto the fourth hole and birdied it with a twisting 40-foot putt. Four holes: four birdie 3s. A par on the fifth, a birdie on the sixth, a birdie on the seventh: six birdies on seven holes. I finished the first nine holes in 30 strokes, just one short of a record.

'Damn!' I said to Bob Drum when he finally caught up to us. 'I really wanted that 29.' Bob exhibited deplorable self-control: 'Well,' he murmured consolingly, 'maybe next time.'

By the tenth hole, I was tied with Mike Souchak. By the twelfth, I was ahead of him. But it was not all over: There had been fourteen men between me and the lead, and before the afternoon was over, a half dozen or more held or challenged for the title. 'This was, to put it mildly, the wildest Open ever,' said *Sports Illustrated*. For me, the birdies disappeared, but the pars survived. The final five holes at Cherry Hills are a punishing finishing stretch: Ben Hogan, then forty-seven, felt it, and he faded here; Nicklaus was twenty-one, and so did he. I managed to play each of those last five holes in par and to come in with a 65 for the eighteen-hole round. Boldness had paid off: That surge at the start was, in the words of golf writer Herbert Warren Wind, 'the most explosive stretch of sub-par golf any golfer has ever produced in the championship. . . .' I finished the tournament with a seventy-two-hole score of 280. That was enough to give me the US Open championship and, as it developed, a certain hold on history.

For the 'charge' didn't stop there. It was not, in the long perspective, to be confined solely to one round or one tournament. It became a sort of phenomenon that marked my career: In the period 1960–63, I was to win thirty-two tournaments – and go on to become the first million-dollar winner in golf history.

From *Go For Broke!* by Arnold Palmer with Barry Furlong
(William Kimber, London, 1974).

The Genius of Nicklaus – Greatest of Them All?

Herbert Warren Wind

Nicklaus was determined to be the greatest golfer that ever lived from the time he was a teenager. He has won twenty major tournaments in a career that has spanned a quarter of a century, including five Masters over three decades from 1963 to 1986. He was the prodigy who didn't burn himself out. He could falter in sight of victory as he did in the 1963 Masters against the main contender Sam Snead, and then come scorching back to regain the lead, which is the hardest way to win any tournament. The first time we played together he didn't say much, his game was off. But there's always a great atmosphere playing with him. His unique blend of temperament and will to win, of technique plus deep golf thinking about the course and shot, is analysed by Herbert Warren Wind, writing in 1963.

I.W.

When golf authorities rank the great golfers of all time, a sizeable percentage of them place Nicklaus on the top level, along with Harry Vardon, Bobby Jones, and Ben Hogan, who were as preeminent in their eras as Nicklaus has been over the last two decades. While I am inclined to go along with this point of view, I can readily understand why many people close to the game consider Nicklaus nothing less than the greatest golfer ever. To a large extent, a golfer's place in history has traditionally been determined by his achievements in the major championships. Played on long, rigorous courses that require expert shotmaking, these championships are the British Open (established in 1860); the British Amateur (1885); the United States Open and United States Amateur (1895); our Professional Golfers Association (1916); and the Masters (1934). Professional golfers, of course, cannot play in amateur championships, and amateurs cannot play in the PGA. Before Nicklaus came along, the highest number of major championships any golfer had won was thirteen. This mark was set by Jones in the eight-year period between 1923 and 1930, and was thereafter believed to be out of reach. Nicklaus, who should be competing for several years to come, has already won nineteen [now twenty with the 1986 Masters].

To my mind, the most effective way to convey what Nicklaus has done is simply to set down the dates of those nineteen victories, championship by championship. Before turning professional, in 1961, he won the US Amateur twice, in 1959 and 1961. He has won the British Open three times, in 1966, 1970, and 1978; the US Open four times, in 1962, 1967, 1972, and 1980; the PGA five times, in 1963, 1971, 1973, 1975, and 1980; and the Masters five times, in 1963, 1965, 1966, 1972, and 1975.

Moreover, Nicklaus has been close to victory in these events on many other occasions. He has finished second or in a tie for second three times in the PGA, four times in the Masters, four times in the US Open, and no fewer than seven times in the British Open. It is hard to believe, but for fifteen straight years, from 1966 to 1980, he finished among the top six players in the British Open. Altogether, in a total of eighty-four major championships he played from 1962 through 1982 he failed to finish in the first ten only twenty-three times. And Nicklaus has been as all-conquering and consistent in tournaments other than the majors. A golfer who travels well, he has, for example, taken the Australian Open six times. He has won sixty-nine tournaments on the PGA tour – a total approached by none of his contemporaries. He was the first to win more than $4 million.

Golf may be the most difficult of all games to play well. For one thing, it is the only major outdoor game in which the player must generate his own power as he strikes a stationary ball from a stationary position. To do this and at the same time hit the ball accurately toward a target requires mastery of a very sophisticated technique. For another thing, since the game is played on natural terrain the player must continually adjust his hitting action to the lie of the ball, not to mention the wind and weather. All the great champions have necessarily been extremely sound shotmakers, but what really separates them from the talented golfers on the level just below them is their deep, unshakeable belief in themselves. This engenders the determination and the self-possession that enable them, in this game where the slightest faulty movement can lead to a costly error, and even to disaster, to rise to the occasion and produce their finest golf at the most important moments. For all the gracefulness of his swing, Jones was a high-strung young man who felt the stress of tournament play so acutely that during one championship he lost eighteen pounds. He had the ability, however, to gather his concentration as he prepared to play each shot. Hogan, from the beginning to the end of a round, could insulate himself from the world and go about his golf with white-hot intensity. He was oblivious of everything else. Nicklaus's mind works unceasingly during a tournament round, but at the same time he appears to be cooler and calmer than any other golfer of the modern era. He seems to actually thrive on pressure. Out on the fairway, surrounded by thousands of exuberant fans, he wears the tournament golfer's invariable frown of concentration, but he seems completely relaxed – as much at home as if he were taking a solitary walk in the country over a pleasant stretch of land he has known all his life.

In a word, Nicklaus has the ideal temperament for a golfer, and, combined with his physical stamina and phenomenal will to win, it helps to explain the miracles he has performed at many critical moments. Let me briefly describe three that come to mind. In the playoff for the 1970 British Open at St Andrews, he held a one-shot lead over Doug Sanders as they came to the eighteenth, a straightaway par 4 only 354 yards long. When there is a good following wind, as there was that afternoon, a big hitter like Nicklaus can drive the green. Sanders, with the honour, played a fine tee shot that ended up a few yards short of the green. Nicklaus then removed the sweater he was wearing – he did not mean this action to be as dramatic as it was – and swatted a huge drive dead on line for the pin. He had, in fact, hit the ball too well. It bounced onto the green and rolled over the back edge into some fairly high rough. Sanders had his birdie all the way, so it was up to Nicklaus to get down in two to win. From a difficult downhill lie in the rough, he played a delicate wedge chip that stopped eight feet from the hole. His putt looked as if it might be slipping a shade too much to the right, but it caught a corner of the cup and fell in. By and large, Nicklaus has been a very solid putter throughout his career – an invaluable asset.

In the 1972 US Open, at Pebble Beach, Nicklaus, with two holes to go, apparently had the championship won, for he led the nearest man by three strokes. Still, anything can happen on the last two holes at Pebble Beach. The seventeenth, a par 3, 218 yards long, is tightly bordered on the left by Carmel Bay, and the green is severely bunkered. With the wind in his face, Nicklaus chose to play a 1-iron. He ripped a beautiful shot through the wind which almost went into the hole on the fly. The ball landed inches short of the cup, bounced up and struck the flagstick, and came to rest inches away. He tapped it in for his birdie, and that was that.

Three years later, in the Masters, Nicklaus was involved in a tremendous battle in the fourth, and last, round with Johnny Miller and Tom Weiskopf. Throughout the long afternoon, all three played some of the most spectacular golf shots imaginable, and the outcome was not decided until the final green, where both Miller and Weiskopf, who were the last twosome, missed makeable birdie putts that would have tied them with Nicklaus. In retrospect, Nicklaus had played the winning shot on the sixteenth. When he came to that hole, a 190-yard par 3 over one of the largest and loveliest water hazards in golf, he trailed Weiskopf by a stroke. The pin was set that day, as it usually is on the fourth round of the Masters, in the hardest position – near the front of the narrow terrace at the back right-hand corner of the green. It takes a superlative shot, with true backspin on it, to hit and hold that terrace, because there is little margin for error: a large bunker sits in wait just beyond the green. Nicklaus, going with a 5-iron, played a so-so shot that ended up on the left side of the green well below the slope of the terrace and some forty feet from the pin. He took a long time studying his putt, to make certain he had read the line correctly. He then rapped the ball firmly up the slope and watched it break some eighteen inches to the left in a gradual curve and dive into the cup. That birdie put him in a tie for the lead with Weiskopf, and when Weiskopf three-putted the sixteenth for a bogey 4 Nicklaus was out in front to say.

Nicklaus is unquestionably the best fourth-round golfer there has ever been. Even when he starts the last eighteen so many strokes off the pace that his chances seem hopeless, it is not his nature to think for a moment of conceding the tournament to anyone else. He is never more dangerous than at these times, and it takes a stout-hearted competitor, such as Lee Trevino or Tom Watson, to stand up to the threat that Nicklaus poses. For most golfers trying to protect a lead on the last day, there is nothing more rattling than to look up at one of the leaderboards positioned around the course and see that Nicklaus, who has slowly mounted one of his celebrated rushes, has picked up three birdies in a row and, now in full flight, is within striking distance of overtaking them.

Nicklaus's awesome career impresses on one how valuable it is in golf, or anything else, to start with the proper fundamentals. His father, Louis Charles Nicklaus, Jr, a warm, companionable man who was a successful pharmacist in Columbus, Ohio, made his home in the suburb of Upper Arlington, and was a member of the nearby Scioto Country Club, the scene of Jones' victory in the 1926 Open. His son began golf at ten. Jack played some with his father; he joined the Friday-morning class for junior members that Jack Grout, the Scioto professional, held in the summer; and every two or three weeks he took a private lesson from Grout, a gifted student of the golf swing.

As Grout saw it there were three main fundamentals. First, the head must be kept still throughout the swing. It is the balance centre, and if a golfer allows it to move it throws everything else off: the movements of his body, his arc, his timing. Second, balance also depends on footwork. The basis of footwork is rolling the ankles correctly. On the backswing, the left ankle and heel roll in toward the right foot, and the right foot remains firmly planted. On the downswing, the left ankle and heel roll back to their original position, where they remain planted, and the right ankle and heel roll in toward the left foot. Golfers with analytical minds, such as Jones, realized early that good golf is played on the inside of the feet. Third, when a golfer is young and limber he should try to develop the widest possible arc by making a full shoulder turn and fully extending his arms on the backswing, downswing, and follow-through. That way, he will be able to utilize all his latent power. The boy who learns to hit the ball hard and far can work on improving his accuracy when he is older. Nicklaus learned very quickly from Grout. The two not only communicated well but liked and respected each other, and they became fast friends.

Like Jones, who was only nine when he won his club's junior championship and only fourteen when he first played in the US Amateur (and won his first two matches), Nicklaus was a prodigy. At twelve, after shooting eight straight rounds of 80, he broke the barrier with a 74. At thirteen, he broke 70 at Scioto for the first time. To do this, he had to eagle the eighteenth, a good par 5, which he did by reaching the green with a drive and a 2-iron and holing a thirty-five-foot putt. That was also the year he made his début in the US Junior Amateur championship. At fifteen, he qualified for the US Amateur. He played well in his first-round match but lost on the last hole to Bob Gardner, a golfer of Walker Cup calibre. At sixteen, he won the Ohio State Open from a field of experienced professionals after take the lead on the third round with a 64. At seventeen, he qualified for the 1957 US Open, which was held at Inverness, in Toledo. He played two loose 80s and failed to make the thirty-six-hole cut by ten strokes. In the summer of 1958, he strengthened his chances of making the Walker Cup team the next year by winning the Trans-Mississippi Amateur, a top tournament, and finishing twelfth in his first PGA tour event – the Rubber City Open, in Akron, in which he was paired with such stars as Julius Boros, Tommy Bolt, and Art Wall. Many boy wonders in sports fade away when they are still young men. Sometimes they lose the precocious skill that had set them apart. Sometimes they lose their enthusiasm – they have had enough of the spotlight and wish to lead an altogether different kind of life. When Nicklaus, at nineteen, was named to the American Walker Cup team for the 1959 match in this biennial series against a team representing Great Britain and Ireland, it was as clear as could be that here was one young man who, given his background in golf and his ardent and justified ambition, would almost surely mature into a much more proficient player and possibly go on to become an authentic champion. In that Walker Cup match, which was played at Muirfield, outside Edinburgh, he adjusted splendidly to the demands of linksland golf and won both his singles and his foursomes.

That summer, he captured his first national championship, the US Amateur, at the ease course of the Broadmoor Golf Club, in Colorado Springs, beating the defending champion Charlie Coe on the last hole by sinking an eight-foot birdie putt. He was on his way.

Grout is the only teacher Nicklaus has had. Since boyhood, Nicklaus has understood the workings of his swing extremely well, and as a rule he has been able to take care of small adjustments himself. He is one of the few golfers who can often do this even during a vital tournament round. There have been times, though, when he has accepted knowledgeable friends' suggestions, and these have proved helpful in correcting some faulty movement of a minor nature which he had been unable to pinpoint himself.

But down through the years, whenever something basic about the way he was hitting the ball was bothering him, or if he simply wanted to have his setup at the ball or his swing checked out, he has always gone to Jack Grout. When they are on the practice tee together, it generally takes Grout no time at all to spot the minutest departure from Nicklaus's customary swing pattern, suggest a remedy, and begin to work on it with Nicklaus.

In 1975, Nicklaus asked Grout to become the professional at the Muirfield Village Golf Club, in Dublin, Ohio, outside Columbus. Muirfield Village is a real-estate development in which Nicklaus has an interest; he was a co-designer of its golf course, the venue each May of the Memorial Tournament. Grout has been at Muirfield Village since 1975, except in the wintertime, when the course is closed.

When old golf hands discuss when it was that it first occurred to them that Nicklaus might turn out to be not just a first-class golfer but a rare champion, more often than not they cite his performance in one or another of three events that took place early in his career: the 1960 World Amateur Team championship, at Merion, an exacting course near Philadelphia, in which his four-round total of 269 (66, 67, 68, 68) was thirteen strokes lower than the runner-up's; the 1960 US Open, at Cherry Hills, outside Denver, in which he was second, only two strokes behind Arnold Palmer, then the premier golfer in the world; and the 1962 US Open, at Oakmont, outside Pittsburgh, where he caught Palmer with an almost flawless last round of 69 and defeated him the next day in their playoff. While I concur that this cluster of events was significant, I would like to add some personal comments. At Merion, Nicklaus hit the ball so squarely and sweetly over the seventy-two holes that I thought he must be having one of those improbable streaks in which people play way over their heads – no one could be that good at twenty. I failed to appreciate the significance of Nicklaus's showing at Cherry Hills, because a large share of my attention was appropriated by Hogan's gallant bid for a fifth Open title and by Palmer's dashing last round of 65. And I must confess that Nicklaus's victory at Oakmont also surprised me. It was as if it had happened a bit ahead of schedule: I'd thought that it would take even a Nicklaus a year or two to win the Open. I had underrated not only his skill but his fortitude.

After winning the 1963 Masters, Nicklaus had established himself as a golfer who could play all the shots, but, understandably, it was his thunderous power off the tee that attracted the most attention. He was the Snead of his generation – the longest driver among the players who were regularly in contention in the big events. He lacked the ineffable rhythm and tempo that made Snead an aesthetic treat, but he was thrilling in his own way. Watching him unload on the ball and smash it three hundred yards down the fairway packed an excitement that never lessened, no matter how often an admirer had been in his gallery. Until 1969, when he went on a diet that radically altered his appearance, Nicklaus, who stands five feet eleven and three-quarters inches, weighed about two hundred and ten pounds. This young Percheron had especially heavy legs and thighs, which helped to explain his power, but the distance he hit the ball was not the result of brute force. Growing up under Grout's guidance, he understood from an early age the four main sources of power. He listed them like this in his book *The Greatest Game of All*, which was published in 1969: '1. a club of proper weight and balance; 2. a long, wide arc; 3. speed of movement from the right side to the left at the start of the downswing; 4. the speed with which the left hip, having stopped its move forward, spins to the rear in the hitting zone.' As goes without saying, the body movements involved in a power swing are infinitely complicated, and few players succeed in mastering them. Nicklaus was able to because of his extraordinary talent and his willingness to put in the untold hours on the practice tee that finally made the synchronization of the multiple movements almost instinctive.

When Nicklaus's colossal power comes up in conversation, golf fans tend to recall different tournaments. Some go back as far as the 1960 World Amateur Team championship. (It was then that people started to speculate about Nicklaus's possibly being the longest driver in the game.) Others immediately think of the 1965 Masters – perhaps the most popular choice. That April, Nicklaus flew the ball such great distances that he made the Augusta National, which measures 6,905 yards from the back tees, seem like one of those little nine-hole courses that used to be operated at old summer hotels in New England. He broke the previous Masters record total of 274 by three strokes, with rounds of 67, 71, 64, and 69, and finished nine strokes ahead of his nearest competitor. On his third round, in particular, he was driving the ball so far that on the ten par-4 holes – only two are under four hundred yards long – he had only a pitch left on his second shot: he used his 6-iron once, his 7-iron once, his 8-iron three times, his pitching wedge four times, and his sand wedge once. Jones, the founder of the Masters, and its host, summed up Nicklaus's performance perfectly when he said at the presentation ceremony, 'Jack is playing an entirely different game – a game I'm not even familiar with.' When I think of his power, as a veteran Nicklaus watcher, I think of the shots he tore through a bitter wind off the North Sea when, in a losing cause, he chased Gary Player down the final holes at Carnoustie in the 1968 British Open.

Nicklaus's victory in the 1966 British Open, at Muirfield, also comes vividly to mind. This takes a little explaining. That summer, Muirfield was modified a bit to keep the big hitters in check. At about the 250-yard mark, the fairways, which were narrow to begin with, were gradually pinched in so that at the 275-yard mark they were scarcely twenty yards wide. Furthermore, the rough bordering the fairways was allowed to grow almost two feet high. Nicklaus made the adjustments called for. Over the seventy-two holes of the championship, he used his driver only seventeen times. He drove with his 3-wood ten times, and the rest of the way he went with either his 1-iron or his 3-iron off the tee, depending on how the wind was blowing. His decision to put accuracy ahead of distance and his discipline in refusing to stray from this strategy was the basis of his victory. At the same time, from the point of view of power the most sensational single hole I have ever watched Nicklaus play was the seventeenth hole of the 1966 British Open. The seventeenth at Muirfield is a 528-yard par 5 that bends sharply to the left about two hundred and twenty yards from the tee and then runs more or less straight to a smallish green tucked in a hollow beyond a daunting mound. As Nicklaus stood on the tee, he knew that he would have to birdie either the seventeenth or the eighteenth to win. With the wind blowing from right to left, he drove with a 3-iron, to make sure the ball didn't carry too far and end up in the rough on the right-hand side of the twisting fairway. On his second shot, with the wind directly behind him, he selected a 5-iron. He played a superb shot. The ball landed on the small front apron about fifteen feet short of the green, as he had planned; it then hopped up and rolled to within eighteen feet of the pin. He was down in two for the crucial birdie. Even allowing for the helping wind and the lively British ball, imagine reaching a 528-yard hole with a 3-iron and a 5-iron!

While Nicklaus has a genius for hitting a golf ball, it should be brought out that he possesses uncommon physical coordination for sports in general. He got his size early: at thirteen, he stood five feet ten and weighed a hundred and sixty-five pounds. In junior high school in Upper Arlington, he was the quarterback, punter, and placekicker on the football team; the centre on the basketball team; the catcher on the baseball team; and, surprisingly, a sprinter on the track team, who could run the hundred-yard dash in eleven seconds flat. He might well have had a career in baseball or football, but in high school he gave both of them up and concentrated on basketball, his favourite team sport.

In college – he went to Ohio State, his father's school – he limited himself strictly to golf. His range of sports interests is wide. He has been a devoted fisherman since boyhood. In conjunction with his golf travels, he has fished the world over. (For example, before playing in the 1978 Australian Open he fished for black marlin off the Great Barrier Reef, and last summer he stopped off in Iceland after the British Open to fish for salmon.) At his home in North Palm Beach, he has two grass tennis courts – a rarity in Florida. They are part of a grassed-over plot adjoining his house which serves Nicklaus, his wife, Barbara, and their five children as a playground. After the golf season ends, he plays a lot of tennis. The workout he gets from a couple of sets helps to keep him in shape, but, in addition, he is fascinated by the game, and he plays it well. (On most Saturday mornings in the autumn and early winter, Nicklaus and seven middle-aged friends, each wearing a special 'Day Camp' T-shirt, assemble at his courts for doubles and singles.) At the side of the house, attached to the garage, are a basketball backboard and hoop. When the spirit moves him,

Nicklaus still goes out and practises shooting by himself or with his kids. He also still enjoys throwing and kicking a football. He can be called, with no exaggeration, a brilliant passer and an astounding punter. (I have seen him boom kicks that were forty yards high and carried sixty yards.) During the last decade, he has developed one new sports passion – skiing. Since 1975, the Nicklaus family has spent nearly every Christmas holiday skiing at Vail, Colorado, or Park City, Utah. All seven Nicklauses are of one mind: skiing is the ideal family sport.

Nicklaus inherited both his love of sports and much of his athletic ability from his father. In high school, Charlie Nicklaus – he was always Charlie to his friends – starred in football, basketball, and baseball. From the start of Jack's career, his father was always on hand at major events. His greatest joy was to watch his son play golf. Until his death, in 1970, he was a familiar figure at the championships, his name purposely removed from his tournament badge as he hurried along in Jack's gallery with his pals from Columbus. Of all the stage mothers and sports fathers I have met, I would put Charlie Nicklaus right up at the top. He was careful, for instance, to inculcate a deep sense of sportsmanship in his son. 'My dad knew how to get his points across,' Nicklaus recalled not long ago. 'One day when I was eleven, I was playing with him at Scioto. We were on the fifteenth, and I had an 8-iron to the green. I put the shot in a bunker, and then I threw my club almost to the bunker. My father turned to me and said, very clearly, "Young man, that will be the last club I'll ever see you throw or hear of you throwing, or you're not going to be playing this game." I've never thrown a club since.' He was silent for a moment, started to laugh, and added, 'I must admit that I've tossed a few over to the bag, but never with any kind of force behind them.'

Nicklaus has given more and more time in the past decade to building courses. He has found it stimulating and fulfilling. When he elects to retire from competitive golf, the bulk of his time and energy will undoubtedly go into golf-course architecture.

He has expanded his vistas in many directions, developing a good mind, through exercise, into an excellent one. His memory can be astonishing. He has learned to understand other people better, and has become more generous of spirit. All in all, he has matured very well – particularly when one takes into account how long he has been in the spotlight and the disruptive effect that this kind of thing has had on many celebrities. My guess is that Nicklaus has always been a much more complicated man than most of us recognized. A profoundly private person of considerable sensitivity, he prefers to keep his problems to himself. He has had his share of them. To name only one, he could not have picked a worse time to burst onto the golf scene. The reigning hero in 1962, Nicklaus's first full year as a professional, was Arnold Palmer, the most popular golfer since Bobby Jones' heyday. A handsome, magnetic man who approached golf with a dramatic boldness, Palmer, who is ten years older than Nicklaus, had the gift of communicating his feelings to his galleries. He had another extraordinary gift: He was at his best when the going was hard, and would come charging down the stretch on the last round with a barrage of birdies that often carried him to victory. Small wonder that his galleries were so immense they became known as Arnie's Army. After winning his first major championship, the Masters, in 1958, Palmer won the Masters and the US Open in 1960, the British Open in 1961, and the Masters and the British Open in 1962. In between these feats, he had torrid streaks on the tour, during which he performed his magic almost on a weekly basis, cheered on by his army and by the enraptured millions who watched him on television. Palmer continued to play fine golf for many seasons, but by 1965 it was clear, if it hadn't been before, that, remarkable as he was, he was not as good a golfer as Nicklaus. In the eyes of Palmer's fans, Nicklaus, the corpulent, expressionless kid who had supplanted their hero, was an unwelcome usurper. Nicklaus took all this in, stoically, and got through it. For several years, even when he stood alone at the top, he had a limited appeal for the average golf fan. Most of the regulars in his galleries were people who had been close to golf all their lives and could appreciate the beauty of his shotmaking. Then, slowly, starting in about 1970, the situation began to change. Nicklaus not only earned an ever-increasing esteem at home and throughout the world but also emerged as one of the most popular figures in modern sports. I can remember no occasion in golf quite like his victory in the US Open at Baltusrol in 1980, eighteen years after he won his first Open. The upstart kid had become a venerated champion among champions. In Nicklaus's own opinion, he has never played a better nine holes than the second nine on the final round of that 1980 Open. The ecstatic, roaring thousands who greeted his sure progress down the last few holes seemed to me at the time to have something of the quality of the worshipful multitudes in Cecil B. De Mille's motion-picture extravaganzas about the heroes of the Bible and early Christian Rome.

On reflection, the comparison is not inapt. If ever there was what has come to be known in sports jargon as a 'living legend,' it is Nicklaus. At Baltusrol that June afternoon, three generations of golf fans – most of them had often watched his exploits on television, but only on television – were ecstatic at being present to witness Nicklaus, in all his glory, once again outplaying and outscoring a strong field of challengers.

Since we live in the age of the 'image' as well as the 'living legend,' it is perhaps not surprising that one factor in the new popularity Nicklaus gained was a drastic change in his appearance. In 1969, he let his blond hair, which he had worn rather short, grow longer, as other young men were doing. The reaction was very favorable, and this naturally pleased him. That autumn, when he and Barbara were flying home from London after the Ryder Cup match, the last event on his schedule that year, he began to think about his weight. He had always had a hearty appetite and had steadily become heavier. He now weighed two hundred and ten pounds or thereabouts. To his admirers, he was the Golden Bear, but to the claques of his rivals he was Fat Jack or Ohio Fats. He had let things go too far and too long, he told his wife on the plane, and he was determined to do something about it immediately. Once back home, he went on the Weight Watchers diet, and he stuck to it. The results were startling. In little over four weeks, he dropped twenty pounds, and in just the right places: He lost six inches around the hips and an inch and a half around the waist. The extra weight around his chin and neck also disappeared. The new Nicklaus was a younger-looking and much more attractive man. Realizing this, he watched his eating habits as vigilantly as a ballet star, and has continued to. The rise in Nicklaus's popularity rested on some things more meaningful than his new look, however. During his first years as a professional, when he sensed that the loyal followers of Palmer and other established stars begrudged him his sudden prominence, his reaction when he was playing tournaments had been to go into a sort of shell. In the nineteen-seventies, he began to relax more on the course and, at length, to be entirely himself. Watching him work on a round became an enchanting experience: one could follow his thinking practically step by step as he prepared to play each stroke, and this made the brilliant shots he brought off all the more spectacular. (Nicklaus believes that setting up correctly at the ball is ninety percent of golf.) As the years passed and the pressure of tournament golf became more and more intense, most of the new young stars flashed for only a brief period. Nicklaus continued to roll on and on, though. His longevity has been the product of his pertinacity no less than of his skill. He has been able to endure several long, discouraging slumps and play his way out of them. Four times, he has done this by winning a major championship – the 1967 US Open, the 1970 British Open, the 1978 British Open, and the 1980 US Open. There is nothing like carrying off one of the four majors to renew a golfer's confidence, and, apparently, there is nothing like confidence to restore the timing in a golfer's swing.

Few golfers know their swing as well as Nicklaus knows his. 'In 1961 and 1962, I was very pleased with the way I hit the ball,' he said the evening of my visit, when he was reflecting on his play during different phases of his career. 'I hit it long and straight those two years. In the middle sixties, I wasn't quite as good with the driver, but I was very sound with the irons. Then, toward the late sixties, my iron play went off. I played on power for several years. In the nineteen-seventies, I had some new problems. When I lost twenty pounds in 1969, I lost twenty yards. Being lighter was only incidental – I lost distance because my swing was starting to deteriorate. I got too upright. During the seventies, I wasn't a good striker of the ball at all. Oh, I won a lot of tournaments. In both 1972 and 1975, I won two major championships – my game happened to be at its best in those important weeks.'

By working on his swing he got back the twenty yards he lost. 'Of course, I practise now more than I used to. You have to when you get older. But I'm more excited about playing golf than I've been in a long time. I suppose the real reason for this is that I know I'm not going to play tournament golf that much longer. I don't want to go out of golf having let my game just dwindle away. I want to make sure that each year that I play I give it everything I've got. As long as I play tournaments, I'm going to work at it, I'm going to make it happen, and if I can't make it happen then I won't play.'

When the day comes that designing courses replaces playing tournament golf as Nicklaus's chief occupation, he will be remembered for his sportsmanship as well as for his achievements. Considerate and gracious in victory, he stands alone in his time as a golfer who is able in defeat to go out toward his rivals with warmth and a genuine understanding of what winning means to them. Nicklaus's father instilled high precepts in him, but there is also something at the core of Nicklaus's character which underlies his attitude and conduct. He believes that there are definite ways a golfer must act in specific situations, and that if he fails to, the failure detracts immeasurably from the essence and worth of the game. There have been many examples of this in his career, but I will note just three. In the 1969 Ryder Cup match, at Birkdale, in

England, the three-day competition came down to the last singles – Nicklaus vs. Tony Jacklin. All even as they played the eighteenth, a short par 5, Nicklaus lay 3 five feet from the cup, and Jacklin 3 two feet from the cup. Nicklaus's putt was a testing one. He took his time over it and holed it. He then turned to Jacklin and told him his putt was good – he was conceding it. This halved singles made the final score of the team match 16–16. Some people thought that Nicklaus should have made Jacklin hole out, but Nicklaus felt that what he did was the right thing in those exceptional circumstances.

In the 1977 British Open, at Turnberry, in Scotland, the championship turned out to be a two-man fight between Nicklaus and Watson, who, as it happened, were paired together on the last two rounds. Nothing in the history of golf quite matches their scoring and shotmaking over those thirty-six holes. Tied for the lead at the start of the third day, each was around in 65, six under par. On the fourth day, Nicklaus, despite a heroic birdie on the last hole, took 66 strokes – one stroke too many, for Watson had another 65. As they walked off the last green, Nicklaus flung his arm over Watson's shoulder and, smiling broadly, told him how wonderfully he had played. The two were involved in a similarly unforgettable moment at the close of the 1982 US Open, at Pebble Beach. Playing three twosomes ahead of Watson, Nicklaus moved into contention on the last round with a string of five birdies on the front nine. Coming down the stretch, they were tied for the lead, but on the par-3 seventeenth Watson played what proved to be the winning shot: he holed a little wedge pitch from the greenside rough for a birdie. When Watson completed his round, there was Nicklaus, waiting off the eighteenth green to greet him heartily and congratulate him. Golf is one of the rare sports in which there has been no drop in the level of sportsmanship over the last decade, and I imagine that the example Nicklaus has set has had something to do with this happy state of affairs.

From *Following Through* by Herbert Warren Wind
(Macmillan, London, 1986).

Mind Over Matter

Gary Player

Gary Player is three times winner of the British Open, in 1959, 1968 and 1974. He and Vardon are the only two players to have won it in three different decades. He is three times winner of the Masters, winner of the US Open and twice winner of the US PGA. Player is the doughtiest fighter in the game of golf, which is why I admire him so much – and, of course, he is another little 'un (5 feet 7 inches tall) who hits the ball a long way. I don't subscribe to all of Gary's habits, such as not drinking alcohol, tea or coffee. Nor do I wear black to absorb the heat of the sun, or do lots of hard-graft exercises from press-ups to running which he reckons enabled him to summon the extra strength to hit the par 5s in two. His attitude to practice is more rigorous than mine. But his 'never say die' spirit is exactly what I believe in. He also believes, as I do, that medal play is better than match play because in medal every shot counts and it makes for better golfers.

To the purist Gary's swing may seem a bit flat. When, on his first trip to Britain in 1955, he asked one well-known player his opinion of his golf, the man advised him to go back to South Africa! Gary, of course, thrives on adversity and on adverse comment. When he went seven down to Tony Lema in the World Match Play in 1965, he heard a spectator say: 'Player has really had it now.' That was enough to spark one of the most spectacular recoveries in golf which, he said, 'contains my whole life story'. Here's how he puts his philosophy of mind over matter.

I.W.

In the make-up of a professional golfer, I would say that only seventy per cent of his success is due to his ability to hit the ball – the rest comes from his superior mental approach to the game, his ability to relax and to out-think his opponent on the course.

How often have you heard it said of an athlete: 'He would be the best of them all, if only he would train harder,' and of a golfer, 'He is undoubtedly a great player, but he takes the game far too seriously.'

I have learned that in sport there are no 'ifs' and 'buts.' It is very simple to me: the fact that a certain athlete does not train hard enough is the reason why he is not as good as others who do. The grim-faced golfer would not be half as good if he went round the course laughing and joking with everybody. It is very much a matter of temperament, and you can no more ask a champion to change his mental approach than you could tell him to alter his style. Both are very much a part of him and both are responsible for his success.

In other words, the athlete who trains hard can be thankful for that capacity for hard work that might be denied his opponents. A man without this gift, or whose nerve cracks under strain, must accept this as a basic weakness in his make-up, for in many cases no matter how hard he tries to overcome these handicaps, he cannot succeed completely.

Temperament is very much a matter of birth I feel, although, like many other aspects of the game, when it is applied to golf it can be cultivated to an extent.

Still, I doubt if the man afflicted with nerves under pressure can ever really be taught to control his emotions. I might add that everybody feels pressure, even Bobby Locke and Ben Hogan, who have the best temperaments I know, although they are totally different in character: Hogan grim and often scowling, with determination written in his every action, Locke expressionless, unruffled and patient but no less determined to win.

These men, like Bobby Jones and Byron Nelson, although the latter's progress ended sooner than one would have expected, had the ability – perhaps gift is a better word – to remain apparently calm and force themselves to function normally even with their nerves screaming.

There are also examples at the other end of the scale, good golfers in every other respect but who fail in the moment of crisis. These attacks of nerves are apparent even in amateur golfers, who find themselves hooking the last putt that would have won them a couple of balls, or breaking down after playing the first few holes in par or better. When this happens in America they say the player 'choked.'

It is perhaps rather a callous way of putting it, but it describes the action aptly. These players do in fact choke on the surge of emotion that in the end overwhelms them.

If I have not exactly choked, I have come pretty close to it in my early days, so I know what the feeling is like. And I won't easily forget missing a three-foot putt on the last green to lose the 1959 South African Open to the then amateur Denis Hutchinson. So unexpected was the lapse that there were those who said I missed the putt on purpose to avoid a play-off, because I was due to leave the next day for America.

Perhaps I should have been flattered by these views, but in fact I always play golf to win: I tried for my life on that putt and when it missed I was as shocked as anybody.

Afterwards I was not as upset as I might have been, for when I looked back on the tournament I realised it was not the putt that had lost me the title but the fact that I had scored seventy-five in my last round, compared to Hutchinson's seventy. When I score seventy-five in perfect conditions I reckon I deserve to lose. Perhaps that does not sound so nice in print, but I have set myself a high standard in this game and when I fall below it I really hate myself for it.

I think one must always be greedy in golf, even in amateur golf. If you are not always striving might and main for the biggest win or the best possible score, your thinking must be negative.

I found this out in a 'challenge' series in my own country against the former American Open champion Tommy Bolt. I had Bolt's temperament in mind when we met in the first match in Johannesburg, where conditions of nap on the greens and altitude are almost unique in world golf. I got two holes up on Bolt very quickly and I began worrying that if I went too far ahead the American might stop trying to fight the strange conditions and allow me too easy a victory, thus spoiling the series.

You might say at this stage that I was presumptuous in thinking that I had a walk-over on my hands when my opponent was a man who had proved himself to be one of the best golfers in the world. In many ways you might be right, but let me assure you that my misguided reasoning was not the result of an exaggerated opinion of my own capabilities. Rather was I overconscious of the fact that all previous visitors to South Africa, including Sam Snead and the British Open champion, Alf Padgam, not to mention a host of others, had floundered in the conditions and had never really shown their home form.

Anyway, that is how I thought and, walking along with my two-up lead, I began telling my friends that it might be a good thing for Bolt's confidence and the match if he were to take a lead. I began hoping that his game would improve. For the first time I did not want to crush my opponent into the ground.

I was not feeling too friendly at the end of the match after I had congratulated Bolt on his one-up victory, nor at the end of the series which the American won by four games to one.

I will admit that Bolt's victory in my own country and within months of my winning the British Open, took me down a peg or two, and I am not making any excuses now, but I am convinced that I contributed towards my own defeat by my negative thinking in the first match. I never at any stage attempted to pull a shot to allow Bolt an advantage he might otherwise never have won, but in feeling sorry for him as it were, I allowed the devil to go out of my own game. Instead of exerting all my concentration upon each and every shot, so that they drove like arrows into Bolt's failing confidence, I became subconsciously content with the not-so-good shot. When it became apparent that Bolt needed no encouragement to play better in South Africa than any previous visitor had done, and my lead began to slip away, I fought as hard for victory as ever I have, but I never again in that match recaptured the 'killer' instinct which I consider necessary to winning golf.

In other other matches of the series Bolt beat me fair and square, but I have often thought since what the result might have been had I hammered away at Bolt when I had the best chance of gaining mental and practical superiority – when he was still new to the conditions.

Like a boxer who wades into a helpless opponent against the ropes, or a Rugby captain who orders his flankers to harass the opposing fly-half, a golfer is also entitled to take the greatest possible advantage of any weakness in his opponent's game.

I have mentioned this incident against Bolt at some length as I want to stress the importance of playing to win, especially if a golfer hopes to improve his game. Also, the killer instinct, which this attitude is sometimes dramatically called, helps to cultivate temperament, the subject with which we began this chapter, and it certainly helps to overcome those periodic fits of choking I mentioned.

A golfer who plays one round light-heartedly, knocking up putts without taking proper care, or who does not mind hitting a bad shot because he is so far ahead of his opponent that it does not really matter, cannot logically expect to sink crucial putts or play his best when he really needs to.

Winning golf, like everything else in the game, has to be practised and, I advise all club golfers to strive as hard as possible at all times for victory, even if they are playing with members of the handicapping committee. Obviously, an amateur golfer does not want to become known around the club as a pot-hunting, ball-grabbing so-and-so, always on the make, or even as a fanatic with whom it is no pleasure to play. One can still play the game hard and pleasantly. One can still win graciously, although you will find that if you win often enough you are bound to excite some criticism.

I have another reason for saying you should always play hard to win, apart from the fact that it improves your golf. I think you owe it to your opponent. For my own part I should feel insulted if I found out that my opponent had purposely eased up because he felt sorry for me. If I am in for a six and five hiding, then that is the way I would like it to be. I want no quarter and I expect none. Anyway, a man who cannot take a thrashing in good part is usually intolerable when he is doing the thrashing.

I do not recall a really good player who does not play the game seriously. The top tournament players who blow up during a round very rarely do so through careless-ness or because they funk a particular shot or situation. They are not suddenly overawed by the prospect of victory, because they have trained themselves to accept it, even to expect it. With them it is not so much a case of nerves as imagination, and this applies to nearly all amateurs. I have often heard it said that to be a great golfer you must be just a little stupid – no brains, no imagination. When I hear this I know that the speaker is merely embittered at the success given to others.

Still, I am always reminded of the story told about Hogan. Somebody asked him if it was necessary for a champion golfer to be stupid. He replied: 'No, it is not necessary, but it helps!' What Hogan perhaps meant was that if a golfer cannot control his imagination it would be better that he had none at all.

This applies particularly to amateurs, who generally think too far ahead. If they play the first couple of holes well they immediately begin thinking of how best they can pick up more strokes on par on holes still to come. The standard joke of the golfer who throws away shots towards the end of his round, that he forgot to play the shots because he was thinking of what to say at the prize-giving, is much nearer the truth than many of his listeners realise.

Many amateurs never realise what most professionals learn early in their careers: that a golf-course must be played as it comes, that your score should be recorded faithfully on each hole and then forgotten. It is bad enough trying to sink a four-foot putt or to hit a straight drive without torturing yourself with the fact that 'this putt means another birdie,' or 'if I make the rough now I'll never reach the green.' However hard it may seem at first, forget about such things. Remember what I said earlier. If you always try hard to sink the putts and hit straight drives, you have no reason to panic when a very important shot comes up.

I know when I was younger and had been practising putting without much success, I used to say to myself: 'All right, so you've missed. Now this one is to win the British Open. If you don't sink it now you never will.' But for all the boyish determination and gritting of teeth, I don't think I ever got one of the putts that was going to win me the British Open. When I really had a putt to achieve my greatest ambition, I will not say that I regarded it as just another stroke, but my previous determination to hole every putt, no matter what the circumstances, certainly helped me overcome the worst attack of nerves I have yet experienced.

If it is essential for a golfer to accept the good scores without them turning his head with visions of glory, when such glory has not even begun to be deserved, it is perhaps even more important that he accept bad scores calmly, for just a few indifferent strokes at isolated holes never completely ruined a card yet. It is when these few lapses eat into the soul, creating the ill-tempered or defeatist or don't-care golfer, that the game is lost.

Even I as a professional, who is supposed to have reached greater proficiency than any amateur, expect two bad shots in every round. A scratch golfer is entitled to have five bad shots without cursing his form, and a handicap golfer many more. I reason this way. The same scratch player is entitled to expect two good chip shots, a good bunker shot, and two putts that drop but could just as easily have stayed out. In this way the balance is restored to his game. If he keeps his head and does not become upset at his lapses, he will be in a position to take advantage of his luck. If he allows his game to disintegrate, however, all the luck in the world later on will not help him.

If I had to give just one definition of a good golfer it would be: *the man who has the determination to win and the patience to wait for the breaks.*

Locke is the living proof of this maxim, and if ever I needed convincing of the truth of it, I had it in the East Rand Open in South Africa against Locke in 1959. At the turn in the last round I led Locke by seven strokes, and I think you will agree that I was entitled to feel confident of victory. Not even Locke's many ardent admirers gave him a chance, and who could blame them, either? I would have had to crash like a novice to allow anyone to make up seven strokes on me in only nine holes.

I did not crack. In fact, I did not drop a shot to par on any hole, yet as I stood on the last tee my lead of seven had been cut to one! I think Locke's bid for victory that day in the face of seemingly overwhelming odds is the greatest I have seen. In the end he needed a three-footer for a par four to be home in six-under-par twenty-nine. That he missed the final putt was due more to the fact that I was assured of a four and victory by a stroke than anything else. To me, that tremendous recovery at a time when most golfers would have been inclined to give up the ghost proved Locke's greatness just as conclusively as his four victories in the British Open, or his fine record in America, had done earlier. During all the time I had imagined myself cruising to an easy victory, Locke had never given up hope, so that when the breaks started to come his way in the end, he was mentally equipped to take advantage of them.

This ability to fight is really more the hall-mark of a champion than any technical excellence in the swing. It is apparent in all the best golfers to-day, and never more so than in a man like Doug Ford, who at first sight would hardly excite comment until one had studied the determination and grit with which he plays every shot. In fact, the amateur purists should see in the flesh many of the great players they know only through the cold statistics published in the record books. They would be in for a shock. Perhaps then they would realise that the 'sweet singers' in their own countries for whom they have so much misplaced respect are completely lacking in many of the other, more important, aspects of a champion.

If this were not so and temperament played no part in golf, a player like the Italian, Aldo Cæsera, or the Englishman, Peter Alliss, would have achieved far greater success, for certainly very few golfers I have seen strike the ball better than they do. In Cæsera's case he suffers like many other Europeans on account of his Latin temperament, which is not easy to apply to a cold, calculating sport like golf. I can never mention Cæsera without thinking of the time I saw him carrying no fewer than three putters in his bag – such was his mental approach to putting.

An excitable person, no matter that he becomes that way through success or failure, is immediately at a disadvantage. At all times one should be relaxed, both in mind and body.

I know that I have drawn heavily upon Bobby Locke as an example to the reader, perhaps because I have had more opportunity to study this great player, but also because he possesses nearly all the qualities I consider necessary for success. I have no option but to mention him again now, because of all the great players I have met, none has been more relaxed on the course than Locke. With Locke this studied relaxation, his refusal to do anything in a hurry, is almost exasperating. I know his leisurely ritual after a tournament has been the despair of many a club official who has urgently sought him for the prize-giving.

Yet it is one of the secrets of his success. No man could be as relaxed without a conscious effort to be so. No doubt it is now second nature with Locke, but it could not always have been so. I think even if Locke was dying of thirst, he would stretch out slowly and unhurriedly for the water that would save his life. When he ties his shoes, his actions are those of a surgeon attempting a difficult operation. On the course his movements are so deliberate as to be almost aggravating, and often when playing with him I get a strong urge to creep up behind him and shout 'boo!' Although Locke is not a slow player once he decides on his club, his lagging gait between shots has often been the subject of controversy. But who is to say that Locke is wrong? This tremendous ability to relax of Locke's is part of him as a man and a champion golfer, and as such must be taken into consideration whenever his success or technique is examined, just as certain other players' tantrums are part of their golfing character. I do not believe either Locke or Bolt is very conscious of his actions on the course, or that they are done deliberately as part of an act. I don't say that Bolt has not found his natural bad temper to be a wonderful 'gimmick,' but he cannot be too conscious of it on the course, or his concentration would be divided between the necessity to act and to play golf. His golf would be the first to suffer – and the same goes for Locke and every other golfer with some pecularity which spectators are all too quick to criticise.

In order to relax properly, a golfer's mind should be completely at ease. Before a round or during a tournament nothing should be allowed to upset his tranquillity or to intrude upon his singleness of mind. Because of this, most top golfers I know appear self-centred without really meaning to be – and I include myself in this. They have set routines and they allow nothing to interfere.

Confidence, too, plays a big part in learning to relax; confidence that one has the right equipment and the right clothes. One of the most miserable rounds of golf I have ever played was in borrowed trousers in an exhibition match with Peter Thomson and Locke very early in my career. My own trousers were not good enough, yet the ones I borrowed were miles too big for me round the waist and far too long in the legs. I had to hitch them up with a tie for a belt and I wore a jersey to hide the folds, even though it was the middle of summer. I know people remarked on the jersey and although I felt uncomfortably hot, I dared not take it off. Throughout the round I was conscious of my borrowed pants and could not concentrate as I should have.

I was often criticised in the Press for my slovenly dress when I first began to play the circuit, but in those days I could not afford anything better. Now my golfing wardrobe is bigger than most and my critics say that I am too ostentatious. Even so I would not dress the way I do if I did not feel confident and relaxed. Incidentally, I wear black often because in the hot South African and American sun, it gives me the feeling of strength.

As with clothes, so with clubs. If you are not confident that your clubs are absolutely right for the job, you can hardly expect to hit the ball well with them. That is why I never agree with beginners who suggest that they need only a few clubs to start with. The feeling of inadequacy is bad enough when they make their first clumsy attempt to hit the ball without the feeling that they have not all the necessary implements.

For the same reasons I never harp on the necessity of a matched set of clubs. Confidence should always be the main consideration in golf, and if you feel confident with an odd driver salvaged from the attic, or an ancient mashie-niblick, then you hang on to it, for that is all that matters. In other words, if you feel that a club is right for you, it usually is. If you feel it is wrong, it most definitely is wrong.

Although I am a strong believer that only bad golfers blame their tools, one cannot overlook the part played by the mind in golf. Because a round takes three hours and more to play, the mind gets plenty of exercise. Obviously, much depends on how the mind works. If you are given to dreaming and imagining, you will not play very well. On the other hand, if you mind is a blank – a popular misconception of professionals among amateurs – you will play worse still. Perhaps a professional does not give much thought to the execution of a shot, but he has to think very hard in his preparation for it. And that is another big difference between the good and the average golfer. I personally think that I play better in major championships and on difficult courses because I think harder than at other times.

It is for a similar reason that the doyen of South African golf professionals, Sid Brews, is reported to have purposely used a driver from a very bad lie at a crucial stage in a tournament. He said afterwards that by choosing his driver, the most difficult club in such circumstances, he forced himself to think and concentrate harder than was actually necessary.

It is for this reason, too, that I always play medal golf, even if I am in a match play event. Medal forces you to think all the time, match play does not, because the value of a stroke is not as important. Only a couple of strokes separates the near-champion from the champion, the good golfer from the not-so-good golfer, and in match play this difference is often not apparent. The costly lapse on one or two holes is swallowed up in the course of the match and in the end the fives and the sixes are not reflected in the result. Being brought up to regard medal as the premier form of competition is one of the big reasons why Americans are better golfers than we in the Commonwealth, where match play has always been said to be more in the spirit of the game. Perhaps it is, but then we must accept that it does not make for better golf. The Americans prove this time and again when they play us at our own game in the Walker and Ryder Cup matches.

Obviously, there are times in match play when it would be plain foolish to try for a score, or to play safe, when your opponent is much better placed. Then you can be forgiven for trying the impossible, or having a go to sink the only putt that matters. But remember this. The bad shots that one sometimes plays in the enthusiasm of match play are not always easy to overcome, to wipe from your mind. In fact, *the swing should never be jolted out of its groove in an effort to achieve something spectacular*.

Funnily enough, although match play produces many dramatic happenings in golf, spectacular scoring is seldom required for victory. All too often match play contests are reduced to the level of a dog-fight, with the better golfer subconsciously being pulled down to the standard of his lesser endowed opponent. I know that in the normal course of events, if I can score a medal card of sixty-eight, or just a couple under par for that matter, I can win most match play contests in which I compete.

I would go so far as to say that a golfer who hopes to improve his game, and train himself to think, should *never* play without religiously keeping his score: golf is a constant battle against par, and if you play it any other way, you are encouraging sloppy thinking and sloppy strokes. Ignore the social or business engagement on the golf-course, therefore, and play medal whenever possible: play against lower handicaps than yourself when you can and play in as many serious tournaments and on as many different courses as you can.

There is nothing like a change of course to make you think. Familiarity with your own course undoubtedly breeds contempt, and a two-handicap at 'home' is sometimes nearer a seven or eight when he is invited out.

The competitive argument should speak for itself. In tournaments you train yourself in all the things we have spoken about in this chapter – temperament, determination and concentration. Golfers who have burned up courses in practice and then scored in the eighties in the first round of the tournament will know exactly what I mean.

From *Play Golf with Player* by Gary Player
(Collins, London, 1962).

Player's Incredible Last Nine Holes in the Masters

Herbert Warren Wind

Even when he was in his forties, Gary Player was equal to the very best. In 1978 he surprised the golfing world as much as Nicklaus did in 1986 by winning the Masters when all seemed lost.

I.W.

Ever since Gene Sarazen holed out a 4-wood shot for his double-eagle 2 on the fifteenth hole in the last round of the second Masters tournament, in 1935, and went on to tie Craig Wood for first and to defeat him in a play-off, the Masters has been known for the high number of dramatic finishes it has provided. At the same time, a certain law of averages has obtained, and golf fans have learned that, after they have been treated to an especially thrilling Masters, more likely than not a few years will follow in which the tournament will probably be relatively placid, like the PGA Championship or a George Eliot novel. For example, after the 1975 Masters, which was perhaps the most exciting three-man battle in the history of the game – as you may remember, on the last day Jack Nicklaus holed a twisting, uphill birdie putt of some forty feet on the sixteenth green to edge out Johnny Miller and Tom Weiskopf by a stroke in a four-hour struggle crammed with the most dazzling kind of golf, which was not concluded until the last green, where Miller and Weiskopf barely missed birdie putts – no one was really surprised when the 1976 Masters proved to be one of the most soporific tournaments ever: Ray Floyd took the lead on the opening day and was never seriously challenged thereafter. In 1977, however, most Augusta regulars, conditioned by the percentages, were unprepared for that year's Masters' tremendously stirring stretch duel, in which Tom Watson, playing half a hole behind Nicklaus and watching all the marvellous strokes that Nicklaus summoned, managed to stand up to the man who is the most awesome competitor in golf (and possibly in all of sport) and, finally, carry the day by sinking a curling birdie putt on the seventeenth green. And certainly none of us expected yet another historic tournament this April, but for the third time in four years we had an extraordinary Masters – one that will be discussed and dissected as long as the game is played.

The 1978 Masters had a different pattern from any of its predecessors. Four men, each with a chance to win, were bunched during the final hour and a half. I am not sure, but I don't think that there has ever been a four-horse race quite like it anytime, anywhere. During most of the afternoon, the interested centered on whether or not Hubert Green, the current United States Open champion, could hold off the challenges of Watson and Rod Funseth, both of whom had started the round three strokes behind him.

Very little attention was paid to Gary Player, of South Africa – the ultimate winner – since he had started the final round seven shots off the pace. Slowly, quietly, almost indiscernibly, Player, the fourth horse, crept into contention. He was out in 34, two under par. This put him five under par for the tournament, and his name then went up on the leader boards, but he was still so far back that no one thought that even Player, a nerveless man who thrives on pressure and the big occasion, could mount a serious challenge on the last nine. Well, he did. In an incredible display of solid shotmaking and some fantastic clutch putting, he proceeded to birdie the tenth, the twelfth, the thirteenth, the fifteenth, the sixteenth, and the eighteenth holes while parring the other three. This gave him a 64, eight under par, for the round, and a seventy-two-hole total of 277, eleven under par. When he posted that score, there was no assurance that it would hold up and gain him a third Masters title, since Watson, Green, and Funseth were still out on the course with a chance to beat his total or tie it and send the tournament into a sudden-death play-off. While it would be completely wrong to say that Player did not *win* the forty-second Masters – I don't remember any previous golfer's playing the last nine holes of a major tournament in thirty strokes, as he did – Watson, Green, and Funseth also had, in effect, to lose it. For the most part, the decisive shots were played on the last hole, before an enormous horseshoe-shaped gallery that watched the drama in hushed silence. This, it should be noted, was one of the best-run Masters tournaments ever.

Of the men with a chance to tie or defeat Player, Watson, a twenty-eight-year-old Stanford graduate who is probably the most literate golfer on the pro tour, was the first to come to the eighteenth, a 420-yard par 4 on which the fairway swings to the right and runs steadily uphill to a two-level green that slopes from back to front and is protected by two bunkers – a shallow one on the right, and a deep one before the green.

Watson, in trouble with a hooked drive could only make a 5, his eight-foot putt for par slipping by just above the cup. What a hard way to lose after all the fine shots he had played throughout the tournament, and all the course he had shown!

Then Green and Funseth, who were the final twosome, came to the eighteenth. Both needed birdies to tie Player. Both failed. Funsett lipped the hole from eight feet. Poor Green, after a superb 8-iron second to within two and a half feet missed to the right without touching the rim. He had been distracted by the voice of a radio announcer.

It seemed like ages before Green walked over and made the tap-in that didn't count. While he did this, the gallery remained transfixed. Then it slowly dawned on the vast assembly that what they had seen had actually occurred: The tournament was over, and Gary Player had won it.

In most record books, Player is listed as standing five feet eight, but he may be nearer to five-seven. He does not, however, give the impression of being a small man. He has a splendid physique, which he has built up and maintained by constant attention to diet and exercise. He weighed a hundred and fifty pounds when he turned professional, in 1952, and he still does. In 1957, when I first saw him play, I was terribly disappointed. He had an ugly swing, for he was intent on hitting the golf ball as far as the big men did, and in his pursuit of length he set up in an overly wide stance, wrapped the club around his neck going back, and practically jumped at the ball at impact. Besides this, he had a defective grip, and on many rounds he was all over the course. Nevertheless, he contrived to bring in some surprisingly good scores, for he used the wedge well and putted like an angel. (In those days, he employed a locked-wrist method of putting, with the movement of his shoulders controlling his stroke.) He was also aided incalculably by his persistence: Success at school sports had convinced him that he had athletic co-ordination, and he was determined to be a golf champion. When I saw him in action the next year, 1958, I barely recognized his swing. I don't know how he managed the change so quickly, but he had transformed it completely. He now had a good-looking orthodox American-type swing, and he hit the ball nicely and far. Over the last decades, he has had his hot streaks and his slumps, but he has never stopped working on the technical nuances of hitting the golf ball as well as he can. Since he understands clearly what the proper movements should be in the vital part of the swing – when the golfer moves into the ball and hits through it – he has been able to remedy bad habits (all golfers fall into them periodically) and come back ready for the next big event.

Today, when practising, he works mainly on tempo. Unquestionably, he has long been and still is the best bunker player in the world. In temperament, he is somewhat like Arnold Palmer, in that he can concentrate during the heat of tournament play on at least three different levels simultaneously. There is also a helpful theatrical streak in his personality, which enables him to respond well to the strident galleries, the spur of competition, and the dramatic moment.

Player lives with his wife, Vivienne, and their six children in a suburb of Johannesburg called Honeydew, where he raises race horses. He has won the South African Open eleven times. There has never been a golfer who has performed outside his own country as well as Player. This is an index of his remarkable talent, for the game is played under subtly different conditions in every land, and so requires the ability to adjust and readjust. Player has won more than a hundred tournaments around the globe. He has won the Piccadilly World Match Play Championship, at Wentworth, outside London, five times. Teamed with Harold Henning, he won the World Cup for South Africa at the Club de Campo, in Madrid, in 1965; that year, too, he won the trophy for the lowest individual total score, and he won it again last year, at the Wack Wack course, in Milana. He has taken the Brazilian Open twice. He has won in Egypt and in Japan, and he has carried off the Australian PGA Championship twice and the Australian Open no fewer than seven times. He looks much younger than he is, possibly because he has never been out of top condition. 'I believe that if a man takes care of himself, then, all things being equal, he should be as competent a golfer at fifty as he was at thirty,' he said at the conclusion of the Masters.

From *Following Through* by Herbert Warren Wind
(Macmillan, London, 1986).

8

THE AGONY AND THE ECSTASY

When Just One Shot Can Make or Break a Career

Angus MacVicar

I can't resist another look at Gary Player and his great comeback against Tony Lema in the World Match Play in 1965, here described by journalist Angus MacVicar, a self-confessed Fairway Fanatic. Sometimes, of course, a medal game comes down to virtual match play as in that contest of the titans, Nicklaus versus Watson, at the British Open at Turnberry in 1977 where not even a defiant birdie was good enough to save Jack at the last hole. In that game there was probably one crucial shot that shattered Nicklaus when Watson holed a putt of 'obscene length up and down the hills of short fourteenth for a 2'. Similarly, one shot changed the life of poor Doug Saunders at St Andrews in 1970. He missed a 3½-foot putt at the eighteenth to win the Open – and then lost the play-off to Nicklaus the next day. He was never the same player again and nor was Tony Jacklin after the 1972 Open at Muirfield when Trevino's chip into the hole at the seventeenth caused Tony to three putt and cost him the title.

I.W.

In a chapter mainly about heroes – and remembering that heroes do not always win – it would be unthinkable to leave out Gary Player. Pound for pound, Gary is the greatest golfing competitor who has ever lived. He is never more lethal than when he is down.

Some doubt his sincerity at times because of his insistence upon talking in glowing terms about players, courses, in fact anything that catches his fancy at any particular moment. But this is part of the Player philosophy of black and white. In his mind there are no greys.

The little man has never been more positive than in the 1965 semi-final of the World Match Play Championship at Wentworth. It was a thirty-six-hole match and after eighteen holes he was six down to the American, Tony Lema, who, in the previous year, had won the Open Championship at St Andrews.

Lema had come home in 32 over the treacherous Burma Road, and Player looked a forlorn figure, particularly when he lost the first hole after lunch to go seven down with seventeen to play. This was surely the end for Gary against a thoroughbred like Lema. But the South African birdied the 2nd and 3rd holes to win both, halved the 4th with another birdie, and promptly birdied the short 5th as well to be only four down with thirteen holes to play.

When he missed a short putt on the 6th green, however, to slide five down again I was sure it was all over. The pendulum had swung back again. But Gary has never been one to follow an old script. He was determined to write a new one for himself.

He was still five down with nine to play. But he won the short 10th with a 3, then birdied the 11th. Three down with seven to play: Lema's beautiful swing was beginning to quicken ever so slightly. The 12th was halved. Then, at the 13th, the American hooked his drive, could only hack his second a few yards along the fairway and barely reached the edge of the green with his third.

After great deliberation, Lema holed his putt, from fully 30 feet, for a miraculous four. Now Player, on with two great woods, had to hole a ten-foot birdie putt to cut Lema's lead to two when only seconds earlier two putts would have been good enough. It was a curly putt, a nasty putt, but Gary gave it every ounce of concentration he possessed and in went the ball. Two down, with five to play.

The next two holes were halved, but at the 16th Lema snap-hooked his drive into the trees. One down, with two to play.

The 17th was halved with birdies, and so on to the 18th, with the light fading fast. Both hit good drives, but Lema was short with his second and Player slammed into a 4-wood, which he struck so hard that he almost swung himself off his feet. The ball, however, soared away with a slight draw and landed in the heart of the green, rolling to within ten feet of the flagstick. Gary reckons it was one of the best shots he has ever hit, and Lema failed to respond with a pitch and a putt. All square and on to the 37th.

Thousands of spectators, spellbound by the drama, charged towards the first fairway, anxious not to miss one second of this awesome struggle. The light was now almost gone, and it looked to me as if Lema, too, was almost gone, in a physical sense.

And indeed he was. Whereas Player found the green in two shots, Lema drew his second into a bunker and failed to get up and down to match his opponent's 4.

A match that is now a legend was over. Player sank to his knees on the edge of the green and wept. He told me later he had had a sudden vision of his farm near Johannesburg, his family, his farmhands, his horses, his home. It had inspired him. His resolute will to win had defied a mountain that had looked impossible to scale.

I have witnessed a great number of memorable moments in golf, both amateur and professional. Some were uplifting, others involved players in the crushing disappointment of having the prize whipped away in the cruellest of circumstances.

Two such occasions stand out especially for me: the 1970 Open Championship at St

Andrews and the Open Championship two years later at Muirfield. Perhaps I did not quite appreciate it at the time, but in those two championships two strokes of a golf ball completely changed the lives of Doug Sanders and Tony Jacklin.

The scene at the 18th in the last round of the 1970 Open remains as clear in my mind as if it had happened yesterday. Thousands had gathered round the historic setting to witness Sanders edge out Jack Nicklaus for the most coveted title in golf. I had squatted down at the top of the clubhouse steps as the colourful Georgian prepared to play his second shot. Doug's personality was as sparkling as his attire. But this time I did not need binoculars to see the tension on his face. He required only a par 4 to beat Nicklaus, but in front of him was the Valley of Sin. I could almost hear him telling himself not to be short. Inevitably he was too strong, and the ball scampered up to the back of the green.

Nicklaus had no hope of getting a birdie 3. Sanders, therefore, had two putts for his first major title and lasting fame.

The downhill putt from the back of the 18th green at St Andrews is notoriously difficult to gauge for speed, and Sanders made the classic error. He left his first putt short by about three and a half feet.

The old grey town waited in silence. Sanders, his face now pale and drawn, hunched himself uncomfortably over his second putt. Suddenly, however, he stood up again, and picked an imaginary impediment from his line. The tension was killing him. It seemed that he couldn't bring himself to strike the putt that meant so much to him.

Finally, his concentration gone, he made contact. It was a diffident putt; his right hand came off the putter grip and the ball trundled to the right of the hole and remained above ground. Though he accepted the bitter disappointment with a dignity few others could have mustered and fought to within a stroke of Nicklaus in the play-off the following day, Sanders was never the same player again.

Two years later Tony Jacklin was within two holes of capturing the Open for a second time when his playing partner, Lee Trevino, perpetrated the most stunning – and the luckiest – shot I have ever seen in championship golf. It was lucky because, as Trevino admitted later, he had not given it his full concentration after bunkering his drive at the 17th, blasting his second shot out sideways, hitting his third into rough and his fourth over the green.

Meanwhile, Jacklin was not far short of the green in two and required only a pitch and two putts for a par 5, followed by a par at the last to beat Jack Nicklaus, who had charged in with a final round of 66. Tony elected to play a chip and run shot, expecting the ball to move quickly on the firm, fast green. But it didn't: it stopped 16 feet short of the hole.

Trevino, obviously angry with himself, then pulled a wedge quickly out of his bag, had a cursory glance at the flag and struck his chip from behind the green. To everyone's amazement the ball went straight into the hole.

'By tenfold that was the worst shock I've ever had on a golf course,' admitted Tony afterwards. Concentration ruined, he took three putts. The title had been snatched away from him.

It was a shattering mental blow from which he has never fully recovered. 'I went into a state of shock, and it definitely took me a long time to get over it, if I ever did get over it,' he admitted some years later.

In the autumn of that year Jacklin again found himself face to face with Trevino in the semi-final of the World Match Play Championship at Wentworth. Tony was four down at lunch, but with a fine exhibition of precision golf, he hauled Lee back in the second round with an outward half of 29. He got round in 63 but still lost the match by a hole. Truly the talkative Texan was Jacklin's executioner.

If the Hollywood moguls had been there they would have bought the film rights of the 1977 Open Championship at Turnberry Hotel, the Open in which no one can ever remember who was third. This was a championship about two players. Tom Watson and Jack Nicklaus. They stalked each other for four rounds, through blistering heat and a thunderstorm. Neither gave an inch. All that was missing was John Wayne, a saloon bar and a musical score by Dimitri Tiomkin.

The final act, had it been scripted, would have been returned to the writer for being too corny, for having gone over the top. But it did happen, and Opens in the years that followed suffered by comparison.

I tipped Watson that year in the *Express*. In fact, half the press tent had put money on him, and so the final hour was doubly tense for us. After all, it was our chance to be right at last!

One shot, more than any other, won it for Watson. This was his putt of obscene length, up and down the hills and valleys of the short 14th, for a 2. When the ball vanished into the hole Nicklaus winced.

If it is possible to break Nicklaus, he was broken then, though he summoned up a miraculous birdie 3 at the last hole in a desperate attempt to catch the man whom he had always regarded the most likely to replace him. He was inches from destruction in the bushes after coming off his drive. But he found the green with his second and holed an enormous putt that owed more to his extraordinary will than to technique. Watson never looked like missing his tiddler, but in retrospect the 18-incher *was* in the missable range, considering the circumstances.

But even before the ball disappeared we in the press tent were congratulating ourselves for an all too rare success in the forecasting business. Next morning, when I caught up with Watson at Prestwick Airport on his way home to Kansas, he was wearing a large pair of dark glasses. Obviously, like ourselves, he had spent little of the night in bed.

> From *Golf in My Gallowses* [Scots for braces]
> by Angus MacVicar (Hutchinson, London, 1983).

The Long and the Short Handicapper

Given that he understands the game's customs and courtesies, the bad player can play with acceptance alongside the good, because golf so lends itself to handicapping.

> Norman Mair.

Tony Jacklin – the Price of Success
Liz Kahn

After winning the British Open in 1969 and the US Open in 1970, Tony Jacklin was the hero the British golfing public had been awaiting for so long. He was still in the forefront for two or three more years – and then it all went wrong. My own feeling is that Tony didn't pace himself after his extraordinary success, that he did too much off and on the course, got stale and lost his real hunger for success in the game. This surely was an element of his failure, but Tony, in the soul-searching book he wrote with Liz Kahn, narrows down the possible causes to that traumatic episode at Muirfield when Trevino chipped in at the seventeenth. Jacklin promptly three-putted and turned what looked like a certain lead into a deficit. Arnie Palmer told a dejected Tony as he came off the last green: 'Whatever you do, try not to let it affect the way you think.' But it did. Triumph turned to dejection and despair. Jacklin tried Valium to help him sleep and he tried Scientology, but he rejected hypnosis. 'Drink and pills dull the senses, and if you think they will change the way life is, you're an idiot.' Ultimately the enjoyment of the big-time game left him. 'Normally you only get so nervous at a tournament and you control it but to be nervous and out of control as I was, that's the end of the world – there's no future in it.'

I.W.

After winning the 1970 US Open at Hazeltine, Tony was on a high. His next major event was the Open Championship at St Andrews, where he was defending his title.

By now, Tony was a household name, an international star, shining bright. He was also heavily involved with all sorts of promotions and commitments, which kept him on a hectic schedule round the world, and which gave rise to plenty of criticism that he was far too stretched to be able to give of his best on the golf course.

The first round of his defence at St Andrews began in amazing fashion: 'I played magical golf. The putts started going in – it was as though I had a hot-line to the hole. On the first three holes I drew back the putter and those three putts, two from 15 feet and one from five feet, went straight into the hole and I was three under after three holes.

'I had a par at the 4th, birdied the 564-yard 5th, where I was on in two and had two putts: I just missed a birdie at the 6th, birdied the 7th from six feet, and had a par at the 8th. At the 9th, I hit a one iron off the tee, pulled it slightly into the rough, and had just over 100 yards to the flag. I took a wedge, and the ball bounced slightly short of the flag, then hit it and dropped right into the hole. I was out in 29 and seven under par for the first nine holes.

'I went eight under as I birdied the 10th from six feet. I just missed chances to birdie the 11th and 12th, and had a par at the 13th. I drove well at the 14th, then, as I swung the club back on my second shot, I heard someone in the crowd shout out "fore" – I don't know why but my concentration wavered and I heaved off the ball and hit it into a gorse bush.

'It had been terribly sultry and quiet, and the sky was looking really threatening. Suddenly, there was thunder and great flashes of lightning, and by the time I reached my ball, after my second shot on the 14th – the course was under water. The greens were unplayable and there was no question of going on, it was a freak storm.

'It was a significant moment when you consider that finally I missed a putt of 10 feet on the 72nd hole and came fifth – if I'd made it I would have tied Lee Trevino and Harold Henning in third place. I was on 286, three shots behind Nicklaus and Sanders.

'I had to go back at 7.30 am the next day to finish my round. I had to drop out of the bush and on the 14th and I made six on that hole. I dropped two more shots on the last four holes, but whereas the day before it had been a drive and pitch to the 15th and 16th, and it had been possible to drive the 18th, now it needed a four and five iron for the second shots, and it was impossible to hit the 18th with a driver. I finished with 67, which was disappointing when something like a 62 had seemed possible.

'I continued with ever-increasing scores in the Championship, taking 70 in the second round that same day; then 73 in the third round to tie me with Nicklaus and Sanders, two strokes behind the leader, Lee Trevino.

'I was in with a chance on the last day, until I bogied the 16th by three-putting, then found myself in loose stones near the Road at the 17th and took five on that hole. I finished in 76, with a par at the last hole, and it was just not good enough.

'It was awful to have your momentum going as I did on that first day, and then not be able to finish your round. People say the whole round should have been wiped out and that I was lucky. Many people think that because it was me we were brought back the next day, when in fact it is the tournament ruling.

'Obviously if I could have finished that day, even in 65 . . . but there I'm dreaming – it's all castles in the air.'

That Open Championship ended not only in disappointment for Tony, but with Doug Sanders becoming a tragic figure, missing his short putt to win on the 72nd hole, followed by the anti-climax of a play-off and victory for Jack Nicklaus.

The following year Tony's schedule was no less hectic, and in June he defended his US Open title at Merion but missed the half-way cut.

He went to the Open Championship in July at Royal Birkdale, where he put up a strong challenge to finish third, two shots behind winner, Lee Trevino, who had just won the US and Canadian Opens, and one shot behind the smiling, hat-doffing Liang Huan Lu from Formosa.

Tony had been fighting a hook all week, and after the third round he was tied with 'Mr Lu' just one shot behind Trevino. Pulling his shots the last day, Tony dropped three shots in the first nine holes, but managed a birdie spurt on the inward half that gave him a creditable round of 71, a total of 280, but not quite good enough to win.

Tony's record in the Open Championship at Muirfield was to prove one of the most devastating moments of Tony's life, and of his golf career. The 1970 and 1971 Open Championships had been major disappointments in not providing Tony with another victory, but they paled in comparison to the shattering experience of 1972.

Earlier in the year Tony had achieved a further milestone in his career by winning a second Jacksonville Open, showing the talent was still there, giving his status in golfing terms another boost and doing wonders for his natural self-confidence. He knew he still had it in him to make the effort for the big occasion, to stand up to the pressure of another Open win, and at Muirfield the scene was set for what so nearly became his second Open win. But in reality it turned out to be a nightmare and a turning point for Tony, which to a great extent undermined that wonderful self-confidence. 'Nothing really good ever seemed to happen after Muirfield,' he claimed.

Tony's constant source of worry with his golf was his putting. He began the first hole of the Open Championship at Muirfield by three-putting for a bogey and ended the round in similar fashion, as he charged a 30-foot putt at the 18th for his birdie, went four feet past, and missed the return. But he played some great golf between the first and 18th, reflected by the five birdies in his round of 69, where he holed some very good putts which prompted him to comment, seemingly forgetting Jacksonville: 'They were the sort of putts I haven't been holing this year, and the sort a winner must hole.'

Tony's opening round in the Championship put him one shot behind Yorkshireman Peter Tupling, one ahead of Jack Nicklaus, and two ahead of Lee Trevino.

After a second round of 72 Tony shared the lead at the end of the day with Lee Trevino who had scored 71, 70, for his 141 total. It had been a scorching hot day at Muirfield but only one person had broken 70, and that was Johnny Miller whose five under par 66 set a new course record and put him one shot behind the leaders. Jack Nicklaus said he had not played well for his 72, and he was tied two shots behind the leaders.

On the third day Tony was paired with Lee Trevino and they were last out in the field. Tony was three under par at the turn, having holed some magnificent long putts to keep abreast of Trevino who was slotting them in from all over the greens.

At the short 13th Tony hit his ball into the bunker on the left of the green. He left it in the sand with his next shot, then hit it out into the bunker across the other side of the green: he got that out and finally two-putted for a three over par six. 'In the third round of the God-damned tournament, I'm in contention and I take a triple bogey and you know what that's going to do to anybody. Well, I was fantastic – I really was. I'm not talking about what anyone else thinks, that's from my own point of view. I can remember saying to myself, somehow you're not going to let that worry you, it's nothing. It was a six on one hole, but it's finished and it's not going to help worrying. I had a great attitude towards it. I can say I was fantastic because I know how I've been since, in letting things affect me.

'I went on to the next hole. Trevino birdied the 14th and I birdied; he birdied the 15th and I birdied; he birdied the 16th, thinned the ball out of the trap, where it hit the bottom of the flag and went in the hole, and I parred. We both birdied the 17th – Trevino nearly eagled the hole. At the 18th we were both five under par. Trevino hit a fantastic drive straight down the middle and put a five iron through the green. I drove into the left rough, then took a six iron and hit it on the front of the long green. It was me to putt as I was further from the hole. But it's a dumb thing to do in professional golf, to let the other player off the green play first, usually you offer him the option, but on this occasion Trevino said, "I'll come up" and I agreed. Then he chipped the damned thing in the hole again for another birdie. By now I was wishing I hadn't let him play – but the guy had asked and you don't like to refuse. I putted up to six feet and made it for a four, and it really was a big putt to make.

'So he finished with five successive birdies for a 66, holing two wedge shots and I think I'd done pretty damned well to stay with him for my 67, especially after my six on the par three. You can only do so much and I really did a good job there that day – I hung right in and felt good about it, and I'm saying to myself, patience lad – your time will come.

'We were out together again the next day and I was one shot behind Trevino who was on 207. It was the most fantastic Open – with Nicklaus six shots behind me, seven behind Trevino, and he was going for the Grand Slam having already won the Masters and the US Open that year. On the first tee Trevino said to me, 'Well, Nicklaus might catch one of us but he ain't going to catch us both.' When we were playing the 9th and Nicklaus stood on the 11th, he had passed us both.

'We both eagled the 9th where we were on the green in two. Trevino holed from 35 feet and I followed him in from 20 feet. There were two tremendous roars, and the film of the 1972 Open shows Nicklaus on the 11th tee backing off for Trevino's roar, then for mine. I continued to play very well, concentrating hard, and when we reached the tee at the par five 17th – we were both six under and needing level par to beat Nicklaus, who had finished with a 66, putting him on 279, five under par for the Championship.

'Trevino hooked his drive off the 17th tee into a bunker. I hit a perfect drive and then put my second just short of the green with a three wood. Meanwhile Trevino had played sideways out of the bunker, hit his third into the left rough, his fourth over the green, and he had given up.

'It was then my turn to play from a good position in the short rough on the left in front of the green. When I hit it, I thought it was a good chip. I know that some long time after, Tom Weiskopf was being questioned about dumb shots in golf, and he said that that chip was one of the dumbest shots he had ever seen. I was mad about that and I never said anything to him, but I thought how little he knew, and that he had never asked me about it.

'The course was very dry at that stage after a week of good weather and the green looked very hard, very fast and very brown. I had a lot of green to go over before I got to the hole, as the pin was tucked in near the back on the right. I played a chip and run with a pitching wedge, and honest to God I thought it was good, I truly did. I expected it to run forwards but instead it slowed down quickly and stopped about 16 feet short. I wasn't too worried, however, as Trevino had played four and was through the back to the green.

'Then he simply took a club out of the bag, never lined it up – took one look and hit the chip just like you would when you want to get the job over. And incredibly it went into the hole.

'My immediate reaction after all the events of the day before was that he'd had all the breaks up to that point but I thought it could be my turn next. When he chipped in, I reacted by thinking I'm not going to let him beat me that way, I'll hole this and still go to the 18th one up. So I gave my ball a bit of a dunk and it went two and a half feet past. I wasn't worried by the one coming back, but I just got quick on the putt through lack of concentration – though really the circumstances were more to do with it than anything – and I missed it. Once I'd three-putted he played the last hole perfectly, while I hit my second shot in the right-hand bunker and took five. The wind had gone out of my sails by then.

'It was one of those incredible situations that happen in life and one hopes that one is always on the doing and not the receiving end. I'm sure if you play long enough most everything can happen to you. But by tenfold that was the worst shock I've ever had on the golf course. It was such an important event, it was in the one tournament that means more to me than any other in the world, and the only saving factor was that I'd already won an Open. If I'd never won one, then it would have been even worse.

'I went into a state of shock and it definitely took me a long time to get over it, if I ever got over it. I was just numb. I didn't weep or cry, knowing that nothing was ever going to change it, knowing that when I awoke the next morning it was still going to be the same. It took a week to realise it, and it was certainly the biggest shock I ever had. Losing that Open to Trevino was like Muhammad Ali must have felt when Henry Cooper knocked him on his arse.'

At the time in 1972, Trevino admitted that he was not giving the chip he holed at the 17th his full concentration. It was for Jacklin, he said, 'the straw that broke the camel's back.' Now, Trevino looking back, comments: 'What a lot of people don't realise is that Tony didn't finish second to me at Muirfield, he finished third and I beat Nicklaus. When I chipped in at the 17th I was aiming at the hole – when you putt and chip, that's exactly what you aim for. If you're saying was I mad when I got over the chip, yes, I was upset at having hit the ball over the green, but you are still trying to hole it. Maybe my chipping in the ball did deflate Tony, but then he bogied the last hole. It's happened to me and I know how he feels about it. But there has to be a winner and there has to be somebody who finishes second. It just happened that I won, that's all.'

For Tony it was obviously not something he could take in his stride. To put so much store by one championship increases the tension to pressure-cooker level. He had given out so much in time, energy, motivation and achievement: the effort and the strain over the years must have been enormous, and when it looked like the reward was there once again the shock of having it snatched from your very grasp must mean that you begin to experience feelings of self-doubt.

'It was the most significant thing that happened in my career and it sure as hell had a big effect. Anything after that may be insignificant, it was a crazy, incredible thing. Anyone who plays sport knows that it can happen, and when I came off the last green Arnold Palmer was there and said to me, "Whatever you do, try not to let it affect the way you think." I knew what had happened to him in the 1966 US Open when he lost seven shots to Casper in the last nine holes, tied, and then lost the play-off. And I think that affected him because he only won odd tournaments after that. Some people can play a whole career and not have that happen to them in a major championship.

'You can say, that's the way it is, you've never won until the last ball is in the hole. But I felt bloody sick. Everyone had talked to me about the law of averages but they don't exist – that confirmed it, there's no such thing. Nothing's fair. Life and golf are for the takers, you've got to take it, grab it and keep it. Never give anything away, it's for taking – there's no question in my mind about that. It may be a hard outlook but life is that hard. There's no room for sentiment while you're doing it. You can like a person but it's very important to have a straightforward outlook because it is dog eat dog whether it's Nicklaus or whoever you're playing against. Nicklaus wants to win so badly and he wants it for himself.

'Of course it can be a matter of who does what and when, but I've never felt a lucky player over the years. I've never won anything without winning it – no one has ever missed a putt on the last green to let me win. If you miss a putt on the last green it's talked about for ever more, if it's the first no one remembers. Doug Sanders will never be forgotten for the putt he missed in the 1970 Open at St Andrews at the 18th, yet in his own heart maybe he thinks about another shot that cost him it more, but he's left looking foolish on the last hole. People play on that sort of thing and you start to believe it – like Oosty (Peter Oosterhuis) believes he's going to flash one to the right under pressure – he's read about it so often and done it so many times, that in the end he expects to do it.

'Until you've won a major championship you don't realise what it means, that the majors are really the only ones that matter. For a British player there's no greater tournament to win than the Open Championship for making money – and that's my profession. I was lucky to win the Open as a young British player with everything going for me. No one could have made more money out of winning one single tournament than I did out of winning that one.

'With the Open being played on links courses and thus having the factor of the consistent bounce, the player who wins is the player who can accept adversity the best – which is what I feel I did that week at Muirfield. When I said to myself, you've made six, let's get some birdies now, when you don't let little things or big ones affect you, realising and putting yourself above them, that's what it's all about.

'There are not many players around who are capable of doing that. There are players who are capable of winning golf tournaments, but very few who can do it when it matters. There always have been very few. Even now in the last 15 years there have only been a handful – and it has nothing at all to do with hitting a golf ball. It's purely and simply an attitude of mind. I think I react well to a crowd. It was always the case in the Open where the crowd would turn me on. I used to expect to hole a long putt because I would anticipate it through the crowd. I didn't have to work at getting up, I was up.

'Motivation and circumstances are crazy things. Winning can be as simple as a putt going in at the right time, or a chip, and thinking, I needed that. Inwardly you always know if it's a lost cause or not – you're honed in to the happenings. When you're on that level, when you know you're going to win, it's like corridors and lots of people banging into each other below you, and the higher the level you reach the more you concentrate and the better you are in control of yourself.

'It's like flying at 45,000 feet where there are no other 'planes and there's nothing to stop you. It's just a question of making your destination. You're not dodging around.'

From *Tony Jacklin: The Price of Success* by Liz Kahn
(Hamlyn, London, 1979).

I thought I'd blown it at the 17th green when I drove into a trap. God is a Mexican.
Lee Trevino, who went on to win at Muirfield in 1972.

How to Lose the US Open

Sam Snead

Sam Snead was the best player never to win the US Open though he was runner-up no less than four times, in 1937, 1947 (after a tie with Lew Worsham), 1949 and 1953. However, he probably came closest to winning in 1939 when the wheels came off in extraordinary fashion, as he relates here. He was only twenty-two with plenty of time ahead of him in which to try for victory, but it was not to be. In 1947 after the eighteen-hole play-off with Worsham, Snead needed a shortish putt for a sure half. He was about to slot it when Worsham queried whether Snead was indeed farther from the hole. It was decided he was, so Snead putted – and missed. Worsham then holed to win.

   Snead viewed his win in the British Open in 1946 with scant pride, hated the icy wind at St Andrews and reckoned that the £150 prize money was such a joke he decided there and then not to defend the title. But perhaps he views it with more pride now. He played forty-four years on the US tour, aided by the smoothest of swings, and in 1979 became the first player to equal then break his age in a full US tour event with a 67 and a 66 at the age of sixty-seven.

I.W.

Going into the final eighteen holes, it looked like I just might win my first [1939] National Open. My 212 score tied me with Denny Shute, Clayton Heafner, and Craig Wood, 1 stroke behind Johnny Bulla's first-place 211.

   I was loose as a goose, mentally. The night before the final day of play, I did some catsprings and some other calisthenics around the hotel-room floor. My roommate, Gene Sarazen, was already in bed and thought my exercises were tomfoolery.

   'This stuff helps me to relax,' I told him.

   'Yes, and you can sprain your back,' said Gene, snapping out the lights and practically ordering me to bed.

   I finished my sit-ups in the dark and then slept like a possum in his mother's pouch. I felt another 68 or 69 coming on when I woke up. Couldn't wait to get out there and win me that $100,000 Open.

   With seventy holes played, it looked like I'd make it. Two pars on the finishing holes would give me a 69 for the final round and a seventy-two-hole total of 281. A 281 seemed good enough, as it would tie the all-time Open record. I went for the first par on the par-4 seventy-first, where I hit a beautiful 300-yard drive. My second shot was over the green into thick clover grass. Chipping out short, I missed a 5-foot putt by an inch and took a bogey 5.

   Right there is where my most famous 'blowup' began.

For some reason, nobody wanted to tell me the facts of the situation I was up against – which wasn't anything to worry about. As matters stood, I needed only a par on the last hole to beat the best score registered so far, Byron Nelson's 284, and win. A bogey would tie Nelson. No one else still playing the course was in shape to beat Nelson.

But I didn't know any of this, and my bogey on the seventy-first had made me nervous. Ed Dudley, my playing partner, and others around me knew what Nelson had done, yet not one of them spoke up. When you're in the dark, your fears close in on you. I felt I had to gamble on a birdie on the par-5, 558-yard closing hole.

People were swarming the fairways and I had a thirty-minute, nerve-racking wait while the marshals cleared the way to build up the decision to play that last hole wide open.

The tee shot was hit squarely, but my right hand turned a bit too quickly and the ball started to hook. I said, 'Whoa, ball, whoa' – but it hooked into trampled rough anyway. The lie was in sandy soil. Up ahead were traps, short of the green and around it. Normally you'd use an iron to make sure of getting out and up. It was still 275 yards to the pin, however, and I still had the idea that the only way to win was to gamble.

Taking a custom-made 2-wood, with several degrees more loft than a driver, one of my favorite sticks, I went for the pin instead of playing safely out. Hit badly, the ball had no height. It was a low liner pushed down the fairway, and I said, 'Giddyap, giddyap,' when I saw it failing near a trap 160 yards away.

It fell into the trap. It was partly buried.

Every expert I've read claims that I played the trap shot before I thought it out. That's not true. With 2 shots used up, I had to reach the green with the next (or believed I did) and the green was still 110 yards away. My bunker lie wasn't too bad. Half the ball was visible. Above me the collar of the trap had been resodded with squares of soil topped by rough grass. This lip had to be cleared at a height of about 5 feet. A heavy sand wedge would get me up but wouldn't give me the needed distance. I asked the caddie for a shallower-faced club. 'Give me the 8-iron,' I said.

Even in 1939, when I was only a two-year touring pro, I knew how risky it can be to use a semilofted iron from a semiburied lie. The danger is that you'll catch the ball too clean. If you don't take enough sand, you don't get it up. Weighing that against the need to reach the green in 3, I gambled.

The ball went 4 feet, slammed into the collar, and struck in a crack left by the resodding. The moans and groans that went up were nothing to my feeling when I caught it too clean and saw it plug in there. In hitting too clean, you don't get under the ball; you hit too high on it and lose the lofted effect of the club. Now I had to chop sod, grass, ball, and all, while standing on sand below the ball.

To cut it out required a sideswiping blow, and she slashed out to the left 40 yards into another bunker. I was sick all over. Still thinking I needed a birdie on No. 72 to win, all my hopes were gone. In landing in that second trap, I'd used up my birdie shot. And now I was shooting 5 from another tough lie in sand.

Just then somebody stepped out of the gallery and said, 'Nelson finished at 284. You've got to get down in two more to tie him.'

I thought I'd explode at this news. All those gambling shots had been needless. 'Why didn't somebody tell me that back on the tee,' I snarled, 'so I could play it safe?' I was mad enough to plow through that crowd, swinging a club right and left. People will give you nine million miles of advice when you don't need it, but here in the clutch, they had dummied up on me.

If there's anything in this story I'm not ashamed of, it was the 9-iron recovery I made then. I was shaking all over. But I was still thinking. My ball rested 4 or 5 inches below my feet at the bunker's edge. In any situation where you must stand in the trapside grass with the ball below you, the danger is 'falling into' the shot and slicing it. Unless you're careful, because you body is tilted forward, you tend to shift weight too soon from your right leg, on the backswing, to the left leg, on the downswing. Which gives you a push or slice. A photo I have of this Spring Mill explosion shows how I avoided that. I bent my knees more than usual, 'sitting down' to the ball. My weight was back on my heels to prevent overshifting. I choked down on the club, to make sure I stayed down to the ball throughout the swing. If you rise up even a little bit on a lie like this, you're ruined. The clubface was closed slightly to counteract any slice. And I scraped the ball onto the green, 40 feet from the cup.

To tie Nelson, I needed the putt, and again I'm not ashamed – the 40-footer came close. It lipped the cup and twisted 3 feet away.

After that, I was an awful sight. I didn't give a damn anymore. The collapse was complete when I missed the 3-footer. One more putt gave me an 8 – the most talked-about 8 ever taken in golf, I guess. Some women were crying and men were patting me on the back as I walked to the locker room. It was worse in there. There was dead silence. The other pros avoided looking at me, to spare me embarrassment. The sportswriters stayed far away, too. All except one, George Trevor of New York, who walked up with a pencil and notebook in hand and asked, 'Sam, what happened on that last hole?'

The boys led Trevor away before I did something I'd regret.

From *The Education of a Golfer* by Sam Snead
(Cassell & Co., London, 1962).

After an abominable round of golf a man is known to have slit his wrists with a razor blade and, having bandaged them, to have stumbled into the locker room and inquired of his partner: 'What time tomorrow?'

Alistair Cooke.

If profanity had an influence on the flight of the ball, the game would be played far better than it is.

Horace G. Hutchinson (the first Englishman to captain
the Royal and Ancient).

I've thrown or broken a few clubs in my day. In fact, I guess at one time or another I probably held distance records for every club in the bag.

Tommy 'Thunder' Bolt.

If you are going to throw a club it is important to throw it ahead of you, down the fairway, so you don't waste energy going back to pick it up . . .

Tommy 'Thunder' Bolt.

Every day I try to tell myself this is doing to be fun today. I try to put myself in a great frame of mind before I go out then I screw it up with the first shot.

> Johnny Miller, the devout Mormon who, from being the most successful golfer in the world (US Open in 1973, British Open 1976 by six clear strokes), plummeted from superstar to also-ran (111th) by 1978. Like the mayfly he shone brilliantly for a brief season and was the best in the world. But unlike Nicklaus he did not have the motivation (or perhaps confidence) to be the best who ever lived. However, he was still a good player.

Arnold Palmer demonstrates bunker power. (*Peter Dazeley*)

Bunker power by Lee Trevino. (*Peter Dazeley*)

Bunker power by Sevé Ballesteros. (*Peter Dazeley*)

Nicklaus at the 18th at Augusta – another Masters almost won for the Golden Bear. (*Peter Dazeley*)

Palmer at the 4th hole of the Burma Road, Wentworth. (*Peter Dazeley*)

Player personifies mind over matter; here he comes to terms with a near impossible lie. (*Peter Dazeley*)

Now comes the triumph. Player's putter holes another long one. (*Peter Dazeley*)

Battle of the giants. The never to be forgotten clash between Nicklaus and Watson, when Watson won the 1977 Open at Turnberry. (*Peter Dazeley*)

They used not to drop . . . But now they do. Bernhard Langer at the 1981 Open. (*Peter Dazeley*)

9

MY FAVOURITE COURSES

Wentworth

Ronald Heager

I first played the West Court or Burma Road at Wentworth in 1977. I got four birdies in the first six holes, and since that includes the 452-yard par-4 third, which demands an accurate tee shot to avoid the bunkers and an equally accurate second to avoid the perils of the two-tier green, I was well pleased. The greens at Wentworth are marvellous – like a snooker table. The course has had happy memories for me ever since and my 1987 win against Sandy Lyle in the World Match Play was a personal pinnacle – so far. The seventeenth, with its sharp dog-leg left, is one of the great par 5s – 571 yards long for tournament purposes. Go too far left and you land up in the trees; too far right and there are trees on the other side. The eighteenth is a left-to-right dog-leg. Greg Norman eagled the eighteenth hole to beat Bernhard Langer by a single stroke in the 1981 Martini International after a birdie on the seventeenth.

   The late Ronald Heager, former golf correspondent of the *Daily Express* and *Sunday Express*, tells us about the history and attractions of what must be the best-known course to all British TV viewers.

I.W.

The Americans have a satirical story about the archetype TV watcher who possesses the blinkered view that Arnold Palmer invented the game of golf and everything flowed from there with the aid of the television studios. It was, however, another legendary American, Walter Hagen, who was captivating an awakening golfing public at the time Wentworth's East Course was opened in 1924. It was laid out by H. S. Colt, who became the first secretary of Sunningdale in 1900 and went on to become one of the greatest of golf architects.

   The Club was just an infant of two years when it first earned a place in golf history, playing host to the unofficial match between Britain and the United States in 1926. This fixture had been tried out at Gleneagles in 1921 and this time was to implant the idea of the Ryder Cup in the mind of millionaire seedsman Samuel Ryder. Britain – believe it or not – won 13½–1½. Another Wentworth 'first' was the launching of the Curtis Cup between Britain and the US women's teams on the East Course in 1932. This time the Americans won 5½–3½.

Through the 1930s the longer and more exacting West Course began to build a reputation that still stands as one of the supreme inland tests of golf in the whole of the British Isles. When the fighting Servicemen were demobilized from 1945 onwards the West Course renewed its climb to international stature. It is easy to visualize a suffering campaigner, having at last reached the haven of the '19th', likening his ordeal to the 'Burma Road', a name so eloquent that it stuck.

The 'Burma Road' received its international hallmark in the 1950s when first the Ryder Cup and then the Canada Cup – now World Cup – were staged there. The legendary Ben Hogan and Sam Snead formed the US team for the 1956 Canada Cup contest. The Americans inevitably won, with Hogan as the individual winner. When golf moved into the age of Palmer, Player, Nicklaus and beyond, Wentworth was ready. The World Match-Play brought the modern giants there and a new chapter of golf history unfolded. Palmer, appropriately, was the first winner. The next year saw Player's epic fightback from seven down and 17 to play, still five down and nine against Tony Lema before winning their semi-final at the 37th.

But even if the Club had never opened its doors to a single tournament it would still possess a special place in golf simply on the merit and the charm of its courses, on the subdued grandness of the clubhouse, and for all the accompanying amenities.

The West Course was also laid out by Harry Colt in collaboration with his partners John Morrison and Charles Alison. No layout has better stood the test of time: the only changes came with the building of super 'tiger' tees for the 1953 Ryder Cup, making the course the exacting test it is today.

The West Course has had so much exposure that even a first time visitor could hardly feel a stranger. You would already know that Arnold Palmer ranks the 17th as one of the world's greatest par five holes and that Bobby Locke includes the par four 11th in his gallery of the best 18 he has played round the world.

The course winds in a vast hairpin through the first six and last seven holes, with a loop of five holes in an undulating clearing of heathery slopes. Neil Coles names the 3rd as one of the supreme holes, as does Bernard Gallacher, the Club professional and latest in a line of distinguished Ryder Cup players to hold the office, with Archie Compston, Jimmy Adams and Tom Haliburton preceding him. The continuity of the World Match Play has provided a fascinating spin-off of statistics and if anything can be proved by figures there is confirmation that the 3rd is Wentworth's toughest hole: it has had the highest aggregate of strokes over par and the lowest yield of birdies.

By the same yardstick the professionals have found the downhill, dog-legged 4th the most rewarding of all the Burma Road stages, for it has the highest birdie yield together with the 12th, and the biggest aggregate sub-par total. But then few can make birdies in the manner I recall Gary Player once achieving here: after a pernicious hook had put him in the trees, he came out sideways, hit a 4-iron to the green and holed a long putt!

Player, as you would expect, was defying the first rule of Wentworth – if you miss the fairway, you are dead; it is certain to cost you one shot, if not more. That is a fact of golf as you thread your way through the trees, heather, sand, gorse and water to the turn, tangling with a well-bunkered 5th green, a tee shot that demands restraint and accurate placement at each of the 6th, 7th and 8th, and the most formidable par fours at the 460-yard 9th.

SCORE CARD: West Course

Hole	Yards	Par	Hole	Yards	Par
1	471	4	10	186	3
2	155	3	11	376	4
3	452	4	12	483	5
4	501	5	13	441	4
5	191	3	14	179	3
6	344	4	15	480	5
7	399	4	16	380	4
8	398	4	17	571	5
9	460	4	18	502	5
Out	3371	35	In	3598	38
			Total	6969	73

Now the 'easy' half is over and one of the most intimidating of par threes starts the par 38 back nine, so difficult as almost to be unfair – unless you have hit the green with a high tee shot. The 11th has its dogleg and two ditches to negotiate, the 12th a line of conifers defying the tee shot and the 13th dog-legs left with a fairway that falls away to the jungle on the right. There just is no respite as you face not only an uphill tee shot but a terraced green again at the par three 14th as the preliminary to the finish of three par fives in the last four holes.

One of the tests of a golf course is how easily the holes are remembered after a casual acquaintance. By this standard the East Course rates as highly as the West. The East possesses five short holes, and such is their quality that it is not one too many. Though measuring only some 6,200 yards, the challenge and variety measures up to the West. Holes particularly to savour are the 2nd – for the glorious panorama from the tee – the 11th and the three finishing holes.

But it is not the courses alone that make Wentworth Club, it is the whole ambience of one of the game's Meccas.

From *AA Golf Guide to Great Britain* (London, 1977).

A Course to Make a Welshman Proud

Peter Allen

I had just turned pro at the age of eighteen when I played my first international against the French at Royal Porthcawl in South Wales and the course has remained a favourite of mine ever since – second only to Wentworth among British courses. In this piece Sir Peter Allen, a former Chairman of ICI and a keen amateur golfer whose business happily took him travelling in the neighbourhood of many fine courses all over the world, describes the special attraction of this Welsh seaside course.

I.W.

I didn't get to Royal Porthcawl in South Wales until late in 1966 and more's the pity, for it is a mighty fine seaside golf course. However, I *did* get there in the end and so completed my tally of all the championship courses of the British Isles, a pursuit which had begun at Deal forty-one years before. True, Porthcawl joined the select band late in the day in 1951 and so became the last but for Ganton to be used for one or other of the major events, but it had its reputation made long before then.

I have called it a seaside course advisedly, for it is indeed by the sea and the club's boast that you can see the sea from some part of every hole is true, but it is not all links-land by any means; the lower holes along the shore and on shore level are links golf, right enough, but there is a distinct hill which you climb at the fifth and on the upper levels from the fifth green to the ninth tee and then again at the twelfth and seventeenth you are on something more like moorland turf with bracken and heather and thick gorse in the rough.

The course is not by any means abominably long, 6,700 yards off the championship tees and 6,400 off the regular tees, so that several of the par fours are under 400 yards, that is until you get stuck into the second half, when the par fours lengthen out and indeed become bogey fives. Don't be deluded, however. The course is not easy, for on the whole the greens are small and the course is richly bunkered; the greens, moreoever, have some heavy curvatures, steps and slopes, so that when the game needs to be tightened up some pretty difficult pin positions can be selected.

The location of the course is excellent, with a fine view over the Bristol Channel towards Minehead and Exmoor twenty miles or so away, and on down the coast to Ilfracombe. Inland are some attractive hills and across the bay the Gower Peninsula, with Swansea on its flank. Industry does not too much intrude, save for the emission at intervals of some pink smoke from below the sheltering hill to the west, which betrays the presence of the Steel Company of Wales's Port Talbot plant.

The Porthcawl Club started its golf on a different site on a piece of common land to the east, but for nearly seventy years it has been where it now is, occupying a rough triangle of land, as good a shape as any for a golf course, and especially if, as here, there is liable to be plenty of wind. Then the straight-out-and-home course is at its worst and a layout on a triangle far better. The first three holes run out to the west along the shore, the third, indeed, so close that you can drive on to the shingle without any trouble at all. Then you turn back and play inland to a short hole, well bunkered, with its green sitting up for you, none the less, then at number five with its long uphill pull to the green you are on the plateau. Here, as I have said, you are off the links-land, and indeed this part of the course reminded me a great deal of Ganton, but, after all, isn't Ganton a links inland or something very like it? Up here there is a very short hole, only 125 yards, but it is not easy, for it is heavily bunkered, the green is long and narrow and has some big slopes and borrows. The ninth, with a drive across a big dip, is a splendid hole, with a small much beset green and with some good slopes on it, an excellent medium-length par four. My Welsh caddie, whose vast ginger moustache and whiskers, extending from ear to ear, reminded me of Sir Gerald Nabarro, declared that it was the finest hole on the course and I'm not disposed to disagree.

The par fours in the second half really stretch you, holes like the thirteenth, fifteenth and sixteenth, which I couldn't reach on a soft November day, and there are two fine short holes in this half, the eleventh, which is longer than it looks – where I bolted a putt for a two – and the fourteenth, which is shorter, where I missed a much easier putt. Only the two long holes in the back nine seemed to me to be rather below standard, but the eighteenth is a beautiful finishing hole, with a downhill drive off the plateau straight towards the sea; there is a scrubby hollow across the fairway about 270 yards from the regular tee which no doubt bothers some, but keeping short of that was no trouble to me. The green is long and narrow and literally runs on to the shore, so a shot hit 'thin' can well end up on the shingle.

The greens throughout the whole layout are excellent.

From *Famous Fairways* by Sir Peter Allen
(Stanley Paul, London, 1968).

The Very Irish Hazard of Maggie Leonard's Cow

Pat Ward-Thomas

Portmarnock Golf Club in County Dublin is one of my three favourite golf courses this side of the Atlantic and it rates with any of the great British Championship links. Even the 'easier' holes become a challenge when the wind blows off the sea and the 192-yard fifteenth with its two little pothole bunkers flanking the entrance to the green can be a real card-wrecker. It was here in his great year of 1960 that Arnie Palmer smacked a 3-iron across the wind which died within a yard of the hole. Though he failed with the putt, he was round in 69. He and Sam Snead went on to win the World Cup (then called the Canada Cup) by eight clear shots, even though Gary Player for South Africa did a 66, equalling Christy O'Connor's record of the previous year in the Dunlop Masters. Christy, incidentally, played the last twenty-three holes of that Masters in 83 or 9 under par to snatch the title from Joe Carr. He even tamed the testing 466-yard seventeenth, which demands a drive of absolute straightness because of the bunkers. The second shot is often a wood because the wind is rarely helpful. If you pull the ball a fraction or drift it, you will be trapped in bunkers round the green. Yet Christy twice birdied the hole in 3, placing a 4-wood for his second to within feet of the pin, on days when 5s were commonplace. Here Pat Ward-Thomas describes the greatness of Portmarnock.

I.W.

In a land where beauty, poetry, conflict and passionate belief in the individual are constantly intermingled, the Irish have found golf to be a ready expression of their character and flair for games. The enthusiasm of the players, the variety of styles and the quality of courses is remarkable. Ireland is not large, but it has several of the finest tests of golf to be found anywhere in Europe.

Except in the country itself, where local feelings might influence judgement, one would be hard-pressed to find agreement as to which was the greatest course – Portrush, Portmarnock or County Down. These three are not alone, for there are Ballybunion and Rosses Point on the far Atlantic shore; Killarney, serene on its lakeside amid the mountains, and Waterville have elements of majesty.

Of all courses, few are blessed with the natural magnificence of Portmarnock. Within the fine sweep of coastline curving to an end at Howth Hill, the northern guardian of Dublin Bay, there is a long tongue of linksland between the Irish Sea and an inland tidal bay. It is thus almost enclosed by water, a private place where a man is alone with the turf, the sea, the sky and the challenge of the wind. It is brave, splendid golfing country.

Portmarnock's moods can vary from a sternness, that can be savage, to wondrous peace. In summer, with a fresh breeze sparkling the bay and stirring the dune grasses, Ireland's Eye and Lambay rising sharp from the sea, there are few more tempting places for a golfer to be. On such a day, long ago, Sam Snead was at practice, pouring a stream of flawless strokes with a 1-iron into the morning distance. Watching golf could offer little more.

Like its great Irish rivals, Portmarnock often changes direction, somewhat after the fashion of Muirfield, with two distinctive and separate trails finishing by the clubhouse, a graceful white landmark from afar. The spectacular quality and unexpectedness of County Down are absent, but Portmarnock's problems are straightforward, even if considerable and often severe. There are no blind shots to the greens and few from the tees, no sharp changes of level yet no monotonous flatness, either. Several holes follow shallow valleys, but they are never as pronounced as they are at Birkdale. They might suggest, but certainly do not afford, protection from the wind.

The design of the course is natural rather than contrived. The 3rd, along a strath of turf, narrow and slightly convex between sandhills on one side and the marshy fringes of the bay on the other, is an example. So, too, is the one bunker guarding the pin at the 5th. The approaches to the shorter par-fours such as the 2nd and 8th, are beautifully shaped. There are only three short holes – the 7th, into a dell, the 12th, high in the dunes, and the 15th, which can be fearsome with a wind from the sea on the right. To hold the narrow table of green, it may be necessary to swing the shot over the beach – which is out-of-bounds – and back again. Even in still air the green, shelving away on either hand, is difficult to hold. Only a true stroke here will prevail.

The three par-fives can be immense. At times the 6th, along its dimpled fairway and valleys, can be three woods for the strongest, yet the second shot can be as little as a medium iron when the course is running fast. The 13th has a long carry from the tee, behind which the waves pound, and there are bunkers to attract and destroy the second shot. The 16th is of similar shape, down from the sea with the approaches swinging in from the left.

These two noble holes are part of a challenging finish, for the 14th, too, is a great hole although less than 400 yards. According to the wind, the second from a rolling fairway can be anything from a wood to a pitch and must carry huge bunkers in front of a long plateau of green in the dunes. Legend has it that Joe Carr, greatest of Irish amateurs, has driven the green, the ball somehow escaping the bunkers; fact in its turn states that Henry Cotton once took seven strokes here – and lost an Irish Open in the process.

As a strong par-four, the 17th takes a deal of beating. Bunkers flanking the straight fairway are cause for thought on the tee and the second demands a long, accurate shot to a closely guarded green. The 18th, a fine hole, owes less to fortune than it did when the home green was hard by the clubhouse. The hole has been shortened and the green moved to a position offering less of a threat to the constantly peppered building.

Portmarnock has been the setting for many great occasions, played in the wildest extremes of weather. When a tempest assailed the last round of the Irish Open in

1927, George Duncan – one of the greatest of inspirational golfers – was round in 74, the only player to break 80. The weather was such that, even with this historic round, his winning score was 312. Christy O'Connor took 36 strokes fewer when he won the Dunlop Masters at Portmarnock thirty-two years later.

The Dunlop tournament won by O'Connor in 1959 was memorable for the golf of Joe Carr. After three rounds, all under 70, he led a strong field by four strokes and was within sight of being the first amateur to win a major professional tournament in a generation until O'Connor passed him with a final round of 66.

The only time the Amateur championship has been played in Eire, in 1949, it was won by Max McCready. His golf had power, authority and great confidence and it disposed of the two most formidable Americans in the field, Frank Stranahan, the defending champion, in the semi-final, and Willie Turnesa in the final. Thunder prowled the distant hills as the inscrutable Turnesa became one up with four to play, but McCready won the next three holes. Ireland rejoiced that night.

None of this might have happened but for the inspiration in 1893 that impelled two men, J. W. Pickeman and George Ross, to row across the mouth of the estuary from the point where the Sutton clubhouse now stands. By some blessing of the imagination they visualized a golf course on what was then a wilderness of dune and bracken inhabited only by a remote and self-sufficient community of farming and fish folk, yet only ten miles from Dublin.

The first clubhouse was only a shack and the greatest hazard Maggie Leonard's cow, which devoured hundreds of balls. Golfers reached the course by crossing the estuary at low tide in a horse-drawn cart, at other times by boat. There is a road now at the far end of the peninsula and this delightful and very Irish way of reaching the 1st tee has gone the way of Maggie Leonard's cow.

From *The World Atlas of Golf*
(© Mitchell Beazley, London, 1976).

10

SOME MODERN HEROES

Tom Watson

Peter Alliss

For a decade at least from the time of his first British Open win in 1975, Tom Watson was the supreme champion, taking over from Nicklaus as the world's leading player – indeed, he is one of the greatest of all time. I've long admired him. At 5 feet 9 inches he doesn't suffer from being too tall and there is immense power in his arms and legs. On top of that he is the world's best short-putter. Peter Alliss, another long-time admirer of Watson, here gives his shrewd assessment of him as man and golfer.

I.W.

'We're vastly overrated.' That's part of Tom Watson's attitude to the fame and adulation that success brings to golfers (and all other athletes) today. It's always been very apparent to me that Tom is one of those who doesn't relish public attention and the praise of genuine admirers or hangers-on alike. True, he has the ambition to be recognized in golfing history as one of the greatest players but that's a very different matter from enjoying all the razzmatazz that goes hand-in-hand with being in the limelight. As I know only too well, much of that brings little more than occasional embarrassment, frequent boredom and always the feeling of being 'on parade' and having to put on a public face.

Indeed, when Tom is actually on parade as one of our Supreme Champions, in one respect he doesn't quite look the part. I'm sure he has a very lucrative clothing contract yet nothing seems to fit. The trousers are usually a touch too long or too short and the labelled shirts and polo necks too loose or too tight. All very different from, let's say, the casual elegance of Jack Nicklaus or Seve Ballesteros. Yet that same Jack Nicklaus 20 years and more ago, in jockey cap and khaki trousers could himself have been competing for the title of worst-dressed golfer. In Watson's case, such disregard for his attire has never been as openly contemptuous – after all, he belongs to a different era when nearly all conform to what is required of them and may well be fined by their PGAs if they don't!

The clothing contract is just one of several that brings Tom's income to something like $1½ million a year, a sum that dwarfs his tournament money winnings which give him a career total of about $4 million. In business, Watson has been very much his own man. It's a family affair with his wife Linda playing a major role though his manager is Charles Rubin, a lawyer who also happens to be Watson's brother-in-law.

Financially, Tom is obviously set up for life but his motivation remains as strong as ever. On the US Tour he restricts himself to about 20 events a year out of the more than 40 possible. He plays more than Jack Nicklaus and Johnny Miller – but not by that wide a margin. Watson's overseas appearances are limited. Of course, the British Open has absolute priority, Watson's favourite and best event, and he is also to be seen from time to time in Australia and Japan. But that's about it. He has learned to protect 'the property', devising a limited schedule which keeps him keen to play golf and competitively sharp.

Of the great and nearly great players, Watson realized early that the majors are what count and was later to say, 'Charisma is winning major championships'. A waning Johnny Miller may declare that a golfer's record in other tournaments is almost as important but, to be blunt, Miller will be remembered for winning the 1973 US Open and the 1976 British Open Championship far more than for the 22 US Tour events he has won to date or even for those couple of years when he played golf at a standard never seen before or since.

Tom appears to me to be a British Open specialist. Oddly, he had won the championship a couple of times before he really understood what was involved or the armoury needed to combat the difficulties of seaside golf. At Carnoustie in 1975, he made his first appearance in Britain, with only two tournament wins under his belt. Surely he had no thoughts of winning as he went to the 1st tee? Yet there Watson produced a performance that has from time to time been a sort of trademark – keep going and it could be the others who will falter. Watson finished a little ahead of the apparent leading contenders and, lo and behold, they all came back to him – Bobby Cole, Johnny Miller, Jack Nicklaus, Neil Coles, and, of course, Jack Newton.

The play-off between this Australian and Watson swung to and fro. It could have gone either way but it was Watson who got his par on the last hole to win. He was on his way and has never looked back, at times making the British Open Championship and dominance of the US money list seem his by right.

I'm sure that victory took Tom Watson by surprise and he was a far more polished player at Turnberry in 1977, a championship which saw the most sustained man-to-man combat since the championship began in 1860. By this time, Watson was a very different player. If the 1975 championship had almost stolen up on him unawares, in 1977 he had come to believe in himself as the most effective scorer in the game of golf. He also sought perfection and, after the third round, was quick to point out to the Press that his 65 was better fashioned than Jack Nicklaus's had been with more tee-shots on the fairway and superior quality of strike on the irons. He didn't mention the putting and hardly needed to for, I believe, Watson is far and away the greatest short putter among the moderns, while his firm-wristed stroke from long range is also highly effective at keeping the ball on line to the holeside and is allied to unrivalled judgement of pace.

Watson is not the thinking man's perfect player. He certainly hits a long ball but some are rather wild. His very strong 'Popeye' forearms should give him an edge in long- and mid-iron play but, if you'll believe the statistics, he virtually never features in the US Tour figures for getting on the greens in regulation figures. In this department Nicklaus, among many others, earns much higher ratings.

That acute observer, Lee Trevino, claims that Tom hasn't got a soft shot. Everything is played with much the same firm, crisp rhythm. Lee believes that Tom can't pitch in with a high fading pattern of flight, that he has, basically, to bang everything at the flag. Well, they used to say that a certain Gardner Dickinson was more concerned about the shape of a particular shot and would be far more delighted to get a delicate fade or a low-drawn ball to 40 feet than something a little more direct nearer the pin. There are players more intent on the perfection of shot than the result, with Tom Weiskopf a clear example. I pass on the truth of these opinions but I can say that I've never seen anyone, lack of a soft shot or not, more adept at getting it close from around the green and then ramming home the putt, almost as an effort of will. His fellow players tend to think that if, at every hole, everyone missed all the greens, Watson would proceed to win all the tournaments. There may be better putters, chippers and pitchers. But no one else can put it all together as well.

Part of this has to do with practice. So many players go to the practice ground occupied with thoughts of the total golf swing. Will that tip about arching the left wrist just a little bit more work? Should the club be kept low to the ground on the backswing for an extra 6 inches? Well you know it all. Tournament golfers seek the magic solutions just as eagerly as the ordinary club player.

Watson goes through the same drills. But he is not so strong a believer. He'd like to be perfect, like Ben Hogan before him, but is much more a realist. Watson knows that, driving the ball well over 250 yards, many of his tee-shots will finish in the rough. The target areas are narrower at that distance. He'll practise and improvise from that kind of territory as much as others will devote time to watching the flight of, let's say, a 7-iron nudged into a perfect lie. How few golfers do this, yet so many shots are, for example, played when the ball is well down in the grass, from worn and bare turf around a green or when the backswing is impeded by a bush, tree or a wall. Watson spends time practising in all these and many other situations. When he gets into them, he's been there before and knows how to cope. Rather like Walter Hagen before him, Tom expects to hit a few poor shots in a round and then briskly confronts the problem and gets on with it.

This briskness is very obvious in other departments of his play. He may not be quite so fast as Lanny Wadkins but there's very little in it. Watson decides on the kind of shot he'll play as he approaches his ball and then simply looks target, ball, target – and swings. And I can detect hardly any difference if he's 20 strokes behind the leaders in a run-of-the-mill tournament or in hot contention for a major championship.

Two shots at such times in recent major championships will go into golfing history.

For both, Watson was as brisk as ever. Needing to par the tough closing hole at Royal Birkdale to win the Open Championship in 1983 and after hitting a poor drive at the 17th, Watson quickly fired his drive straight down the fairway. He was equally brisk playing a 2-iron, held up against the wind, which finished in the heart of the green, making two putts for victory a formality.

An even more famous shot had occurred a little over a year earlier at Pebble Beach in the US Open Championship. Nicklaus had completed his final round; Watson needed a par, par finish to tie over two difficult holes, a long par-3, followed by a par-5 with an intimidating tee-shot and played right around the cliff tops. Watson then proceeded to stand the situation on its head. For a start, he looked as if he'd lost the championship when his long-iron bounced into quite thick rough just to the left of the green. There seemed little or no chance that he could get his tiny pitch shot to stop near the hole. Instead, in it went for a 2 and Tom needed only par on the last to win. The birdie which followed was not necessary but he had won his first US Open by two.

Two quite different stories have been told since about this legendary pitch-in. The first is that a TV company approached Watson with the request that he attempt to re-enact the shot. Watson refused. Why? Well perhaps he didn't want to tarnish his image by failing. The second is that Tom has since tried to do it again and again for his own personal satisfaction – and failed, seldom getting within several feet. You pays your money and takes your choice.

Perhaps that 1982 US Open assured Tom of golfing immortality but it certainly took many observers of golf a long time to concede him this status. Byron Nelson's opinion is interesting and he knows Tom's game better than anyone. He considers that Watson could prove to be better than both Hogan and Nicklaus, superior from the mid-irons through the pitching clubs and a far better clipper and putter. Although this argues supremacy for Watson in approach play and the short game only there's not much left for Hogan and Nicklaus to be good at is there? Just driving, fairway woods and the long-irons! They are departments of the game where Watson himself is no slouch.

Even so, shot-making was never Tom's main problem but learning to win and to manage both himself and the golf course was. He was introduced to golf at the age of six by his father but he did not have an outstanding amateur career. He won the Missouri State Amateur Championship four times and played for the Stanford University team for three years, finishing as their number one. He had no success at the higher levels of amateur golf, however, and with this record could hardly have been worth a thought as a possible Walker Cup choice.

The accepted route to the US Tour was a Walker Cup place and a proven record in national and regional amateur tournaments which players such as Nicklaus, Wadkins and Crenshaw have enjoyed as part of their golf pedigree. Nevertheless, Watson decided to try his luck on the US Tour and turned professional in 1971. His first season, 1972, was immediately reassuring.

The Bing Crosby National Pro-Am was the second event of the season, played over the testing courses of Pebble Beach, Spyglass Hill and Cyprus Point. Watson finished twentieth, seven strokes behind the play-off between Jack Nicklaus and

Johnny Miller, winning a modest $1,400. It was a start and showed Tom that he could compete with the best. He won money in the next two or three events so in his first month on Tour he had gone a good way towards proving, if only to himself, that he could make a living at the game.

Learning to contend and to win were to take considerably longer. In the rest of the season by far his best result was second place in the Quad Cities Open, his 69 and 66 finishing rounds putting him a stroke behind Deane Beman, now US Tour Commissioner. However, the field wasn't of the highest quality and Tom had yet to face the test of being tournament leader and holding onto it with all the big guns there.

That problem came twice in 1973. In the Hawaiian Open he took a three-stroke lead into the final round but then faltered to end with a 75. Much the same happened in the World Open, a strange and short-lived event dedicated to the idea that eight rounds of golf are a better test than four. In the fifth round, Watson played the splendid Pinehurst Number 2 course in 62, which catapulted him into a six-stroke lead, but he dribbled it away with rounds of 76, 76 and 77. However, by the end of the year he'd moved up from seventy-ninth place in the money list to thirty-fifth.

Watson first became a 'name' in 1974. The event which established him was the US Open at Winged Foot. After three rounds he was the leader by a stroke but on the final day staggered home with a 79. Three failures in a row. Among those in the know, it was openly bandied about that Tom Watson had no iron streak. He was a 'choker', a man who lost his nerve when protecting a lead. This reputation was only partly changed a short time later when Watson won for the first time at the Western Open. This time he had a weak third round but came past the leaders with a 69 on the last day to win by a couple of strokes from J. C. Snead and Tom Weiskopf.

He was by then an established player, and finished the year tenth in the US money list, which made him roughly equivalent to Ryder Cup status. In 1975 Tom Watson became a star but there were still problems along the way. After winning the Byron Nelson Classic in May, he had a second bad experience in the US Open at Medinah. His start of 67 and 68 equalled the championship record for the first 36 holes. Although his finish of 78 and 77 sounds like another total collapse it was a high-scoring event and his total of 290 was only three strokes worse than the winner's. (Lou Graham and John Mahaffey tied and Graham won the play-off.)

Later in the year, after his British Open title, Tom won the World Series and finished seventh on the US money list. Jack Nicklaus commented: 'He knows exactly where he's going. Straight ahead. Nothing distracts him. He has great abilities, super confidence and just enough cockiness. He's not a comer. He has arrived.'

Watson was indeed soon to take over from Jack Nicklaus as the world's leading player though that wasn't to be fully clear for some years yet. His progress was distinguished in the immediate future by being leading money winner four years in a row, 1977–80, with wins in the 1977 and 1981 Masters, but most of all by his extraordinary achievements in the British Open with five championship victories in the space of only nine years. If his victory at Turnberry over Jack Nicklaus remains the most memorable, Muirfield in 1980 saw Watson at another peak. After the first round he was tied for the lead with Lee Trevino and a 64 in the third round took him into a four-stroke lead. Thoughts of whether or not Watson might 'choke' were long gone. We all thought it was inevitable he would win. The final day was indeed rather dull as Tom put together a cast-iron 69 for a four-stroke victory.

By this time, Watson had made another move forward in the major championships. Almost always he was a contender, able to raise his game for the great occasions of golf even when not on his best form. Others may beat him, as Seve Ballesteros did when he started his final round so strongly in the 1983 Masters. Yet a month or so later, Watson produced form so devastating in the US Open as to leave the Spaniard in his wake. It should have been enough to give Watson his second US Open had that vast putt from 62 feet by Larry Nelson not gone in on the 16th hole.

If Tom has had to learn how to compete and withstand pressure, he has physically always been very well suited to the game. He has almost the perfect golfing body, with magnificent forearms and very strong legs, hands and shoulders and all at what I consider the right height, 5 feet 9 inches. If a player is 6 feet or more the game becomes more difficult. The angles are wrong and many players suffer from a lack of co-ordination. Short men, on the other hand, usually have insufficient power. Watson's physical fitness, like Nicklaus's, has also been vital. I can't remember him having any of the problems with his lower back, wrists and elbows that so many golfers suffer, Trevino and Fuzzy Zoeller, for instance, and whatever has become of those lady stars, Judy Rankin and Sally Little?

As he enters his mid-thirties, it's perhaps the right time to wonder where Watson will go from here. His desire, dedication and determination don't seem to have been diluted by all the success. Unlike so many, he still enjoys playing the game on both the sternly competitive and fun occasions. He was a great success in 1983 on BBC television's Pro-Celebrity series at Gleneagles and aroused great interest with his demonstration of the importance of the constant angle of the left elbow in putting. He could rattle several putts home from a few yards' range without needing to glance at the line again. Watson also enjoys playing with friends and declares he would still make trips to Britain and Ireland even if there were no British Open to play in. He declared Royal Dornoch the most fun he had ever had playing golf and said of the towering duneland of the great Ballybunion course in Western Ireland: 'Golf architects should live and play here before they build courses.'

If Watson keeps that kind of enthusiasm, his tournament and championship successes ought to continue as long as that putting stroke remains firm and decisive. Here he's the early Arnold Palmer, willing to give the hole a chance from long range, confident that he'll be still able to hole those frightening 4- to 6-footers on the way back.

Watson is one of our Supreme Champions who seems to me to have very much benefited from the stability of his family life. It was typical that after his 1982 US Open Championship victory at Pebble Beach he didn't carouse away the night. Instead, he was to be seen on the rocks near the course quietly sharing a bottle of wine with his wife Linda and his two-year-old daughter, Meg. He has also remained in touch with his roots. Although he majored in psychology at Stanford University, he didn't seek the sun of either that state or, another favourite choice, Florida, once success came his way. The golfers who do so aren't necessarily sun-worshippers, of course. It's easier to keep a golf swing in trim during the off-season in warm weather, despite the fact that the golf season is now so long that it's certainly possible to play around the world in a summer climate throughout.

However, Watson has remained faithful to the American Mid-West and his birthplace Kansas City. In fact, he claims actually to enjoy bad weather golf and that has included playing in snow. It's all part of a pattern which has allowed Tom Watson to relish his success but to keep as level-headed as when he's contending for a major championship.

From *Peter Alliss's Supreme Champions of Golf*
(Willow Books, London, 1986).

Super Mex on the British

Lee Trevino

Lee Trevino's is a real rags-to-riches story. A Mexican-American farmboy who started as a caddie at the age of eight, he had a fatherless childhood living rough with his mother and grandfather in a Dallas shack with dirt floors and no plumbing or electricity. He taught himself to play golf well enough to win the US Open with a 275 four-round record in 1968 at Oak Hill and was the first to break 70 in every round. He won the Open again in 1971 in a play-off against Nicklaus and was also victorious in the British Open twice, in 1971 and 1972.

You could call Super Mex (a nickname coined by his agent) a lucky player, especially with that chip that went in and shattered the hapless Tony Jacklin at the seventeenth hole at Muirfield. When Lee is on a high he is brilliant, but not a battler against odds like Player or Nicklaus. His characteristic shot is low and faded, which is why he has never come to terms with the Masters – Augusta demands the opposite. 'Augusta is one type of golf course and I'm another type of golfer. Even on our best days I'd guess you'd say we have our differences,' he admits.

After being struck by lightning in the Western Open in 1976, he recalls, 'I stretched out like a vibrator – your whole life passes before you at that moment. Hey, I never knew I was so bad! I saw a lot of old girlfriends.' His back was affected by a ruptured disc and he had to have surgery. 'I sure as hell wouldn't recommend being struck by lightning, but it turned my life around. It made me appreciate everything I have.' That includes the wise-cracking routine and the chatting between shots which so delights the crowds – though not always his opponents.

In his autobiography Super Mex freely discusses his one-time drink problem, appearing on *The Johnny Carson Show* and falling down drunk, playing tournaments with horrible hangovers, and once winning a championship on the first-hole play-off after staying up till five in the morning. Then in 1974, realizing that this could cut years off his career, he cut down on the hard stuff and limited his beer drinking. He confesses to a love affair with the British and the British courses, as he explains here.

I.W.

Everything went like a dream that week at Royal Birkdale, but that really was no surprise. My experiences with British golf through the years have captured a special place in my heart.

I was introduced to British courses in 1968 and it was love at first sight. My strong showing in championship tournaments just made the romance more glamorous. And after I had played in a dozen British Opens I saw no end to it.

'I'll always play in this tournament,' I said before I teed off in 1981 at Royal St George's. 'I don't care if I shoot eighty-eighty. I'll always play over here. I love this championship. I love the links courses, with the mist and wind sweeping off the sea. I love these people.'

There's nothing quite like playing in the British Isles. Golf is in the air there. You breathe it, like smelling home cooking. It makes you hungry. You want to play.

Now it seems strange that I passed up my first spot in a British Open. I earned that in 1968 when I won the US Open, but I had a commitment to the Milwaukee tournament and didn't think I should break it. I did go to England for a couple of tournaments that fall, then entered my first British Open in 1969 at Royal Lytham and St Anne's. In 1970 we played St Andrews and I led after three rounds, but blew the championship with a final 77. Still, I felt I eventually would win the British Open. Once I got a taste of those seaside courses I knew they were for me.

It doesn't matter if you hit it short. As long as you hit it straight you can run the ball on the greens. And the wind doesn't bother me because I hit a low ball anyway.

As fond as I am of Birkdale, Muirfield, where I won the 1972 championship and finished second to Tom Watson in 1980, is my all-time favorite. I play the courses in Scotland extremely well. I can bump and run the ball better on them than any native. I've told the people there, 'If you believe in reincarnation, I probably was a Scotsman two hundred and fifty years ago.'

I won British championships the last two years they used the small ball. That was one more thing I loved about playing there. The ball was 1.62 inches in diameter as compared to 1.68 for the American ball and that meant less wind resistance, fewer dimples on the ball and less spin. To me, playing with the small ball was like cheating.

While I was always comfortable on the courses, I had some early problems communicating with the people. It took me a while to loosen them up, too. They were pretty damn reserved when I first went over there.

During my first practice round for the Alcan tournament at Birkdale in 1969, my caddie told me, 'You have to be careful here because there's a birn going across the fairway.'

'A what?' I said.

'A birn,' he said.

I hit a drive, then walked down the fairway and found my ball in the water. I looked at him and said, 'Why didn't you tell me there was a creek running through here?'

'I told you, mate. That's a birn.'

The 9th is a blind hole. You go over a hill and down and you can't see the fairway. I stood on the tee for a second, then asked him, 'Where is the fairway going?'

'Hit it straight to the marquee,' he told me.

'Where?' I asked.

'Hit it to the marquee,' he said.

Well, I took my driver and hit my ball into the right rough. 'Damm,' I said, 'I thought the fairway went this way.'

'No,' he said, 'I told you that a straight line off that tee is to the marquee.'

'Let me ask you a question,' I said. 'What the hell is a marquee?'

'That thing over there,' he said, and he pointed at a tent.

I knew right then I had to learn the language.

He wasn't a very good caddie, though, so I got rid of him after nine holes. That's when Willie Aitchison took my bag.

Willie was a Scot who had carried for two British Open winners, first Tony Lema and then Roberto de Vicenzo. Since Roberto wasn't playing in this tournament, I hired Willie and he wound up working for me in Britain and Europe for many years. But first I had to teach Willie how to caddie.

'I've got too many shots and I hit the ball too many different ways,' I told him. 'Look, I want you to go to the drugstore . . .'

'Where?' Willie asked.

'Go to the drugstore,' I said.

'You mean the chemist's,' he said.

'Well, just go there and get a notebook,' I said. 'Bring it out here tomorrow and I'll show you how to diagram each hole and mark down the yardage.'

Willie handled that all right, but there was one problem. He talked more than I do.

'Willie,' I said, 'you've got to be the listener. We can sing together, but we can't talk together.'

He still got involved with talking to too many people. In the Ryder Cup matches at Birkdale in 1969, Miller Barber and I played Tony Jacklin and Peter Townsend and when we came to 18 it was almost dark and we were feeling a lot of pressure. These points were important because the teams were tied and the United States hadn't lost to Great Britain since 1957. When I got to the tee I looked for my bag and Willie wasn't there.

The next thing I knew here comes a guy carrying my bag and I've never seen him before. 'Where's Willie?' I asked.

'He was talking to someone coming up the hill,' this stranger said, 'and he slipped down and broke his ankle.' Now that's got to be a first in the history of golf!

While I was still trying to figure that out, I missed an 8-foot putt to keep us from winning outright and that let Great Britain tie us, 16–16. Hell, the British should have given Willie a team blazer.

When I went to London to play in the Piccadilly World Match Play Invitation in 1968 I didn't know much about the tournament except that it was very exclusive. To play there you have to have won one of the four major titles in the past year, be top money-winner for the previous year or something like that.

Before I got there I played in the Alcan, and the Piccadilly publicity man looked me up. I was wearing slacks, cowboy boots, sports coat and sports shirt with no tie, which is what I liked to wear. He wrinkled his nose.

'My good man,' he said, 'you'll be staying at the Savoy Hotel during the Piccadilly and this is not proper attire.'

I asked him what he meant by that. 'You must wear a solid suit,' he said. I told him I didn't have a solid suit, didn't even have a tie. He gave me a fishy look and walked away.

Well, before I checked into the Savoy, I went to Moss Brothers in London and rented me white tie and tails, top hat, cape and cane – the whole bit. Then I made a big entrance at the hotel and got a whole lot of press.

The publicity man was kind of stunned, but he introduced me to his wife. She told me I must go sightseeing and kept telling me about the Teems. I didn't know what she was talking about.

She pointed out a window of the hotel and said, 'That's the Teems.'

I thought she was pointing at a building, but she told me she was talking about the river that goes through London. I told her, 'Lady, that's a little ol' creek in Texas.' She didn't even know what a creek was.

My British Open victory in 1971 really warmed up the fans, and I think I've had a lot to do with galleries' behavior since then. They've gotten louder, more sociable.

Oh, they were sociable before, but only at the right time and the right place. Galleries were completely different from those in America simply because they have been brought up to believe golf is a very quiet game. You don't talk while anybody is playing, and you sure don't laugh.

Families would come out to watch golf and they might not speak to each other for hours. At my first British Open I was struck immediately by the quietness of the galleries. They were huge, but silent. They were all bundled up in raincoats and boots and they all looked like brothers and sisters. There might be 30,000 people out there, but you never heard a word.

Through the years, because of my strong play in tournaments and the television exposure I've enjoyed with my own show on the BBC, I have gotten the galleries to enjoy themselves more. They have tremendous knowledge of the game. In Scotland once, I hit a beautiful low shot that carried about three or four feet above the ground, right at the flag 190 yards away. The ball hit in the front and just trickled over the green and stopped about four feet off the green but 20 feet from the hole. I got a standing ovation. The guy I was playing with hit a terrible-looking shot that hit the bank and kicked down about four feet from the hole. Nobody made a sound. They knew it wasn't a good shot.

In the United States you'll probably find only 30 percent of the galleries really care about the game. The other 70 percent are just where it's happening, man. It's like a flea market. Look at the Colonial tournament in Fort Worth. It's one of the best in our country, but half the people who go to it never see a golf ball hit. Especially those girls parading around in shorts and halter-tops. They don't give a damn about golf.

When British youngsters come to you for an autograph they never hand you a gum wrapper or a paper bag or a napkin. Every one of those kids has an autograph book. Some of those books go back a hundred years and have been handed down through the generations. I don't mind signing those. They make me a little piece of their family history.

And I've always been fascinated by how the British dress up for golf tournaments. Even the greenskeepers.

All the years I worked on a golf course I always wore the raggediest clothes I could find – old blue jeans, T-shirts, boots. But the guys mowing the fairways and greens there are wearing coats and ties. It's customary. That's why I go to Britain with a coat and tie on and I leave with a coat and tie on.

On a plane I never know if I'll sit next to some chairman of the board who may be looking for someone to endorse his company. If I'm dressed in blue jeans and a

T-shirt and he asks me what I do for a living, he'll look at me and forget it. I'm the last person he wants to endorse anything.

It's none of my business what other athletes wear, but I couldn't believe how John McEnroe was dressed when he flew back to New York from winning Wimbledon. He looked like he'd been working on his car.

Someday these guys are going to realize you don't make nearly as much money in the sport as you can make outside. That's why I carry a three-piece suit and three sports coats with matching ties. A lot of times I have to go to two or three functions in a week and I don't have to wear the same thing. My wardrobe has changed some since I went to that US Open in 1967 and could wash everything for a quarter.

Tradition never changes at the British Open, however. Those people have a tremendous respect for history, rank and honor.

When we played at St George's, I was walking toward the Tented Village, where equipment and clothing companies sell their products, to make an appearance at the John Letters exhibit when I saw an ancient little man totter by wearing a dark blue uniform. Hell, he had a big gold sword buckled around his waist and six or eight rows of huge, fancy medals on his chest.

I thought to myself, 'He better hope there's no lightning around here.'

But if lightning ever did get him, I guess he certainly would want to go in full dress uniform.

Everything is so old there. St Andrews, of course, is the birthplace of golf. It is home of the R&A – the Royal and Ancient Golf Club of St Andrews, which has held the Open since 1860. At Muirfield the Honourable Company of Edinburgh Golfers wrote the Thirteen Articles, the first rules of golf, about thirty years before some of our guys wrote the Declaration of Independence. And St George's, on the English Channel, is only a couple of tee shots from Pegwell Bay, where Julius Caesar first landed in England. There also are a couple of castles in the neighbourhood where Henry VIII hung out.

My locker in that old clubhouse was so small that all I kept in it was a pair of shoes, which I stood on end, and a bottle of whiskey for Seve Ballesteros' father.

'Man,' I told the attendant, 'I can't get my one-iron in this locker!'

But when it's time to play the Open, I don't want to be anywhere else.

The R&A still held the Open championship from Wednesday through Saturday in 1971 and my last day and night there were an unforgettable ending to a wonderful week.

Clyde and I stayed at the Prince of Wales Hotel in Southport that week. Just across the road was the Kingsway Casino, which was owned by George James, a man who treated us wonderfully. We went there every night to have dinner, see a show and then gamble until five in the morning. Then we went back to our room and slept until noon. I'd eat a light lunch and leave for the course around two. I teed off about three-thirty every day so everything worked out. I had some fun, I got some rest and I was always ready to play golf. Then, out of nowhere, Arnold Salinas appeared in the locker room at Birkdale just before I teed off in the second round.

Pete Dominguez, a good friend and a great guy who owns some Mexican restaurants in Dallas and Houston, had made so many bets on me with everyone at the Great Southwest Club that he sent Arnold over to coach me. He bought him a first-class airline ticket and said, 'Go keep Lee company.'

I don't know how Arnold talked his way into the clubhouse because security was extremely tight. But he can get in anywhere. All I know was I was sitting on a bench putting some cleats on my shoe when I heard a voice behind me ask, 'Hey, are there any Mexicans in this tournament?'

I turned around and there was Arnold. 'All right, son!' he said. 'Go get 'em!'

I shot 70 that day, same as Tony Jacklin, and we were tied at 139. I finished strong the next day and my 69 put me one shot up on my old friend from Formosa, Mr Lu, and Jacklin, who was wavering a little. Nicklaus was back some more with 71–71–72.

The weather was beautiful for the final round, just like it was all week. It must have been the best in British Open history: sixty-five or seventy degrees every day. I came out to the first tee in shirt sleeves and Mr Lu, who still had a crewcut, was wearing a straw hat.

We first met in 1959 when I was a Marine stationed on Okinawa and we played a match on Taiwan. Mr Lu beat me, 10 and 8. He was a fine golfer, a great up-and-down player, and a wonderful little man. Those British galleries loved him. He called me Bird, a name he gave me when I was in the Marines because my drives always flew past his.

We shook hands on the first tee and I told him, 'You don't need this trophy. You'd just fill it with flied lice.' He grinned. 'Birrrddd!' he said.

I shot 70 and beat Mr Lu by one shot with a total 278, but the final numbers were deceiving. I had a 5-shot lead with nine holes to play, but I was clowning so much I almost threw it away. It was just one of those times when everything was fun and I figured it was going to work out okay. And it did.

I was so hot on the front nine that I was hitting putts and walking away to the next tee without watching my ball drop in the cup. 'Hey, Bird,' Mr Lu said. 'You want to go through?' I laughed and hit him on the back of the head.

Just before we made the turn I knocked in a long putt and it snaked into the hole. I tossed my putter up, fell to my knees and then face down on the green. That's when the gallery loosened up. They loved it! No one had ever done that on one of their greens.

Well, it was so much fun by then that I almost forgot to finish the tournament. Clyde and Arnold walked along the fairway with me the last three rounds, thanks to the courtesy of an R&A official, so they were right there. On the back nine I would three-putt a hole and think, 'Hell, I've got enough to win.' Then on 17, I hit into a sand dune, knocked it across into the rough, had a hard time getting out of the heather, then stopped a 15-foot uphill putt short and wound up with a double-bogey 7. Suddenly, my lead was down to one!

The last hole at Birkdale is a par-5 of 500-plus yards but my chili was hot and I hit a drive that left me about 200 yards from the pin. Then I smoked a 6-iron to the back edge of the green. Meanwhile, Mr Lu got unlucky. His drive kicked left into a bunker, and when he tried to come out, he hit his ball with the heel of the club and it exploded into the gallery behind him, hitting a woman right between the eyes. She went down like she was shot, bleeding badly. He was sick about it, and I couldn't even bear to look at her. It turned out she was all right but it was terribly unnerving.

His ball bounced back in front of the green, however, and he hit a sensational shot that stopped about six feet from the hole. I had a 40-foot putt but I didn't fear a thing. I knocked it to two and a half feet and I still didn't have any doubts that after Mr Lu sank a birdie putt he forced me to make mine to win. I didn't wait. I just knocked it in and walked away. Clyde and Arnold ran up and hugged me.

'Hey, we did it!' I told Arnold.

'I know you did,' he said.

I won my first British Open championship with a game as good as Jack Nicklaus told me it could be. So in just twenty days I had beaten Jack in our US Open play-off, taken the Canadian Open title and then won in Britain, where Jack was defending champion.

'I wish,' he told a huge crowd at presentations, 'I had kept my damn mouth shut.'

We had a marvelous party at the Kingsway Casino that night. Someone had given us a two-gallon bottle of Bollinger's champagne at the course, so we drank that and then ordered some more. I had some special guests coming – two nuns from the local orphanage.

George James had told me, 'If you win this tournament and give five hundred pounds or fifteen hundred dollars to the orphanage you will really make a hit with them.' Well, my prize money was $13,000 and I told the nuns I would give them $5,000 of it on one condition: they had to come to the casino and drink a glass of champagne with me.

They had never been in a bar in their lives but they did it and had fun. Everybody was raising hell. Mr Lu was there and Jimmy Dean was singing to me. Later that night we raffled off my golf clubs for $1,500. I gave that to the orphanage, too. I wanted to share my joy.

Nicklaus tied for fifth at 283, but he was really fired up when we went to Muirfield for the 1972 British Open. I believe Jack felt if he ever was going to score a Grand Slam of the four major championships he would do it that year because he would play on his favorite courses – Augusta National, Pebble Beach, Muirfield and Oakland Hills, where the PGA was held later that summer.

I had given him a tough battle for the US Open title at Pebble Beach for three rounds but I weakened the last day, which wasn't surprising. I had spent four days in an El Paso hospital with pneumonia before the tournament and got out of bed just in time to fly to California and practise for nine holes. But in the month before I defended my British championship, I trained very hard. I took my family with me to Central Texas, rented a house and trained on Orville Moody's place in Killeeen. I was up at five every morning, running through the hills, and then I played golf. The greens superintendent had a twelve-year-old daughter, a mute who read lips, and she drove the cart with my bag on it. I didn't ride. I ran between shots and I played 36 holes a day. I was determined to be sharp for Muirfield.

Well, I won again at Muirfield with 278 and again I broke out of a 36-hole tie with Tony Jacklin after shooting 71–70. It turned around in the third round. Jacklin had a good edge on the front nine but I sank a 25-footer for a birdie on 14 and that touched me off. I birdied the last five holes and finished with 66 to lead Jacklin by one.

On 16 that day I gave a pretty good example of getting a lemon and making lemonade. I took a 6-iron and just as I got ready to hit my shot the grip unravelled at the bottom. Like a snake, it just tangled up around my hand. It was a funny sight and everyone laughed. I stopped, took a couple of minutes to rewrap it and got my muscles tensed up. When I swung that club it felt like a feather and I hit a bad shot into the bunker, on the back upslope. I had no shot from there so I went with my wedge, hoping to keep it on the green, maybe 30 feet from the flag, and 2-putt for a bogey. I hit the wedge and the ball came out entirely too fast but somehow it hit on the green, took one big hop and went into the cup on the fly. It went in so fast the BBC cameraman missed it.

Coming out of there with a birdie instead of a bogey meant two shots that changed the final outcome because the next day Jack rallied with a 66. But my 71 gave me the championship by one.

That ruined possibly the best shot at a Grand Slam in his career but Jack didn't take that loss as hard as he did losing by one to Tom Watson at Turnberry in 1977. I finished fourth that year, after sharing the 36-hole lead with them, but I was pleased with that because I was working myself back to top form after my back surgery. For me, that was a good tuneup for the Canadian Open, which I won. For Jack, it must have been very tough to play head-to-head with Watson the last 36 holes, shoot 65–66 and see Tom beat him with two 65s. What marvelous golf they played! The whole locker room was out there in the gallery watching them play.

That trip had its special value for me, just as every one to Britain does.

In 1981, for example, I tied for twelfth at St George's and won $10,000, which just about covered expenses for making the trip, but I made deals to play in other tournaments around the world paying a total of $150,000 appearance money.

And there's the pleasure of meeting nice strangers and making new friends I'll always remember.

My golf series on the BBC has gotten me into a lot of homes. I have old women and old men walk up to me on the course every day and say, 'I've never met you and I know nothing about golf but I love your television show. I had to come out and meet you.'

There's so much I like to remember from all those visits. When I played in the 1973 Open at Troon we stayed on a farm where they were harvesting hay. I had no place to practise, so I would go down in the fields and hit balls. The Scot who farmed the place had two sons, about fourteen and eight, and they wanted to play golf, so I got them some cut-down clubs.

The old man looked at them, puffed on his pipe a minute and said, 'I thank you, Mr Trevino, but I don't know when these lads will have a chance to use them. There's w-o-r-r-r-k to be done.'

Those kids worked, all right. The older boy drove the tractor and stored the hay in the barn. The little one fed the cattle and milked the cows. As soon as they got home from school they took off their uniforms, put on their coveralls and worked until dark. And they were up at five in the morning, picking strawberries.

They'll never be kids, just like me. Looking back on my early years, I believe that's why I have such a special relationship with kids and with other people. I'm forty-two years old and I still act like a kid, because I never was one.

There's a kid in me trying to get out. Maybe there always will be.

From *Super Mex – An Autobiography* by Lee Trevino
and Sam Blair (Stanley Paul, London, 1983).

I'm a serious contender this week. How can they beat me? I've been struck by lightning, had two back operations and been divorced twice.

Lee Trevino at Royal Birkdale, 1983.

Seve – the Car Park Champion

Peter Alliss

Seve Ballesteros first made his name in Britain at Royal Birkdale in 1976 when he was just nineteen years old, tying with Nicklaus for second place after Johnny Miller. He is – or was – the boldest, most spectacular player since Arnold Palmer with wildness off the tee accompanied by immense and powerful recovery shots – a technique never better displayed than in the 1979 Open at Royal Lytham St Anne's when he became the first player from the Continent to win in seventy-two years. He was also the youngest winner of the Open since Tom Morris in 1861, and he did it after that sensational visit to the car park. The Americans rather unkindly labelled him 'the car park champion', as if to suggest that he could never do much on a tighter golf course. But he proved them wrong in 1980 at the age of twenty-three when he became the youngest player ever to win the Masters. Here's how Peter Alliss described that remarkable Open win. Today, of course, Seve has a more re-strained game, but still knows more about getting down in par from unlikely places than anyone else. There's another major or two left in Seve.

I.W.

Before every Open Championship begins many words are expended by the nation's leading golf correspondents. There are columns to be filled for some four days leading up to the event while golf magazines seem to use well-nigh half an issue. One of the main themes, of course, is: Who is going to win?

For the first time in many, many years Jack Nicklaus was not the favourite in 1979. He had at last been displaced by Tom Watson in the betting. Watson had been again busying himself in America with four tournament victories by the end of May and had tied for the US Masters before Fuzzy Zoeller took the play-off from Watson and Ed Sneed. He was to raise the US Tour money-winning record by almost $100,000 with his eventual total of $462,636 and more, of course, won outside America.

In the betting, Severiano Ballesteros was also well favoured at 12–1, but the pundits, with almost one voice, felt he had little chance of winning. The Spaniard's fairly frequent wild drives were well known and it was thought that a claustrophobic course like Royal Lytham and St Annes would frustrate even his formidable skills in recovery play. Instead a far 'tidier' player, Hale Irwin, recent winner of the US Open, was thought particularly likely to win.

There was also the often expressed thought that no American had won at Royal Lytham. This was not true. A certain Robert Tyre Jones Junior's name can be seen on the trophy for the year of 1926 and he was, incidentally, followed past the post by

Al Watrous, George von Elm and Walter Hagen, all golfers of unimpeachable American nationality. That championship was the first held at Royal Lytham and St Anne's and no American professional has ever won there.

The news story of the first day was the play of Bill Longmuir who had his lowest-ever tournament round. The Open Championship was the right time to find the inspiration. He played the first nine in 29, only the fourth time this had been done for either first or second nines in a British Open. His total of 65 equalled the lowest score for an opening round, set by Neil Coles at St Andrews in 1970 (since beaten by Craig Stadler's 64 at Royal Birkdale in 1983). Longmuir had never made the top 60 on the European Tour but he had won a couple of tournaments overseas, the 1976 Nigerian Open and the Southland Classic in New Zealand the same year. He birdied five holes in a row from the 3rd to 7th, added another at the 9th and moved smoothly into the second nine with more birdies on the 10th and 12th. Thereafter, on the more difficult run-in, he dropped two strokes.

The round gave him a three-stroke lead on the first day over Hale Irwin, who was very keen to become one of those rare birds who have won the championships of both America and Britain in the same year. Rounds under 70 were rare throughout the championship. The only others on the first day came from Irwin and his fellow American Jerry Pate.

The second day largely belonged to Severiano Ballesteros, who notched up a 65 of his own. He reached the turn in 33 and this did not really foreshadow the score that was to come. At Royal Lytham a really good score has to be made on the first nine (three of the four 29s at that time in the Open had been recorded on this nine – by Peter Thomson, Tom Haliburton and, of course, Longmuir).

It was Ballesteros's brilliant finish that brought the 65. Because of the wind direction that day, it was reckoned that the true par for the lst five holes was 4, 5, 4, 5, 4. Ballesteros finished 3, 3, 4, 3, 3 and had 32 for the inward nine.

He had played with Lee Trevino, which may well have helped his cause because the Mexican American, besides speaking his own brand of Spanish, is also a great admirer of Ballesteros's play. If Lee Trevino is not going to win himself, he likes to see Severiano take first place.

After his first-round 73, Ballesteros was now right up near the top:

> 136 Irwin;   138 Ballesteros;   139 Longmuir;   140 Watson;
> 142 Nicklaus;   144 Crenshaw;   145 Aoki.

Ballesteros was later to claim that his attitude to Lytham was very different from that of so much expert opinion. The many bunkers he felt were no real problem because 'I am the best bunker player.' Probably true and even more likely to be true if the player believes it. He did not consider the rough particularly severe and later claimed that he had deliberately driven into it on his practice rounds both to test it out and to see if wide positions to right or left of some of the fairways gave better lines into the green.

Another Spanish speaker had a great influence on Ballesteros. Roberto de Vicenzo had been one of the first to recognize that Ballesteros was a major talent and did indeed recommend him to Ed Barner, the American agent/entrepreneur, who was to manage him until Ballesteros turned to a Spanish friend and former airline-executive, Jorge Ceballos, several years later. De Vicenzo has often been seen with Ballesteros on practice days and an old master–young pupil relationship grew up between them.

De Vicenzo advised him to attack the course, pointing out that Jack Nicklaus's caution may well have cost him several British Opens. Though he felt Nicklaus was the man to beat, de Vicenzo had noticed that his strategy had been cautious on the practice rounds: taking the safest line from the tee rather than the one more likely to set up a birdie chance. He also felt that, with most severe trouble – particularly out of bounds – on the right, Ballesteros should work on the practice ground to shape his shots from right to left. Not much of a problem, as the Spaniard can fade and draw at will, right-handed or left-handed, on one leg or two or, for a lark, on his knees as well. I am sure it was this ability to manoeuvre a ball that so captured Roberto's imagination, for he had so much of the same ability – but not the putting and chipping finesse to anything like the same degree. How many times I have seen Roberto stroll the length of a par-5 bouncing a golf ball on the face of a 9-iron while discussing the merits of the scenery, the standard of food in the locality and the charms of his breakfast waitress. Try it yourself one day. Just hitting a golf ball well is difficult – but that!

Roberto gave Ballesteros one piece of general advice that I find particularly inspirational: '*Tienes las manos. Ahora juega con tu corazon.*' (You have the hands. Now play with your heart.) How about that for a great line? I think most of us would agree that Ballesteros did just that in the 1979 championship.

For the third round, Ballesteros and Hale Irwin were paired, and I dare say it was an experience that was wearing on the American's nerves. Irwin is an exemplary player, one of my favourites to watch, and in the Peter Thomson mould: hit it onto the fairway, then onto the green and don't three-putt. Here he was confronted by a man whose philosophy that year could be summed up as: 'Hit it as far as you can, find it, get it on the green and then try to one-putt. Never mind the bunkers and the rough. You're used to them.'

Both were round in 75 on a blustery day; both still led the field:

> 211 Irwin;   213 Ballesteros;   214 Nicklaus, James (with his second 69);
> 215 Crenshaw, Byman, Davis;   216 Aoki, Norman, Longmuir,
> Watson;   217 McEvoy, Marsh, D. J. Clark.

With the gap between them only a couple of strokes, Ballesteros struck early, holing a fine putt for a 2 on the 1st to Irwin's par 3. On the 2nd, Ballesteros took the championship lead, parring the hole with a 4 while Irwin took 6 after half-hitting his tee-shot.

The Ballesteros immortalized in this championship was at his most characteristic on the 486-yard 6th hole. With a drawn tee-shot needed to this right-to-left dogleg, he hooked wildly across the 14th fairway. He reckoned he was some 90 yards off-line. From this unaccustomed position, it was no surprise that neither he nor his caddie had much idea which club to use for the second shot. Ballesteros hit about 50 yards through the green. He still got his par and reached the turn in 34.

The 10th, a relatively short par-4, had given Ballesteros trouble in each round. This time he was in rough short of the green in two. He played a weak third and was still not on the green. Rather uncharacteristically he chose to putt and ran it some 3 yards past the hole. A double-bogey threatened, but Seve holed the crucial putt that could have cost him the championship.

The 13th is another short 4 of 339 yards. De Vicenzo advised boldness as the right tactic here. Ballesteros should use his driver and attempt to carry to the green. In the first three rounds, however, he had taken an iron from the tee. On the final day he gave it every ounce. The result can be seen in a well-known photograph by Bert Neale: the momentum of the club was so extreme that there is a kind of recoil from the finish of the follow-through. But what happened to the ball? It hit a mound to the right of the green and ran into a bunker. The carry was a yard or so under 300 yards. From there, the Spaniard's bunker shot was on the fringe, perhaps a dozen yards from the hole. On and on the putt went as he pointed his club, matador-like, at the hole. It dived in; a decisive moment indeed.

There remained the celebrated tee-shot to the 353-yard 16th. Conventionally, the drive should be down the left of the fairway but, because of the flag position well to the left that day, Ballesteros claims he decided to play to the right – and finished in what has often been described as a car park. This gives the impression that Ballesteros must have been about as far off-line as he had been at the 6th, or had carried the clubhouse at the 1st and put it in the road. Yet it was hardly a car park at all, just a reserved area for our BBC vehicles, little more than 30 yards from the edge of the fairway. Nevertheless, it gave certain partisan Americans the opportunity to refer to him as 'the car park champion'. From there, Ballesteros hit a sand wedge 6 or 7 yards from the hole and got the putt. He was poised for almost certain victory.

But what had been happening to the other contenders? Hale Irwin, after his poor start, seemed to lose heart and became almost invisible in contrast to the panache of the Spaniard's play. In the end he staggered in with a 78, not after all to be one of the select band who have won both American and British championships in the same year. His card showed six 5s and two 6s. Seldom can two more contrasting styles have been paired at an Open climax. The Australian Rodger Davis, playing in elegant socks displaying his name in diamonds, was at one time championship leader, having reached the turn in 32. He went in a spell of 6, 5, 6 on the 14th to 16th holes. Crenshaw also played well that last day. When he stood on the 17th tee he was level with Ballesteros, who at that time had five holes to go. But Ben Crenshaw took a 6 – and that was that. Yet another major championship had slipped from his grasp.

Ballesteros's progress was now triumphal, for here was one of the most popular winners of modern times. The British public, of course, want a British winner but Seve was easily the next best thing. He was young, handsome, smiling, a cavalier, with an almost amateurish air about him. On the 17th he was in his last bunker and once again was down in two strokes to save his par. In the championship as a whole, he reckons he was fifteen times in greenside bunkers and just once failed to be down in two, possibly a record.

The diagonal line of bunkers on the 18th fairway has dashed the hopes of many players over the years. Ballesteros, however, was rather more worried by the gorse on the right. Naturally, then, he aimed for the left rough, to avoid both hazards, played a 5-iron to the front of the green and was down in two putts to be champion by a comfortable three-stroke margin.

Said Hale Irwin, shaking his head in disbelief, 'I cannot understand how anyone can drive as badly as that and still win an Open Championship.' There was, indeed, justice in the American's criticism. In his final round, Ballesteros had found the fairway only once with his driver and only eight times in previous rounds. Yet his power and touch from the rough had proved wrong all the pundits who had thought that Lytham would yield only to the man who could keep the ball on the fairway.

Ballesteros had come a long way from his first championship appearance at Carnoustie in 1975. Then he had rounds of 79 and 80, probably confirming his dislike of links courses for, a little earlier, he had scored even higher at Royal St George's in the PGA Championship. Even now that course is no favourite of his, even after winning the 1983 PGA Championship there.

The 1976 Open, however, had brought him to the fore and his Lytham triumph was his 17th in world golf. The Americans who labelled him 'the car park champion' had the smiles taken from their faces by Ballesteros's dominance in the 1980 Masters. His 1983 Masters victory and fine play in the US Open that year were needed before all were prepared to concede that here was a great player.

From *The Open* by Peter Alliss (Collins, London, 1984).

Steady as She Goes – the Way to Win the Open

Nick Faldo

Some major championships have been won by sheer exuberant aggression – like Balles-teros's victory in the 1979 Open at Birkdale where he even played a shot out of the car park. But just one shot that's too aggressive can always lose a championship: just ask Arnie Palmer. The Nicklaus approach has always been one of steadiness and patience, waiting for the right opening to notch a birdie or even an eagle and trying never to drop more than one shot to par at any hole. That was the method that Nick Faldo committed himself to at Muirfield in 1987 and here he explains how it won him a dramatic British victory and his first major championship. His thorough approach and dedication, including the remodelling of his swing to become slightly flatter and more reliable, had finally paid off.

I.W.

The trick with Muirfield is to adhere to a chosen game plan. The premium is placed on driving the ball into the correct position, as the fairways are ingeniously bunkered, and the choice of club – driver, three wood or one iron – is critical off the tee.

It is, of course, easier said than done. Yet I felt that over the first two days of the 116th Open Championship I came as close as one could hope to carrying out my own preconceived plans. My opening 68 provided a sound foundation on which to build, though the Australian Rodger Davis moved smartly into the lead with his 64, but I had more regard for my second round of 69. I was out early in the day and the persistent rain meant that it was all the more important to concentrate on steering a safe passage around the 6,963 yards which make up Muirfield's par-71 Championship examination.

The plan, quite simply, was not to take any gambles. One wayward shot on a course such as Muirfield can, if you are unfortunate, lead to a penalty which is too severe for the 'crime' committed. Coincidentally Arnold Palmer admitted on the Friday at Muirfield to 'taking a gamble and paying for it'. He tried to force something out of the 14th hole after driving into a bunker, and he eventually walked off the green with a *ten* on his card. It had taken him five shots to escape from a greenside bunker. He had, at the age of fifty-seven, turned back the years to be in contention and then, after that 14th hole, he was out of the Championship.

I made mistakes at the 14th and 15th holes in the second round, but on each occasion it cost me only the one shot. Mostly I was happy with the way I swung my way around Muirfield's two splendid loops of nine holes. I hit a seven iron to four feet for a two at the 180 yards-4th. My five iron to three feet for another birdie at the 8th filled me with confidence.

I had brought over David Leadbetter from Florida the previous week in order to fine-tune my swing during the Bell's Scottish Open at Gleneagles. We took a video of the swing and I kept that to turn to for confirmation after David had sorted out a couple of things for me.

Then a 69, for a halfway aggregate of 137, was sufficient at the end of the day to earn me a share of second place alongside the American Payne Stewart, who had an equal best-of-the-day 66, Australia's Gerry Taylor (68) and Davis, who faltered with a 73. The leader now was Paul Azinger, who was seeking to emulate his American compatriots Ben Hogan (1953) and Tony Lema (1964) by winning the Open at the first attempt.

I was to partner Azinger on the third day, when we both scored 71s despite being buffeted by 25-mph gusts. It was a difficult day and Paul continued to defy logic, for he had never seen a links course before setting foot that week on the first tee at Muirfield. It must have seemed so incredibly foreign to him, and yet he played the kind of commonsense golf that suggested he might have been reared on the east coast of Scotland.

So as the final day dawned Azinger was still one shot ahead of David Frost of South Africa and myself. One stroke further adrift was the American trio of Craig Stadler, with whom I was paired, Payne Steward and Tom Watson. All three appeared to me to be threats, but it was Azinger who continued to bowl along in front.

He began the fourth and final round as if it were just a walk in the park. He holed a putt of fully 25 feet for a birdie at the 4th and another of ten feet at the 5th. He was out in 34. I could do nothing but make pars, although I was within inches of birdies at each of the first five holes, but I feel that it was the kind of round, looking back, of which Jack Nicklaus would have been proud. I recall Tom Watson once explaining how early in his career he had partnered Nicklaus in a US Tour event. Nicklaus did nothing spectacular. He simply played conservatively, because he felt that was the order of the day, and when he finished he had won the tournament.

I was pleased at the way I remained composed. On three occasions, in four holes from the 7th, I kept my score intact by getting up and down from bunkers. Andy Prodger, my caddie, thought that the one at the 8th won me the Championship: I exploded out of the sand from 30 yards to three feet. The four-foot putt which I holed at the 11th, after playing an adroit chip round a hillock, was also an important recovery. Azinger had wriggled three shots clear of me but now he dropped a shot at the 10th by being bunkered and another at the next which he three-putted.

I knew now, as the mist began to clear and as I edged closer towards the clubhouse of the Honourable Company of Edinburgh Golfers, that I was within sight of the most elusive prize in the game. I stuck to my game plan when it mattered most, so that without taking a gamble I limited the risk of one destructive shot ruining what could be the most important day in my career. I parred my way through to the end and a 71 gave me a five under par aggregate of 279. It was enough to put Azinger, playing behind me, under pressure.

We have all been in that position before. It can be so important to have your score on the board. Paul Azinger will have his day, of that I am sure, but on this occasion he was to meet his nemesis.

I had been nervous, of course, over the closing holes. I knew that during my last hour on the Muirfield course one mistake could ruin everything. Yet my lasting memory is of my five iron to the last green. I knew as I stood over that shot that it could make all the difference. I didn't want to sit back at the end of my career and accept that I had come close without actually winning the Open Championship. I knew that when that five iron shot – one which I had rehearsed on many occasions – deposited the ball on the green, I had done everything humanly possible to engrave my name alongside the greats of the game on the silver claret jug that is the Open Championship trophy.

> From *On Course for the Open* by Nick Faldo with
> Mitchell Platts (Stanley Paul, London, 1987).

Tony Jacklin looks worried. Is it going to trickle into the rough? (*Peter Dazeley*)

After the agony, the ecstasy. The putt which recorded Tony's last major golfing prize – the 1982 PGA Championship (*Peter Dazeley*)

Greg Norman – at last a Major. Greg celebrates his 1986 Open victory with his wife Laura. (*Peter Dazeley*)

Rivals since schoolboy days in Shropshire. Ian wins a close game against Sandy Lyle in the World Match Play Championship. (*Peter Dazeley*)

Lyle wins the Masters. Oh, the joy and relief after the tension and anxiety of the last few holes when the shots began to dribble away. Then came that brilliant 7 iron bunker shot at the 18th to within 10ft of the hole and a majestic birdie putt to become the first Briton to win the US Masters. (*Associated Press*)

Peter Alliss. If you can't beat the Yips, at least let's have a laugh about them. And come to think of it, Peter hasn't done too badly out of the game, has he? (*Peter Dazeley*)

Ballesteros in killer mood, as he wins the 1984 Open at St Andrews (*Peter Dazeley*)

Nick Faldo . . . steady as she goes. Faldo on the way to winning the 1987 Open with a patient, consistent performance over four rounds. (*Peter Dazeley*)

Gene Sarazen . . . the old maestro makes one of his last tournament appearances at the Masters. (*Peter Dazeley*)

11

HEROES WITH PROBLEMS

The Yips – and How to Beat Them

George Plimpton

The yips are a terrible thing – that awful nervous affliction on the short putts which results in a convulsive jab and a missed putt. The yips have afflicted the greatest in the game, including Vardon, Snead and Hogan, and some of the greatest strikers of the ball like Peter Alliss. He, poor chap, had a total disaster on his first visit to Augusta in 1966. 'I played one round with Gene Littler and took five putts from 6 feet at the 11th hole,' he recalls. 'Shattering!' It really finished him for the big game. The yips caused Henry Longhurst to throw his clubs into the loft – forever and with no regrets, as he describes in the second piece in this chapter. George Plimpton, the long-handicapper who wrote so amusingly in *The Bogey Man* about 'the world of big-time golf experienced by and reported by the 18-handicap author', investigated the downside of the problem thoroughly.

However, I still insist that where there's the will there's a way, as Bernhard Langer found. From being the worst putter in big-time golf, by sheer dedication – and the reverse grip – he's made himself into one of the best, if not *the* best. He found himself so at home on the super-fast greens at Augusta with their tricky borrows, where four- or five-putting is always possible, that in 1985 when the greens were never faster, and when Watson three-putted four times in one round, Bernhard three-putted just once in four rounds. Not surprisingly, he became the triumphant winner of his first major. He's now so good he's even written a whole book, *Langer on Putting*, from which I take the third and final of these extracts on the yips.

I.W.

One evening in San Francisco I heard for the first time about the 'yips' – a phenomenon talked about rather uneasily by the pros, and with wary respect, as one might talk about a communicable disease ravaging the neighboring township. The yips (a name invented by Tommy Armour, who had them) was the term given the occupational malaise of golf – a nervous affliction that settled in the wrist and hands, finally, after the years of pressure and the money bets and the strain. It was what ultimately drove the pros out of the game to the teaching jobs at the country clubs, setting the balls on the tees for the girls in the Pucci pants who came down for their two free gift lessons of the summer.

The legs don't give out, as in so many other sports, or the wind, or the sense of timing, or the power, but the *nerves*, so that one could see the hands of great golfers beset by the yips tremble visibly on the putting greens, the greatest names in golf completely at the mercy of short putts of 4, 5, 6 feet.

I said I had never heard of such a thing.

Dave Marr told me that he had seen Byron Nelson stand over a 4-foot putt at Florida's Seminole golf course, and, finally, after swaying back and forth several times, he had stabbed at the ball desperately and sent it *40 feet* past the hole.

At that same club, Seminole, Craig Wood had them so badly during an exhibition match, which should have relaxed the pressure, that he hit the first nine greens right on target in regulation strokes, but then putted so badly that his first-9 total was *44*. His dismay was such that he refused to putt out at all during the second nine; when he reached the greens he stooped and picked up the ball and stuffed it in his pocket and walked on to the next tee. The rest of his foursome, sympathetic, allowed him double gimmes, the regulation two putting strokes, and marked him down as such.

There was someone, a curious youngster, unaware of the ravages that the yips are capable of committing, who had gone up to the golfer and had the temerity to ask: 'Why aren't you putting out like the others, Mister Wood? I mean, I don't understand . . .' and then he had stopped in mid-sentence because Wood had such a murderous look on his face.

It seemed to get them all. Leo Diegel had an awful time with nerves. He fussed around with a pendulum stroke with his putter but most people thought he was afflicted with a spastic tic. A great golfer, he never had the right mental equipment and he knew it: 'They keep trying to give the championship to me,' he once said, 'but I won't take it.' In the British Open in 1933 at St Andrews he faced an incredibly short putt, just a foot or so, and he wandered up to it shaking like a leaf and stubbed it past the hole to lose the championship. Vardon, at the end of his career, in 1920, when he was in his fifties, got the yips. They were blamed on two attacks of tuberculosis. He called them the 'jumps' and recommended putting in the dark as effective treatment. Apparently it didn't work. Gene Sarazen (he eventually got them, too) recalls Vardon as the most atrocious putter he had ever seen. 'He didn't 3-putt, he 4-putted.'

Rod Funseth . . . said that one of the saddest examples of the yips he had seen were those infesting the person of Jon Gustin, who was known for owning one of the prettiest swings on the tour. Funseth went on about him at some length. Apparently, he was a great dresser – he had been a former flag-bearer in the Honor Guards in Washington. Very snappy. 'So you had,' Funseth said, 'the fine combination of a great swing, smooth and pretty as Snead's, and a guy who *looked* great as a golfer, like he stepped out of the advertising pages of *Esquire*, and yet what would happen, because of those yips, was that he would stand over the ball to swing – his irons, drives, putts, any shot – and his hands would come back, but the *club head wouldn't*. It would stick there right behind the ball like it was cemented to the ground.'

'Lord Almighty,' I said.

'He had to give up the tour.'

'Worst case I ever saw.'

'No cure, I don't suppose, for the yips.'

'Golfers who have the yips *try* to cure them, God knows,' Funseth said. 'Gene Sarazen found one – at least one that worked for him. Watch him in the Senior tournaments. He steps up to the ball and hits it all in one motion – almost like he's hitting a shot off a polo pony. He doesn't dare stand over the ball, because he knows he'll freeze. Snead had the idea you could drift into a sort of "pleasant daydream" to get back to the fundamentals of the practice swing. And then I recall that Bobby Locke had an idea that the yips could be cured by holding the club very loosely. If the yips had him bad, why you wouldn't be surprised to see his club just slip out and fall on the grass. Really no thing to have,' Funseth said. 'There's no sure cure. The yips can get so bad that you hate the idea of being in the lead in a tournament – where the pressure can bring on an attack. You begin to crave for a fair round, even a mediocre one, where the pressure isn't so stiff.'

The great distinction to make was that there was no similarity between the yips and 'choking' – though every once in a while the younger pros, who looked on the yips as something that couldn't possibly happen to them, would say that yips was just a fancy word that the older pros thought up to hide the fact that pressure got to them too.

'Who told you that?'

'Oh, one of the younger professionals.'

'That figures. If you want to see choking on a vast scale – I mean, what the caddies call the Apple Orchard for the big lumps that turn up in the throat – and if you want to see the eye-staring and those clammy foreheads, then you got to take in the qualifying tournaments that the rabbits play in. Ludicrous. Or you'll see one of those kids play in the high 60s for a round or so in the Open, and then what happens to him? The pressure gets to him. He skies to an 80. He chokes. He's so scared he damn near closes his eyes when he swings.'

Someone said: 'Pee Wee Reese, the shortstop, used to have a good phrase for the choke. He'd say, "I know I'm choking when I'm chewing and can't work up a spit".'

'Sometimes a particular hole will cause a choke – a choke hole,' said Marr. 'Like the 18th at Cypress. It's like walking into a certain room in a big dark house when you were a kid – you get this fear that hits you.'

Johnny Pott said: 'That's why we spend so much time on the practice tee. You're down there trying to groove the shot, to tone up the muscle memory, so that when you get out on the golf course and the pressure's really on – the choke at hand, and you can sense your eyes popping, and the jaw shaking – the muscles can still perform in their usual groove and you can get your shot off. You practise to get the muscles moving almost automatically.'

'Doesn't that work for putting as well?'

'No, because muscle memory doesn't have anything to do with putting. Take Sam Snead. He's got the most famous swing in golf – you wouldn't find a differential of a millimeter in the circle of his swing if you took a thousand stop-action films of the guy. Perfectly grooved. Great on long putts, where the demands on muscle and swing are slightly more. But short putts! Give me someone out of kindergarten! His hands come back fine, but then the blade seems to go out of control just at the stroke. Sometimes he hits the top of the ball so that if it drops, it bounces every which way to get in there. Snead has had the yips for years. That's why he took that pro's job at Greenbrier way back in 1937. He thought he was going to have to quit the tour because he had the yips so bad. Or take Hogan, the most tragic case. Best tee-to-green player there ever was. Ever. I mean he put the balls *there* off the tee, then *there*, just where he wants, then *there*, right on the green. You might as well *give* him those shots. But once on the green his troubles begin. He had those two holes to go at Oak Hill – just par-par, that's all he had to do to tie for the 1956 Open, but the yips got him. You know the guy got ten thousand letters from people trying to help him.'

'Ten thousand!' I said.

'That's right.'

I once asked Claude Harmon about those ten thousand letters, and whether he thought I would get an answer if I wrote Ben Hogan and asked him what the most ridiculous of the suggestions received had been – I thought that might be interesting.

'You wouldn't get an answer,' Harmon said, looking at me sharply. 'Because I'll tell you one thing. Hogan would have *tried* every damn one of them – I don't care how "ridiculous" – to rid himself of those things.' He repeated what I had heard so many people say: 'If only Hogan could have putted – Jesus, he'd've made every record in the book look silly.'

Hogan's miseries with the yips reached a climax in the 1954 Masters when, leading the field, he went to pieces on the final holes of the tournament. He 3-putted the 13th, missed a 4-foot putt on the 15th, 3-putted the 17th, and then came to the 18th needing a 6-foot putt to win the tournament. Claude Harmon said that Hogan went off to the side of the green and he made about one hundred practice strokes with his putter, all markedly different – changing his grip, the position of his hands on the club, the stroke itself. Whe Harmon asked him about it later, Hogan said that he had been trying to find a stroke, any stroke at all, in which he felt comfortable – a last-minute desperate search – and after the experimenting at the edge of the big crowd around the green, he had taken one of the styles back out on the putting surface and, perched over the ball, he used it, and not unsurprisingly he missed the putt.

Claude Harmon had an interesting notion that a golfer's control over those shots, putts especially, which were conducive to the yips, was at best fragmentary since the ball traveled over the *ground*, and was at the mercy of irregularities and worm casts and the rubs of the green and beetles sticking up their heads to look round and minuscule pebbles and so forth.

'Even a machine will miss half the time from six feet. It's been tried,' Harmon said. 'Golf is really two games. One is the game in the air. The golfer can lick that part of the game. It sounds like quite a feat – I mean, you've got to get all those parts of your body moving absolutely correctly to send that ball off the tee at over 200 miles an hour. But once the ball is up in the air, there's not much that can happen to it. The air is a medium a golfer can control, as easy as fish in water: he can move the ball in it just where he wants to – fade it, or hook it to his liking, if he's good enough – and he's never going to be surprised unless he makes a mistake himself. Or unless he hits a bird. But the other part of the game is across the ground. It sounds easy. You hardly move a muscle to hit a putt. A child can do it easier than nothing. But the medium controls the ball, that's the difference; the golfer can get the ball moving, that's all. After that, the ball moves and turns and dies by reason of the ground surface. What you can't control gets the best of you after a while – death and taxes, the old song – and that's what the yips are.'

Harmon's story reminded me of Bernard Darwin's anecdote about the famous billiard professional who saw his first game of golf and remarked on it as interesting enough, but wondered why (as he said) 'do golfers on the green first knock the ball up to the hole, and *then* put it in.'

Some golfers felt that any prolonged absence from the game resulted in such a loss of confidence that an infestation of the yips would result. Bobby Cruickshank remembered that when his great rival Bobby Jones returned to competition in 1934 after a four-year layoff, his putting had deteriorated to such an extent that he wandered around the Masters that year asking his fellow golfers if they could spot what was wrong. 'It looked the same,' Cruickshank said. 'I mean you'd see him address the ball, then set the putter in front of the ball, and then at the back of the ball again, and then the stroke – that was the famous procedure he went through. But you could see he had no confidence.'

Claude Harmon told me of a more recent example of the damage a layoff could do – the decision of Mike Souchak to take his family for a month's vacation on the beach after he had a remarkable succession of wins and near-wins on the tour. 'I told him he was crazy. You got to keep at it. When he came back it was gone – it had floated away on him, and what he had was like the yips.'

Occasionally, though, one heard of cures. Roberto de Vicenzo, at one time afflicted with the yips so badly that he had the reputation of handling the spookiest putter on the tour, had been able to do something about it. It had not been easy. In the throes of the disease he had changed putters every week, picking out a new putter every time he went into a pro shop. He looked in a closet at home in Argentina not long ago and found fifty putters standing there, a total not counting many he had given away. No one of the putters seemed better than another. Each seemed utterly unreliable. In 1967 in Australia he blew an eleven-shot lead in the last fourteen holes because of his putting and lost to Alan Murray in a play-off. He talked about an occasion in England when his putters had let him down – his accent heavy, his big hands moving artfully in the air to describe his meaning, his chair squeaking under him, his face expressive under the white baseball-style golf hat he wears to cover his thinning hair.

'In the British Open, in 1965, I think, we are playing the final day, which is thirty-six holes, and in the morning I am leading. I have had one bad green, number 9, which I three-putt in the morning, but I still in very good position. So we come to number nine in the afternoon and I say to myself, "Roberto, you no three-putt this green this afternoon, do you?" I didn't. I make *four* putts. I was so mad I wanted to break all my clubs and quit the game and never play again. I had no confidence. I look at the cup and she look like a little spike mark. I tell myself, "Roberto, you no can put the ball in there." So I lose my confidence and I lose the tournament right there.'

Vicenzo's cure turned out to be a matter of self-application – finding the right type of putter, the correct style of hitting a ball with it, the regaining of confidence, and practice, endless practice. Many golfers go through an equivalent regimen of experiment and practice without finding the answer: Snead had tried a number of putters and such grotesque putting styles – the 'sidewinder' in particular, in which he faces the hole and strokes the ball just off the outer edge of his golf shoe – that only his great grace as an athlete keeps him from looking ludicrous. Vicenzo was lucky. He found his putter two years ago. A mallet putter that he says is appropriate for his big hands. He watched other golfers' putting styles and decided that all the good putters (with the exception of Billy Casper and Doug Ford) use their *arms* primarily in the putting strokes, not the wrists, which had been his style. So he changed his style and found his sense of 'feel' increased immeasurably. His confidence began to return. He practised endlessly – especially to get what he refers to as the 'head in rhythm . . . to work the head and the hands at the same time.' He began to collect some tournament wins – notably the British Open, and then a close run at the Masters which he would have taken to a play-off had he not handed in a mistotaled score card. But he was phlegmatic himself about the future. 'The putt is a funny game. You can't think you got it for always. You can lose it tomorrow. But for the moment,' he said, 'I feel better when I step onto the golf course. I no feel scared to step onto the green. Not any more. Or maybe for the time being, eh?'

Another older player I talked to about the yips was John Farrell, once the great rival of Bobby Jones and now a teaching professional in Florida. He said that if you play in competition long enough you're sure to get the yips. 'Walter Hagen,' he said. 'If you had to vote for the player with the best temperament, well you'd *have* to vote for him. Hell, he had such confidence that there wasn't a shot that held any terror for him: they used to say that when he had a particularly tough shot to make, and he'd stepped up and made a great one of it, why then he'd whisper at his caddy, "Did I make it look hard enough?" and give him a wink, y'see. Well *he* got them. The yips. He got them so bad that he tried strokes and grip styles you could scarcely *believe*: cross-handed putting; or sticking the elbows way out so that the wrist action was throttled down and his whole body moved as stiff as a derrick. He even tried putting in the dark – thought that might cure him. Nothing did. . . .'

I asked the question I had put to the others – if there was any connection between the yips and losing one's nerve.

'It's that you lose *nerves*, not nerve,' Farrell said. 'You can shoot lions in the dark and yet you can quiver like a leaf and fall flat over a two-foot putt.'

'I would think,' I said, 'that years of experience standing over two-foot putts, and gaining all the know-how of reading greens and distance, and the competition – that all of that would be to a golfer's advantage . . . confidence.'

'Oh, I wouldn't want to be so sure as that,' Farrell said. 'I always remember Waite Hoyte, who pitched for the Yankees, you'll recall, and what he used to say about "experience". He said experience *punishes* you. A veteran player *knows* what can happen to him: he comes onto a pitcher's mound and he knows the batter waiting for him can pop the ball right back to the bullpen where he's just come from for a home run. He's gone through it before. So he's something of a fatalist. It's the same in golf. "Experience" punishes you as you continue with the game. That's why in golf we speak of someone being "competitively young" or "competitively old". Craig Wood, you see, he was "competitively young" at forty-three because he started playing serious golf when he was well into his thirties. Then on the other hand Bobby Jones was "competitively old" at twenty-three – he had started at fifteen, you see, which gave him early "experience" but it aged him good and quick as a golfer.

'Experience,' Farrell went on ruefully. 'I won the Open in 1928 at Olympia Fields, and then in 1929 I missed the cut at the Open at Winged Foot. Dropped from the tournament I had *won* the year before! D'you think *that* experience did me any good! Well, I'll tell you. The next year at Interlachen, Minneapolis – in the 1930 Open which Bobby Jones won to fetch himself the Grand Slam – I stepped up on the first tee with the "experience" gained from those bad rounds the year before, and what did I do but get myself an 8 on that first hole. I managed to pull myself together after that and I finished eighth behind Jones, but don't talk to me about *experience*. Snead can't win the Open because of his memories – missing that two-footer in the 1947 Open. Palmer won't win the PGA. He has that block. No; it's the kids, the strong young golfers who have it all. They make great big errors – I mean, a kid like Marty Fleckman coming up with an 80 after leading the Open into the last day in 1967 – but he's at the age when mistakes are easily forgotten; those kids' imaginations aren't jumpy with crucial flubs – y'know, disaster, that's what they don't know about. Not yet. It'll come. They'll get there. Experience will come. Oh yes.'

From *The Bogey Man* by George Plimpton
(André Deutsch, London, 1970).

Pressure is something every golfer feels at one time or another. . . . Sometimes when I putted I looked like a monkey trying to wrestle a football.

Sam Snead, 1970.

How to Give up Golf Without Really Trying

Henry Longhurst

As my travels, writings and broadcasting increased, to say nothing of my age, my golf fell away and it became less and less fun to do progressively more badly something that one had once done reasonably well. I had had every reason to believe that I should turn out in middle age, and even later, to be an accurate and crafty player, always liable to beat an undergraduate, but it was not to be. My swing disintegrated and I became quite pathetically bad. I kept meaning to take myself in hand and go in for a fortnight's serious practice, which I knew was all that was needed, but somehow, with all the travelling about, I never got down to it. If I played on Sunday mornings, I did not enjoy it, and, if I didn't, I had it on my conscience that somehow I ought to be. What settled the problem for me was what we call the twitch and the Americans the 'yips'. This is so ridiculous a disease that non-sufferers can scarcely credit it. It attacks the victim almost always on short putts, though one great professional who might otherwise have beaten the world had it on short pitches. It does not come on all short putts, but you always know in advance when it is coming. You then become totally incapable of moving a piece of ironmongery to and fro without giving at the critical moment a convulsive twitch. Some people simply stab the ground and move the ball a few inches. Others catch it on the twitch and send it shooting past the hole. Bobby Jones has recounted how he was playing with an American professional called Wild Bill Melhorn, who suffered from it, and on one green Melhorn, trying to hole a yard putt, actually putted it off the green and into a bunker. I was reminded only the other day of an occasion I had forgotten when a caddie had said to me, 'I think it would be better if you stroked the ball a bit more, sir,' and I had replied, 'Dammit, you don't think I *mean* to do it like that, do you?' I am, however, in good company. Jones himself got it – he described the sensation as of the ball 'apparently vanishing from sight just as the club was about to strike it'. The great Harry Vardon got it. Sam Snead, still at fifty-seven one of the finest swingers in the game, actually had to take to putting croquet-fashion between the legs. Ben Hogan, the most determined golfer of all time, not excluding Palmer, wanted two par fours for a record fifth US Open and not only missed a yard putt on the 17th but 'yipped' it. 'Once you've had 'em, you've got 'em,' they say, and he was never the same again. The Americans tend rather unkindly to call the affliction 'whiskey fingers', and so it may be with some, but Snead is a lifelong teetotaller and Vardon was a most abstemious man – though I particularly like his reply to the lady who asked him to sign the pledge: 'Moderation is essential in all things, madam, but never in my life have I been beaten by a teetotaller.'

I am afraid that by constantly writing about it I may have served to spread the disease, in which context I am reminded of my friend and neighbour Tubby Ionides, who incidentally won the Grand National Irish Sweep on Sundew. Some people have only to read about that other ridiculous golf shot, the socket, in which the ball shoots off, knee high, almost at right-angles, to start doing it themselves, yet quite unable to do it on purpose. Confessing to be one such, my friend added, 'I am worse. I am a *carrier*.' So perhaps am I with the twitch. After one piece I had written about it an old Austrian doctor wrote to me from London saying that he knew the answer, so I naturally hurried to see him. The answer, he said, lay in the angle of the right elbow, i.e., neither stretched straight nor fully bent, as in putting, and there may be something in this, for if you stretch your right arm out as far and as stiffly as possible, you can make some sort of stroke at a putt even when the curse is upon you.

What really shook me, however, was when he added casually, 'Violinists sometimes get it.' Here we may imagine the twitch in all its full horror. The hushed Albert Hall and the master, as his elbow bends to the fatal angle, giving a sudden and convulsive jerk and nearly sawing the instrument in half, never to play in public again. I was thoughtless enough to tell this to Hogan in Mexico City once and I have an awful fear that it hastened his downfall.

In the end I think they will find it akin to vertigo, or the case of the rabbit and the stoat. The rabbit can do twenty-five miles an hour and the stoat, I suppose, about four, but the rabbit stands paralysed like a man with a four-foot putt. Similarly you could guarantee, drunk or sober, to walk down a road without touching either side, but put the same road, unfenced, over Niagara and you would be on your hands and knees within a few paces. Thus I came one day to the last green in the Medal needing a four for a net 69 and a faint chance of defeating at last one of the most tight-fisted bodies in the world, the handicapping committee of the R. and A. My second got on the green, only to roll back into the Valley of Sin, in which one stands at about eye level with the flag. I pitched up and the ball ran so straight that I had time to think, 'By God, it's in! 68!' It stopped just short, a few inches perhaps – but when I got up onto the green the eye had been deceived from down below and it was a yard short. I was standing idly thinking of nothing while my partner holed out when suddenly it came over me. *I can't do it.* I looked at this hideous thing – just like the one you may have seen poor Doug Sanders missing to win, or rather not to win, the 1970 Open on the same green. I stood over it and remember with the utmost clarity thinking that I would willingly lay down a five-pound note on the green not to have to make this putt. Suddenly I found that the putter had shot to and fro and the ball was as far away the other side. I scuttled round and a moment later it had shot by again and we were back where we started. I doubled back, jerked at it again and this time by sheer good fortune it hit the back of the hole, jumped in the air and went in – but even as it disappeared I knew that my golfing days were numbered.

I forget where it happened but in the middle of a round, which I was regarding with the usual distaste, a small voice within me said, 'You don't *have* to do this,' and I thought, 'No, by God, I don't.' A great wave of relief came over me and on D-Day, 1968, I put the clubs up in the loft with the water tanks, closed the hatch, removed the steps and walked away. Nor have I for one second regretted it. I had travelled a long and happy road since we had cut the holes with our penknives on the Common at Yelverton, but now it was rather like having sucked a very good orange dry and realizing that you were eating the peel. Why not chuck it away and try an apple instead? Which is what I did.

From *My Life and Soft Times* by Henry Longhurst
(Cassell and Co., London, 1971).

I've gotten rid of the yips four times, but they hang in there. You know those two-foot downhill putts with a break? I'd rather see a rattlesnake.

Sam Snead, 1984.

My Cure for the Yips

Bernhard Langer

For the first ten years of my golfing life I played on slow, bumpy greens in Germany. As a youngster I was always a very good putter and by the time I became an assistant professional at Munich I was virtually infallible from 6 feet and closer. Slow, bumpy greens like the ones we had in Germany are in many ways not very demanding. If the ball doesn't go in you always feel you have an excuse because it may not have rolled very well. In many ways it was, therefore, very easy to be confident on these greens. I could blame any miss on the green and not on me. Like many golfers who play on poor greens, I had developed a stroke with a rather long backswing from which I could hit the ball hard. Once I started playing on fast tournament greens as a professional this stroke let me down. I still used to swing the club too far back, but would then have to decelerate to try to keep the putt rolling slowly. It was only when I first played in top professional tournaments in 1976 that I came across fast greens. It took me a considerable length of time to adjust. Many people believe that I only really conquered my putting in 1985 when I won the Masters. In fact I had probably conquered most of my problems by 1983 after beginning to putt cross-handed.

The Cross-handed Cure

My main difficulty in putting was that my right hand used to take over on short putts and jerk the putter head through. This is usually referred to as the 'yips'. Your right hand gets out of control and jerks the putter forward, pushing the ball out off line and often shooting it too far. The faster the green the more frightening this becomes. The difficulty, of course, if you putt badly is that it tends to put pressure on the rest of your game. I used to find myself hitting a good iron shot into the green perhaps 12 feet away, missing my putt for a birdie, and then would be under pressure on the next iron shot feeling that I had to get even closer to make my birdies. Bad putting puts pressure on chipping, pitching and the whole of the long game if you allow it to.

I soon realized that to become one of the best players in the world I had to conquer my putting difficulties. I was producing some good results but they didn't fully satisfy me. If I hadn't putted well as a youngster, and if I wasn't a good chipper and bunker player, I might have doubted that my hand–eye coordination was good enough to putt really well. But I knew that I had it in me, if I could only find the right technique and discover where I was going wrong.

There are two main principles which seem to be common to the technique of most really good putters. *First, they usually keep a firm and consistent angle in the left arm and the left wrist through the whole stroke. Secondly, they manage to combine this with a light, sensitive grip pressure.* I found that with my usual stroke, setting the right hand below the left in the orthodox way, I couldn't keep my left wrist and arm working as a consistent unit *and* stay relaxed with this light grip pressure. If I relaxed, I was always aware of the left side breaking down through impact. As the angle of the wrist and arm altered I felt my club coming off line or the clubface turning. It seemed to allow the right hand to take over. If, on the other hand, I firmed up my left arm and wrist, it seemed to create too much tension.

I therefore decided that I had to find a method which would allow me to keep my left arm and wrist working smoothly as a unit without creating tension. A conventional grip always seemed to force me to bend the left wrist or elbow more than I wanted. I had occasionally seen other good players putting with a cross-handed grip and I decided that it might solve a lot of problems.

I use two quite distinct techniques for short-putting and long-putting. Short-putting to me, and to most tournament professionals, requires a precise stroke which must be absolutely repetitive. Distance is not much of a problem; what I want is an accurate stroke in which the putter moves back and forwards on the right line, returning the clubface absolutely square. Long-putting is very different. With a long putt the skill lies far more in being able to produce feel and sensitivity in your fingertips to get the ball running the right distance and in reading the greens really well. I therefore use a cross-handed method for my short putts, where I am working almost entirely on a repetitive stroke. For my long putts I use a more conventional method which gives me feel in my hands. There is a distance somewhere between 15 and 25 feet at which I may use one method or the other. Sometimes a putt of 20 feet looks very straight and true and then I see a good short-putt stroke without any real difficulty in the line or length. If, on the other hand, the putt seems very fast or there is a big break, I may well decide that my other method is more appropriate to produce good touch. Sometimes with these medium-length putts I may set up one way and then change to the other style if I subsequently see the putt differently. I don't necessarily expect readers to follow my suggestions on cross-handed putting, but even with a conventional grip there must be two distinct approaches to short and long putts.

Short-putting

My aim with a short putt, having read the green and found the line, is to stroke the ball right on the sweet spot of the putter and to set it rolling smoothly on the correct line. From about 15 feet and closer, distance should not be a problem. Obviously one has to get the correct distance, but usually that is secondary and much easier to achieve than getting the right line. With my short putts I want to strike the ball from the correct part of the clubface – the sweet spot – with the clubface perfectly square and the putter head travelling on line. I see good short-putting as being a question of swinging the putter head back and through on a perfectly straight line from ball to target.

On putts of perhaps 5–6 feet or more I am aware of the putter head moving slightly inside this line on the backswing, but my predominant idea for short putts is to obtain a straight swing path.

I know, after hours of research and practice, that the key to my short-putting is to keep my left arm and left wrist as a constant unit. You will see this in nearly all really great putters. I achieve this by letting my left arm hang loosely and freely from the shoulder, and by gripping the club with the left hand very much to the side of the club, with the left thumb straight down the front of the putter. I always use a putter which has a flat-fronted grip. This helps in getting the hands in the right position, with the palms of both hands predominantly to the side of the club and the thumbs down the front. As I look down at my left hand I can see the left *thumb* running straight down the putter shaft, but *not* with the left *hand* on the top as in a conventional long-game grip. My right hand also holds the club with the palm to the side of the grip, never underneath it. Again, the thumb is virtually straight down the front of the grip and the right wrist and elbow are allowed to bend quite naturally. I use a form of reverse overlap grip, with my right index finger overlapping the little finger of my left hand and fitting snugly between the base of the little finger and the third finger. As I set up to the ball I have my eyes directly over the line from the ball to the hole, ensuring that they are never outside this line, with the ball halfway between the centre of my stance and my left instep and my hands very fractionally ahead of the ball. I like to use a fairly wide stance, with my feet about shoulder-width apart, aiming at stability and as little body movement as possible. My feeling is one of having the weight almost evenly distributed between left foot and right foot, but slightly favouring the left, and nicely balanced flat on the feet, neither towards the toes nor the heels.

The set-up has to be absolutely meticulous. It is essential that the clubface is set square to the desired direction.

I feel the left arm and left hand are absolutely dominant, with the right arm, hand and indeed the shoulder in a passive position. I feel as though there is a complete unit, from my left shoulder through my left arm and hand and down into the putter, which controls the whole stroke. By setting up in this cross-handed position I am able to get rid of the unwanted feeling of the right hand being dominant. The whole stroke feels as though it can take place with the left arm perfectly in control.

Long-putting

My long-putting technique is quite orthodox in that I use a fairly conventional grip rather than a cross-handed one. As I have said, there is sometimes a point between about 15 and 25 feet at which I may at first be in two minds as to which method to use. But once I get beyond 25 feet I am invariably working at acquiring a feeling for distance and good judgement, rather than worrying about direction and being precise and accurate with my stroke. I don't wish to sound misleading in suggesting that the stroke is not important, because, of course, it is. But as a rule it is the distance and exact judgement of the strength of the putt that are so crucial. Failure with long putts – by which I mean a putt which isn't left within a foot or so of the hole – is far more a question of a poorly read putt or of badly gauged distance than one in which the line and stroke haven't been good enough.

Having systematically read the putt, I make a practice swing in which I try to visualize the distance involved and rehearse the length of the backswing and throughswing. All too often I see my pro-am partners making practice swings for long putts which bear no resemblance to the swing they make with the ball. This practice swing is important in giving my body the clue to the length of swing and speed of the roll I want with the ball.

When I am putting well my grip seems light and sensitive, and I easily transfer the feeling from my fingers right through to my putter head, feeling the ball coming off the clubface in a very soft and delicate manner. This is something you have to work on to be able to produce the same feel under the pressures of tournament golf. Again, it is essential to stay relaxed to be able to produce a really great touch in tournament golf.

My long-putting is aimed at perfect touch. Sometimes I set up to the ball and seem to have a wonderful feeling of knowing exactly how it is going to roll, easily visualizing it dropping into the right part of the hole. I have a fairly aggressive approach, trying to hole most long putts, except for those which are exceedingly sidehill or downhill, but at the same time being very aware of where I want to leave the ball just in case I should miss – perhaps to leave myself an uphill rather than a downhill putt on the return.

My long-putt technique centres on producing good feel through my fingers and right thumb, reading the greens well and, as with my short putts, adopting and sticking to a rigid routine to create muscle memory for a repetitive stroke.

From *Langer on Putting* by Bernhard Langer with
Vivien Saunders (Stanley Paul, London, 1987).

How Not to be a Club Thrower

Greg Norman

When I was at school my great ambition was to be a sportsman. Greg Norman was no more keen on his school studies than I was, though as a child of sunny sub-tropical Queensland his mind was always turning to the beach, and as a teenager he says he was in serious danger of turning into a beach bum. He was almost fifteen before he first swung a club – rather unsuccessfully. The ball disappeared up a tree. He then turned his skills to Australian Rules football and got injured in a nasty accident that heavily flattened his nose. Golf still seemed like a quaint activity, but to fill in time he asked his mother, a regular player, if he could caddie for her. He took a few swings, realized the thrill of hitting the ball well – and quite suddenly he was hooked.

He was fifteen and a half in 1970 when he got his first set of golf clubs, and his handicap was 27. Within a little over two years he was down to scratch. Many people, such as the great Australian Peter Thomson, have likened him to Jack Nicklaus, though modestly Greg says the resemblance stops at their fine heads of blond hair. Greg is a fantastic competitor. His driving is so impressive – so long and so straight, which is half the battle. He's bound to have confidence in his irons from where he gets to hit them.

Greg has lost two majors to chip-ins. Larry Mize's 140-foot shot to win the 1987 Masters, coming only a year after Bob Tway's chip-in at the eighteenth hole at Inverness, Toledo, Ohio in the US PGA, might have shattered a lesser man. But Greg is not baby-meat. He said afterwards: 'Hundreds of sympathetic and well-meaning people have told me that Larry would have had no chance of making par and that the tournament would have been mine had he missed that impossible shot from 140 feet. I can't buy that. I am not interested in what might have happened. He holed the damn shot, didn't he? And good luck to him.' You can tell that Greg has had good schooling in the philosophy of the game. It came both from experience and from his father. Here, in this extract from his autobiography, written before he won the Open in 1986, he describes how he had an early lesson from Dad in conquering a fiery temper.

I.W.

When I was very young in golf my father Mervyn once walked off the course in disgust as I displayed my anger in a flurry of club-throwing during a quite unimportant club game at Virginia Golf Club near Brisbane. In my youth I found giving an errant club the good old heave-ho down the fairway a splendidly satisfying method of letting off steam.

The day my father stopped following me at Virginia he left the club without saying a word, but when I arrived home in the evening he sat me down in his study and admonished me in terms that were unmistakable.

As a young man my father was an above-average rugby footballer and played representative football in North Queensland as a second-row forward. He rejected several offers to go south to Brisbane and play, preferring to pursue his career, which has now taken him to a senior executive job with Mt Isa Mines Holdings. He is currently the general manager (engineering services) for the company, and in control of the development of a gigantic new coal-mining enterprise in Queensland involving the building of a town, railway and a port as well as other engineering developments.

There was a wealth of wisdom and experience behind what he had to say.

When my father walked away from me at Virginia on this particular day I had just sent my 7 iron cartwheeling down the fairway with my anger its main propelling force. Club-throwing seemed to me a perfectly natural way to release one's ire.

But I did not stop to think how it looked to outsiders. My father told me, 'If you ever throw a club again I will walk away from you. Son, I do not believe in that sort of thing. No self-respecting golfer or future professional would think of doing what you did today.'

My father's words sank in. I doubt if I have been guilty of throwing a club since, but there is no question that this game of golf can tear at your nerve-ends.

Certainly I have a temper. Sometimes I think I graduated with Straight 'As' in this department, but over the years I have learned to keep it in check. When I look around me there are very few people who play top-level sport who can really bottle up their inner emotions. Take Lee Trevino. He is a nervous type of character, but when things go awry for Lee his comic act is his safety valve. Bjorn Borg did not let a thing upset him, but how different is John McEnroe? Even Jack Nicklaus has those glowering moments when the club is returned to the bag with a force that could send it through the bottom and disgust is written all over his face.

There is a fine line between temper and temperament, and being in control of both these ingredients is an essential prerequisite for success. I am at my angriest on a golf course when I hit a bad shot, because I do not expect to hit bad shots. They upset me. As I am now aware, when I was a kid it got out of control, and I would follow one bad hole with another.

Now I am looking for a birdie, and expect to get it immediately after I have blundered. I can forget my bad shots a lot more quickly.

Sometimes I wonder if golf fans are genuinely aware of the pressures that go hand in hand with golf at international level. I find there is a tendency for them to invade the privacy of the players at the most inopportune times. When I go to the practice fairway before a round of golf I am going to my 'office' where I want to work and concentrate – to sort out any problems that I might have in my swing. That hour or so before the starter calls me to the tee is vitally important, and not the time for answering questions or signing autographs.

To draw a parallel, I can imagine the sort of reception I would get if I walked unannounced into a doctor's surgery and started asking questions, or went uninvited to the cockpit of a Jumbo aircraft and asked the captain for his autograph.

I know other players share my view on this subject.

From *Greg Norman – My Story* by Greg Norman
(Harrap, London, 1983).

It was soon borne in upon me that as a character-builder, or at any rate character-tester, golf left all the virtuous team games standing. Indeed, one could claim without being pompous that this ridiculous game teaches you all the lessons of life in miniature – no sense in losing your temper . . . never give up till the game is lost, and many others – without the disastrous penalties that await failure in higher spheres. For myself, nearing what my friend Leonard Crawley habitually refers to as the 'close of play', I find myself super-tolerant – dust into dust and nothing and nobody really matters, and what business of mine are another man's shortcomings? – but in the early days failure drove me almost out of my mind, so that to this day I sympathize with the silver-tongued, club-throwing golfers of former times so piously frowned upon today. I was in good company, however, for only after similar years of mental anguish did the great Bobby Jones himself become a model of deportment and the best-loved figure in the history of golf. I will not say that I became a model of deportment but I did eventually develop an aptitude for wrapping myself in a sort of cocoon of concentration.

From *My Life and Soft Times* by Henry Longhurst
(Cassell and Co., London, 1971).

The least thing upset him on the links. He missed short putts because of the uproar of butterflies in the adjoining meadows.

P. G. Wodehouse, *The Unexpected Clicking of Cuthbert.*

Why, during those early days on tour Palmer threw them. I have to say he was the very worst club-thrower I have ever seen. He had to learn to play well, he'd never have made it as a thrower.

Tommy 'Thunder' Bolt.

I should throw a provisional if I were you.

John Barratt, captain of Royal Mid Surrey Golf Club,
to a notorious club-thrower whose iron had just
disappeared into thick rough.

12

THE CADDIE

In the early days of the last century, before the term professional was used, a golf club's senior caddie was in effect the pro, green-keeper, club-maker and bag-carrier to the club captain or other important people. The word comes from the French *cadet* (young person) which was imported by Mary, Queen of Scots, who included many *cadets* (or pages) in her entourage when she returned to Scotland after her marriage to the Dauphin. 'Caddie', as the Scots pronounced it, came to refer to people wandering the streets looking for a carrying job.

The normal fee for a caddie before the Second World War was 7s 6d (37.5p) per round plus tip. But when Walter Hagen gave his £75 fee for winning the 1922 Open to his caddie, the pattern was set for much higher fees for professionals' caddies. Lee Trevino once quipped, 'I am going to make so much money this year my caddie will make the top twenty money winners' list'. He added, 'Caddies are a breed of their own. If you shoot 66, they say, "Man, *we* shot 66." But if you shoot 77, they say, "Hell, *he* shot 77." '

Palmer's caddie, Nat 'Ironman' Avery, says, 'We work as a team. I hand him the clubs and he makes the shots.' Sam Snead told his caddie before a tough game, 'When I ask you what kind of club to use, look the other way and don't answer.' Seve Ballesteros grumbled, 'The only time I talk on a golf course is to my caddie – and only then to complain.' My own caddie, Phil Morbey, volunteers information only when I ask him. Sometimes he suggests a different club from the one I have chosen – and more often than not he's right.

The legendary Tommy 'Thunder' Bolt, winner of a US Open in 1958, was known to break irons when he was in a fury. Once, so the story goes, he asked his caddie what iron to take to reach the green. 'An easy 2, Mr Bolt, was the answer. 'Hell, son, I can reach it with a 9, maybe a wedge,' said Tommy. 'There's only the 2 left in the bag, Mr Bolt,' came the reply.

I.W.

My Favourite Caddie

Gene Sarazen

Gene Sarazen, who wrote the following piece, shares with Bobby Jones, Ben Hogan and Tom Watson the distinction of winning both the British and American Open Championships in the same year; 1932 was his big year, but he also won the US Open in 1922 and tied with Lawson Little in 1940, but lost the play-off. Without doubt his most spectacular victory was in the Masters in 1935 when he made up a three-shot deficit at the par 5 fifteenth in the last round with a 'golden eagle' or albatross 2. His drive of 260 yards left him 240 yards from the green. A 4-wood shot cleared the lake in front of the green, bounced twice and rolled into the hole. He did the last three holes in par to tie with Craig Wood, then beat him in the play-off.

In 1960, when he was fifty-eight, Gene returned to St Andrews for the Centenary Open to score a 69 on the Old Course – and he also played in the 1970 Open at St Andrews. He has one of the sagest heads in golf and his philosophy on practice is almost exactly my own. Before a round a player should warm up rather than practise, he believes. Don't practise when you are tired and above all make sure that all your practice is purposive, rather than simply slogging balls. No one has ever put better the bond of loyalty and affection between caddie and player than Gene's moving description of how he won the Open at Sandwich with a then record score of 283 – with the help of the faithful Daniels.

I.W.

After a few days in London, I went down to Prince's to practise. The first person I met, right at the gate, was Daniels. He was overjoyed to see me. While we were exchanging news about each other, I could see that the last four years had taken a severe toll of him. He had become a very old man. His speech was slower. That shaggy mustache of his was much grayer, his limp was much more obvious. And his eyes, they didn't look good.

'Where's you bag, sir?' Daniels asked, hopping as spryly as he could toward the back seat of my auto.

'Dan,' I said – I couldn't put it off any longer though I almost didn't have the heart to say it, 'Dan, this bag is too heavy for you. I know you've been in bad health, and I wouldn't want you to try and go seventy-two holes with it.'

Dan straightened up. 'Righto, sir, if you feel that way about it.' There was great dignity in the way he spoke, but you couldn't miss the threads of emotion in his voice.

'I'm sorry, Dan,' I said, and walked away. I had dreaded the thought of having to turn old Dan down, but I had never imagined that the scene would leave me reproaching myself as the biggest heel in the world. I attempted to justify what I had done by reminding myself that business was business and I couldn't afford to let personal feelings interfere with my determination to win the British Open. It didn't help much.

I was a hot favorite to win. The American golf writers thought that I had a much better chance than Armour, the defending champion, and the veteran Mac Smith, the other name entry from the States. George Trevor of the *New York Sun*, for example, expressed the belief that 'Prince's course, a 7,000-yard colossus, will suit Sarazen to a tee, if you will pardon the pun. It flatters his strong points – powerful driving and long-iron second shots.' The English experts were likewise strong for me until, during the week of practice, they saw my game decline and fall apart. The young caddy from Stoke Poges did not suit me at all. I was training for this championship like a prizefighter, swinging the heavy club, doing roadwork in the morning, practising in weather that drove the other contenders indoors. My nerves were taut and I was in no mood to be condescended to by my caddy. He would never talk a shot over with me, just pull a club out of the bag as if he were above making a mistake. When I'd find myself ten yards short of the green after playing the club he had selected, he'd counter my criticism that he had underclubbed me by declaring dogmatically, 'I don't think you hit that shot well.' I began getting panicky as the tournament drew closer and my slump grew deeper. I stayed on the practice fairway until my hands hurt.

Something was also hurting inside. I saw Daniels in the galleries during the tune-up week. He had refused to caddy for any other golfer. He'd switch his eyes away from mine whenever our glances met, and shuffle off to watch Mac Smith or some other challenger. I continued, for my part, to play with increasing looseness and petulance. The qualifying round was only two days off when Lord Innis-Kerr came to my hotel room in the evening on a surprise visit. 'Sarazen, I have a message for you,' Innis-Kerr said, with a certain nervous formality. 'I was talking with Skip Daniels today. He's heartbroken, you know. It's clear to him, as it's clear to all your friends, that you're not getting along with your caddy. Daniels thinks he can straighten you out before the bell rings.'

I told his Lordship that I'd been thinking along the same lines myself. Daniels could very well be the solution.

'If it's all right with you, Sarazen,' Lord Innis-Kerr said as he walked to the door, 'I'll call Sam the caddymaster and instruct him to have Daniels meet you here at the hotel tomorrow morning. What time do you want him?'

'Have him here at seven o'clock . . . And thanks, very much.'

Dan was on the steps of the hotel waiting for me the next morning. We shook hands and smiled at each other. 'I am so glad we're going to be together,' old Dan said. 'I've been watching you ever since you arrived and I know you've been having a difficult time with that boy.' We walked to the course, a mile away. Sam the caddymaster greeted me heartily and told me how pleased everybody was that I had taken Daniels back. 'We were really worried about him, Mr Sarazen,' Sam said. 'He's been mooning around for days. This morning he looks ten years younger.'

Dan and I went to work. It was miraculous how my game responded to his handling. On our first round I began to hit the ball again, just like that. I broke par as

Dan nursed me through our afternoon round. We spent the hour before dinner practising. 'My, but you've improved a lot since 1928!' Dan told me as he replaced my clubs in the bag. 'You're much straighter, sir. You're always on line now. And I noticed this afternoon that you're much more confident than you used to be recovering from bunkers. You have that shot conquered now.' After dinner I met Dan by the first tee and we went out for some putting practice.

The next day, the final day of preparation, we followed the same pattern of practice. I listened closely to Dan as he showed me how I should play certain holes. 'You see this hole, sir,' he said when we came to the 8th, 'it can be the most tragic hole on the course.' I could understand that. It was only 453 yards long, short as par 5s go, but the fairway sloped downhill out by the 200-yard mark, and eighty yards before the green, rising twenty-five to thirty-five feet high, straddling the fairway and hiding the green, loomed a massive chain of bunkers. 'But you won't have any trouble on this hole,' Dan resumed. 'You won't have to worry about the downhill lie on your second shot. You have shallow-face woods. You'll get the ball up quick with them. I should warn you, however, that those bunkers have been the graveyard of many great players. If we're playing against the wind and you can't carry them, you must play safe. You cannot recover onto the green from those bunkers.' Yes, I thought as Dan spoke, the 8th could be another Suez [the hole at Sandwich which cost Sarazen the 1928 Open when he took a wood from the rough, and then another . . .].

That evening when the gathering darkness forced us off the greens and we strolled back to my hotel, Dan and I held a final powwow. 'We can win this championship, you and I,' I said to Dan, 'if we do just one thing.'

'Oh, there's no doubt we can win it, sir.'

'I know, but there's one thing in particular we must concentrate on. Do you remember that 7 at the Suez Canal?' I asked.

'Do I!' Dan put his hand over his eyes. 'Why, it's haunted me.'

'In this tournament we've got to make sure that if we go over par on a hole, we go no more than one over par. If we can avoid taking another disastrous 7, Dan, I don't see how we can lose. You won't find me going against your advice this time. You'll be calling them and I'll be playing them.'

Mac Smith and Tommy Armour were sitting on the front porch when we arrived at the hotel. 'Hey, Skip,' Armour shouted. 'How's Eugene playing?'

'Mr Sarazen is right on the stick,' Dan answered, 'right on the stick.'

The qualifying field played one round on Royal St George's and one on Prince's. There isn't much to say about my play on the first day at Prince's. I had a 73, one under par. However, I shall never forget the morning of the second qualifying round. A terrific gale was blowing off the North Sea. As I was shaving, I looked out of the window at the Royal St George's links where I'd be playing that day. The wind was whipping the sand out of the bunkers and bending the flags. Then I saw this figure in black crouched over against the wind, pushing his way from green to green. It was Daniels. He was out diagramming the positions of the pins so that I would know exactly how to play my approaches. I qualified among the leaders. You have to play well when you're partnered with a champion.

The night before the Open, the odds on my winning, which had soared 25–1 during my slump, dropped to 6–1, and Bernard Darwin, the critic I respected most, had dispatched the following lines to *The Times*: 'I watched Sarazen play eight or nine holes and he was mightily impressive. To see him in the wind, and there was a good fresh wind blowing, is to realize how strong he is. He just tears that ball through the wind as if it did not exist.'

On the day the championship rounds began, the wind had died down to an agreeable breeze, and Daniels and I attacked from the very first hole. We were out in 35, one under par, with only one 5 on that nine. We played home in 35 against a par of 38, birdieing the 17th and the 18th. My 70 put me a shot in front of Percy Alliss, Mac Smith, and Charlie Whitcombe. On the second day, I tied the course record with a 69. I don't know how much Dan's old eyes could perceive at a distance, but he called the shots flawlessly by instinct. I went one stroke over on the 9th when I missed a curling 5-footer, but that was the only hole on which we took a 'buzzard.' We made the turn in 35, then came sprinting home par, par, birdie, par, par, birdie, birdie, birdie, par. My halfway total, 139, gave me a three-shot margin over the nearest man, Alliss, four over Whitcombe, and five over Compston, who had come back with a 70 after opening with a 74. Armour had played a 70 for 145, but Tommy's tee-shots were giving him a lot of trouble – he had been forced to switch to his brassie – and I didn't figure on too much trouble from him. Mac Smith had started his second round with a 7 and finished it in 76. That was too much ground for even a golfer of Mac's skill and tenacity to make up.

The last day now, and the last rounds. I teed off in the morning at nine o'clock. Three orthodox pars. A grand drive on the 4th, and then my first moment of anguish: I hit my approach on the socket. Daniels did not give me a second to brood. 'I don't think we'll need that club again, sir,' he said matter-of-factly. I was forced to settle for a 5, one over par, but with Daniels holding me down, I made my pars easily on the 5th and the 6th and birdied the 7th.

Now for the 8th, 453 yards of trouble. So far I had handled it well, parring it on both my first and second rounds. Daniels had given me the go-ahead on both my blind second shots over the ridge of bunkers, and each time I had carried the hazard with my brassie. On this third round, I cracked my drive down the middle of the billowy fairway. Daniels handed me my spoon, after he had looked the shot over and tested the wind, and pointed out the direction to the pin hidden behind the bunkers. I hit just the shot we wanted – high over the ridge and onto the green, about thirty feet from the cup. I stroked the putt up to the hole, it caught a corner and dropped. My momentum from that eagle 3 carried me to a birdie 3 on the 9th. Out in 33. Okay. Now to stay in there. After a nice start home, I wobbled on the 411-yard 13th, pulling my long iron to the left of the green and taking a 5. I slipped over par again on the 335-yard 15th, three-putting from 14 feet when I went too boldly for my birdie putt and missed the short one coming back. I atoned for these lapses by birdieing the 16th and the 18th to complete that long second nine in 37, one under par, and the round in 70, four under. With eighteen more to go, the only man who had a chance to catch me was Arthur Havers. Havers, with 74–71–68, stood five strokes behind. Mac Smith, fighting back with a 71, was in third place, but eight shots away. Alliss had taken a 78 and was out of the hunt.

If the pressure and the pace of the tournament was telling on Dan, he didn't show it. I found him at the tee after lunch, raring to get back on the course and wrap up the championship. We got off to an auspicious start on that final round – par, birdie, par, par. On the 5th I went one over, shook it off with a par on the 6th, but when I missed my 4 on the 7th I began to worry about the possible errors I might make. This is the sure sign that a golfer is tiring. The 8th loomed ahead and I was wondering if that penalizing hole would catch up with me this time. I drove well, my ball finishing a few feet short of the spot from which I had played my spoon in the morning. Daniels took his time in weighing the situation, and then drew the spoon from the bag. I rode into the ball compactly and breathed a sigh of relief as I saw it get up quickly and clear the bunkers with yards to spare. 'That's how to play golf, sir,' Daniels said, winking an eye approvingly. 'That's the finest shot you've played on this hole.' He was correct, of course. We found out, after climbing up and over the ridge, that my ball lay only 8 feet from the cup. I holed the putt for my second eagle in a row on the hole, and turned in 35, after a standard par on the 9th.

Only nine more now and I had it. One over on the 10th. Nothing to fret about. Par. Par. Par. A birdie on the 14th. Almost home now. One over on the 15th, three putts. One over on the 16th, a fluffed chip. Daniels slowed me down on the 17th tee. 'We're going to win this championship, sir. I have no worries on that score. But let's make our pars on these last two holes. You always play them well.' A par on the 17th. On the 18th, a good drive into the wind, a brassie right onto the green, down in two for a birdie, 35–39–74, even par. There was no challenge to my total of 283. Mac Smith, the runner-up, was five shots higher, and Havers, who had needed a 76 on his last round, was a stroke behind Mac.

Feeling like a million pounds and a million dollars respectively, Daniels and I sat down on a bank near the first tee and congratulated each other on a job well done. Our score of 283 – 70, 69, 70, 74 – was 13 under par on a truly championship course, and it clipped two strokes off the old record in the British Open, Bob Jones' 285 at St Andrews in 1927. [The record is now 268, achieved by Tom Watson at Turnberry in 1977.] Much as I was thrilled by setting a new record for a tournament that had been my nemesis for a decade, I was even more elated over the method by which I had finally reached my goal. I had led all the way. I had encountered no really rocky passages because I had had the excellent sense to listen to Daniels at every puzzling juncture. Through his brilliant selection of clubs and his understanding of my volatile temperament, I had been able to keep my resolution to go no more than one over par on any hole. The 8th, which I had feared might be a second Suez, had turned out to be my best friend. I had two 3s and two 5s on a hole on which I would not have been unwilling, before the tournament, to settle for four 6s. . . .

After a shower, I changed into my brown gabardine jacket and was going over the acceptance speech I had prepared four years earlier, when the officials told me they were ready to begin their presentation ceremonies on the porch of the clubhouse. I asked them if it would be all right if Daniels came up and stood beside me as I received the trophy, since it had really been a team victory. They regretted to have to turn down a request they could sympathize with, but it was against tradition. I scanned the crowd gathering before the clubhouse, looking for Dan so that I could at least take him down front. I couldn't find him. Then, just as the officials were getting impatient about delaying the ceremony any longer, I spotted Dan coming down the drive on his bicycle, carrying a grandson on each handlebar. On with the show.

After the ceremony the team of Daniels and Sarazen got together for a rather tearful good-bye. I gave Dan my polo coat, and told him I'd be looking for him the next year at St Andrews. I waved to him as he pedaled happily down the drive, the coat flapping in the breeze, and there was a good-sized lump in my throat as I thought of how the old fellow had never flagged for a moment during the arduous grind of the tournament and how, pushing himself all the way, he had made good his vow to win a championship for me before he died.

It was the last time I saw Dan. A few months later some English friends, who kept me posted on Dan, wrote me that he had passed away after a short illness. They said that after the Open he had worn the polo coat continually, even inside the pubs, as he told the golf fans of three generations the story of how 'Sarazen and I did it at Prince's.' When old Dan died the world was the poorer by one champion.

From *Thirty Years of Championship Golf* by Gene Sarazen
(Prentice-Hall, New Jersey, USA, 1950).

A Caddie-ish Trick

Henry Longhurst

At most of the big London golf clubs in the 1930s the regular caddies tended to be brigands in long overcoats, and Walton Heath was no exception. After I had won my single there, my caddie, a man named Wilson, suggested that, as we were evidently so well matched a combination, it would be a good thing if he accompanied me to Rye for the University match, and thus it was arranged. (It was at Walton Heath that there occurred the basis of one of my favourite golfing stories, when Wash Carr hit a drive right up the middle, only to find the ball deep in a divot mark. 'That'd be a nice one to get in the Medal,' he said to his caddie. 'You'd never 'ave 'ad it in the Medal,' said the man darkly.) I mention Wilson because at the critical moment in the singles he put in on my behalf a supreme stroke of gamesmanship. My opponent happened to be an old friend with whom I had often played at Charterhouse, Pat Jackson, and in the morning I was four up at the 16th, well short of the green in three, while Jackson had a five-footer for a four. At this point I holed my chip. I only wish that the Master Gamesman himself, Stephen Potter, had been there to admire the timing by which, not a moment too soon nor a moment too late, Wilson, on picking the ball out of the hole, remarked to the world in general, 'Yuss. I thought we should 'ave one of *them* before long.' Jackson stood staring for a moment and then, having said simply, 'You little worm!' missed the putt. One of the many charms of golf and its infinite variety is that you accumulate over the years a whole host of personal memories – *this* happened here and *that* happened there – and thus in all the times I have played at Rye since, I have never passed the 16th green without thinking, 'It was exactly from *there* that I holed that chip.'

From *My Life and Soft Times* by Henry Longhurst
(Cassell and Co., London, 1971).

The Caddie who Out-earned the Open Champion

Sam Snead

The purse of $600 [for winning the 1946 British Open] was such a joke that I decided then and there not to defend the title. My travelling expenses alone were over $1,000, and nobody but me picked up that tab. On top of that, all my hitting muscles 'froze' in the icy wind at St Andrews. For days I ached in every joint.

Then there was my caddie friend, 'Scotty,' who got himself sprung from jail and begged me to give him the winning ball. 'Maun,' he promised, tearfully, 'I'll treasure it all my days.'

That ball was worth some cash, and Scotty proved it. An hour later he sold it for fifty quid. So he made more off the Open than I did.

For years afterward, British and American writers panned me for passing up the British Open, but like I've always said – as far as I'm concerned, any time you leave the USA you're just camping out.

From The Education of a Golfer by Sam Snead
(Cassell and Co., London, 1962).

Caddie Backchat

Vardon (playing badly) to Caddie: What on earth should I take now?
Caddie: Well, sir, I'd recommend the 4.05 train.

I think it's slightly straight, Mr Faulkner . . .

> Mad Mac, the dirty-raincoated eccentric caddie who 'read'
> the green through opera glasses without lenses, advising
> Max Faulkner (British Open Champion 1951) on a putt.

I've been caddying for him for ten years and he's never had a bad lie yet . . .

> Skeets, caddie for Bob Hope.

He told me just to keep the ball low . . .

> A caddie's putting advice to Chi Chi Rodriguez, the former
> shoeshine boy from Puerto Rica who spent many years in
> the US top sixty. Only 5 feet 7 inches tall, he could drive
> 300 yards. Known as 'the Clown Prince of the Tour' and
> 'the Four-stroke Penalty', he was asked by both Palmer
> and Nicklaus to cut down on the wise-cracking while
> playing.

13

GOLFING INTELLIGENCE

It *Does* Take Brains to Play Golf – or Does it?

Gene Sarazen

It takes some intelligence to play good golf. An ambitious player must think clearly about his practice habits and his equipment. On the course he must know his limitations and not expect to hit eighteen perfect tee-shots. Middlecoff and Mangrum don't. He mustn't destroy his concentration before a shot by wondering if thirty-three anatomical parts are going to perform their appointed functions. If he falls into an error which he does not understand, that's what qualified professionals are for. He must remember that a good grip is the foundation of a good golf swing. If your foundation is right, your house will stand firmly down through the years. If the foundation is faulty, it doesn't matter how well you have decorated the rooms, the house will collapse anyway. I am sincerely convinced that if the average player approaches the game sensibly, he will soon discover that he is well above average.

From *Thirty Years of Championship Golf* by Gene Sarazen
(Prentice-Hall, New Jersey, USA, 1950).

Give me a man with big hands, big feet and no brains and I will make a golfer out of him.

Walter Hagen.

Question: What do you think of when you play a shot?
George Duncan (winner of the 1920 British Open and Ryder Cup captain, 1929): Nothing. Nothing at all.

It is impossible to outplay an opponent you can't out-think.

Lawson Little, US Open Champion, 1940.